Public Finance in Japan

1064. β3.51 (1)
———————————
04

Public Finance in Japan

Edited by Tokue Shibata

UNIVERSITY OF TOKYO PRESS

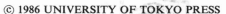

© 1986 UNIVERSITY OF TOKYO PRESS
ISBN 4-13-047028-0
ISBN 0-86008-387-x
Printed in Japan

Fourth printing, 1990

Contents

List of Tables   vii
List of Figures   ix
Contributors   xi
Preface   xiii

1. General Survey
   Tokue Shibata   3
2. The Public Sector in the National Economy
   Makoto Takahashi   24
3. The Development and Present State of Public Finance
   Yukio Noguchi   36
4. National Finance Administration
   Takashi Katō   50
5. The General Account Budget
   Seiji Furuta and Ichirō Kanō   67
6. The Government Credit Program and Public Enterprises
   Hiromitsu Ishi   81
7. The National Taxation System
   Torao Aoki   103
8. Government Bonds
   Masazo Ohkawa   123
9. The Local Public Finance System
   Nobuo Ishihara   132
10. Financial Relations Between National and Local
    Governments
    Junshichirō Yonehara   156

Appendix 1. Organizational Charts 169
Appendix 2. The Constitution of Japan (Extracts) 172
Bibliography 175
Glossary 181
Index 191

List of Tables

Yen Exchange Rate   x
1.1. Land Use by Country, 1981   4
1.2. Population Density per Square Kilometer of Agricultural
     Land, 1980   5
1.3. Life Expectancy   5
1.4. Trends in Age Distribution   6
1.5. Farm Households by Ownership Status   9
1.6. Rural and Urban Populations   10
1.7. Gross National Product and Per Capita National Income   11
1.8. Gross Domestic Product by Kind of Economic Activity, 1983   12
1.9. Output of Selected Products by Country, 1981   13
1.10. Wage Differentials Between Younger and Older Workers
      by Size of Firm, June 1983   14
1.11. Monthly Household Income and Expenditure of Average
      Worker   16
1.12. Public Parks in Major Cities   17
1.13. Exports and Imports by Commodity Groups, 1984   20
1.14. Japan's Foreign Trade Value by Country, 1984   20
1.15. Balance of Payments, 1984   21
2.1. Percentage of World GNP by Country, 1955–79   24
2.2. GNP and Fiscal Sizes, 1885–1980   25
2.3. Government Sizes in Industrialized Countries   28
2.4. Government Expenditures in Industrialized Countries   32
2.5. Government Expenditure and National Burden, 1970–81   34
4.1. Special Accounts (1984)   62
5.1. General Account Budget by Major Expenditure Programs   68
5.2. Social Security (General Account)   69
5.3. Education and Science (General Account)   72
5.4. Public Works (General Account)   74
6.1. The FILP Compared with the General Account Budget   84

vii

6.2. The FILP Compared with GNP   84
6.3. Government Financial Institutions   92
6.4. Borrowings and Subsidies from the General Account   95
6.5. Amounts of Carry-forward and Disuse in Government
     Financial Institutions   96
7.1. Components of Direct and Indirect Taxes, 1982   103
7.2. Components of National Taxes   104
7.3. Revenue from National Taxes, 1985   105
7.4. Tax Burden as Percentage of National Income   105
7.5. Tax Revenue of Main Headings as Percentage of Total
     Taxation in Industrialized Countries, 1983   106
8.1. Transition in the Issue of Government Bonds, 1975–82   124
8.2. International Comparison of Government Bonds   126
8.3. Government Bond Underwriting Share and Available Fund
     Share by Type of Financial Institution   128
8.4. Transition in the Underwriting Ratios by Method of
     Underwriting Government Bonds   129
8.5. Distribution of Government Bond Holders   129
9.1. Expenditures by the National Government and Local
     Governments   135
9.2. Settled Accounts of Revenue, 1982   140
9.3. Local Tax Revenue, 1982   144
9.4. Local Transfer Taxes, 1982   148
9.5. Number of Local Public Enterprises, 1983   153
9.6. Expenditures of Local Public Enterprises, 1982   154
10.1. Vertical Financial Imbalance   157
10.2. Fiscal Transfers in 1982   158
10.3. Distribution of Local Allocation Tax to Prefectures
      and Municipalities   160
10.4. Distribution of Local Allocation Tax among
      Prefectures, 1981   161
10.5. Distribution of National Government Disbursements
      for Specific Purposes, 1982   165

List of Figures

2.1. Organization of the Public Sector   30
4.1. The Budget Process   57
6.1. Basic Framework of the FILP   82
6.2. Sources of Funds in the FILP   85
6.3. The Fund Allocation of the FIL Agencies   87
6.4. Loans by Categories: The Case of the Japan
     Development Bank   94
9.1. The Gross National Expenditure, 1982   133
9.2. Ratio of Expenditures of National and Local Governments
     in Specific Fields   136
9.3. Local Government Expenditures Analyzed by Purpose,
     1982   137
9.4. Local Government Expenditures Classified by Nature, 1982   139

x   *EXCHANGE RATE TABLE*

Yen Exchange Rate

National	Japanese yen per unit of national currency				
currency	1960	1970	1980	1983	1986
French franc	72.94	64.82	48.61	28.53	26.38
West German mark	90.00	98.36	110.79	86.76	80.32
British pound	1,008.00	864.00	515.70	342.61	268.58
U.S. dollar	360.00	360.00	211.50	234.00	193.00

Note: Year end rates given for all years except 1986, with rates for February 5, 1986.

Source: Bank of Tokyo.

Contributors

Torao Aoki is Professor at Niigata University, Niigata. He was formerly Director, International Tax Affairs Division, Tax Bureau, Ministry of Finance.

Seiji Furuta is Professor at Keio University, Minato-ku, Tokyo.

Hiromitsu Ishi is Professor at Hitotsubashi University, Kunitachi, Tokyo.

Nobuo Ishihara is Vice-Minister of the Ministry of Home Affairs.

Ichirō Kanō is Researcher, Distribution Economics Institute of Japan, Shinagawa-ku, Tokyo.

Takashi Katō is Director-General, Yamaichi Research Institute of Securities and Economics, Inc., Kabutochō, Tokyo. He was formerly Director-General, Financial Bureau, Ministry of Finance.

Yukio Noguchi is Professor at Hitotsubashi University, Kunitachi, Tokyo.

Masazo Ohkawa is Professor at Hitotsubashi University, Kunitachi, Tokyo.

Tokue Shibata is Professor at Tokyo Keizai University, Kokubunji, Tokyo. He was formerly Director, Department of General Planning and Coordination, and Director, Institute of Environmental Protection, both of the Tokyo Metropolitan Government.

Makoto Takahashi is Professor at Hosei University, Chiyoda-ku, Tokyo.

Junshichirō Yonehara is Professor at Hiroshima University, Hiroshima.

Preface

The 37th annual Congress of the International Institute of Public Finance, entitled "Public Finance and Economic Growth," was held in Tokyo in September 1981. During the Congress, a number of participants from abroad expressed interest in learning more about how Japan achieved its high postwar economic growth and, particularly, what role public finance played in that process and how the public finance system was developed. However, most of the English-language materials we were able to assemble dealt only with specialized topics, for example, tariffs or corporation tax. Realizing the necessity of a comprehensive book in English providing a balanced outline of Japanese public finance, the Japan Fiscal Science Association proposed the publication of this book in commemoration of the Tokyo Congress.

Today, as Japan's exports continue to expand, problems in trade friction are becoming more serious than ever. The economy is confronted with mounting criticism from abroad. Some of the criticism, however, seems to be the result of misconceptions or lack of information on the practices and systems of this country. It is our hope that this publication will present readers with a clear picture of public finance in Japan and thereby contribute to better international understanding.

This volume consists of ten chapters written by scholars and officials in government agencies. The opinions expressed herein are the responsibility of each individual contributor, but the translations of organizational names and technical terms conform with standard financial or official usage.

In preparing this book, we have received the assistance of many people. We are grateful to Akira Togasaki for his conscientious rewriting of the original drafts, and to Shōgo Hayashi, Deputy Director, Local Finance Bureau, Ministry of Home Affairs, for his expert advice on local public finance. We are also indebted to a number of

American and French scholars and municipal administrators for their comments and advice. Finally, we thank Kazuo Ishii, Director of the University of Tokyo Press, for his efforts which made this publication possible.

Tokue Shibata
International Relations Committee
Japan Fiscal Science Association
(Nippon Zaisei Gakkai)

Public Finance in Japan

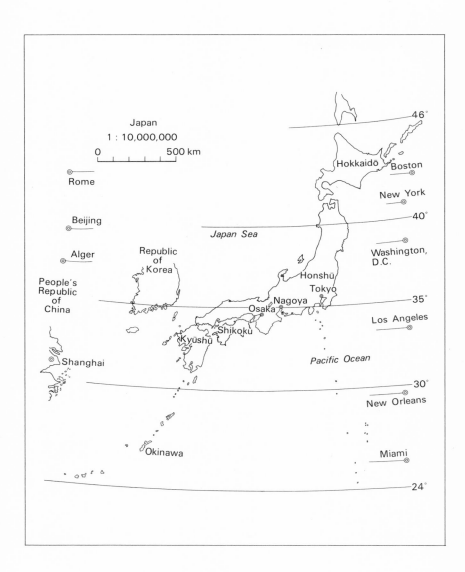

Japan
1 : 10,000,000

0   500 km

Rome

Beijing

Alger

People's
Republic
of
China

Republic
of
Korea

Shanghai

Kyūshū

Shikoku

Okinawa

Japan Sea

Honshū

Nagoya

Osaka

Tokyo

Hokkaidō

Boston

New York

Washington,
D.C.

Los Angeles

Pacific Ocean

New Orleans

Miami

46°

40°

35°

30°

24°

1 | General Survey

Tokue Shibata

This chapter provides an overview of Japan. It begins with a brief description of the geography and population. Highlights of its relations with foreign countries up until Japan's surrender in World War II are then presented. A section on economic development after the war, including the factors which led to Japan's recovery from the devastation of war, follows. The postwar land and educational reforms plus the trends of rapid urbanization and economic concentration are also covered. The third section presents figures on national income and labor. These figures show the change in the nature of the country from a rural based, light-industry society to the urban-based, heavy, and more recently information industry-dominated country of today. A fourth section discusses the effects these changes have had on the country. On one hand, economic growth has given the people a higher living standard and also led to more leisure time. Within the society, improved transportation and communication has led to greater economic efficiency. On the other hand, new social problems have emerged. The fifth section presents figures on Japan's position in international trade, in particular the nature of Japan's imports and exports. A listing of its major trading partners and figures of its international balance of payments are also presented. In a final section the problems and issues that public finance in Japan faces today and in the future are discussed.

Geography

Japan consists of four major islands—Honshū, Hokkaidō, Shikoku, and Kyūshū—and thousands of adjacent islands. These islands stretch for about 2,800 kilometers (1740 miles) from a latitude of 45 degrees 33 minutes north to 25 degrees 25 minutes north. This range is equivalent to: between the northern United States and northern Cuba; or between northern Italy and southern Algeria or Egypt. The archipelago lies off the eastern edge of the Asian continent. As shown on the map on page 2, the western edge of Honshū is about 200 kilometers (125 miles) from the southeastern tip of the Korean peninsula. Western Kyūshū is about 700 kilometers (430 miles) from mainland China.

Japan's land area is 377,765 square kilometers (145,000 square miles), which is slightly larger than Malaysia or Norway, yet smaller than Iraq or Paraguay. It is about the same size as the state of Montana in the United States. Mountains cover about 80% of the nation's land area, thus only a limited amount of land is available for agriculture and industry. The land use in Japan compared with that of other countries is shown in Table 1.1, which compares the percentage of land use for crops, orchards, pastures, and forests in five countries.

Japan is also blessed with many rivers. Beginning in the high mountains and flowing straight into the sea, most of the rivers are short and have rapid currents (the longest is the Shinano which measures only 367 kilometers—228 miles—in length). In the past, flood control was a major task for people living along rivers. These floods occurred quite often during the rainy season (June and July) and during the typhoon season (August and September). Successful flood control promised a good rice harvest and abundant hydroelectric power.

Most of Japan is situated in the temperate, so-called monsoon zone where seasonal winds prevail and rainfall is abundant. Average annual rainfall is about 160 cm (more than 60 inches). A comparison of annual rainfall in some of the major cities is as follows: Tokyo 146 cm (57.5 in); London 59.4 cm (23.4 in); San Francisco 47.5 cm (18.7 in); Cairo 2.5 cm (1 in) (Tokyo Astronomical Observatory). The weather is divided into four distinct seasons. Summer begins with a long rainy period followed by a hot and humid period with strong sunlight. Winters are cold with a great deal of snow falling in northern Japan and on the northwestern slopes which face the Japan Sea.

Rice is the major crop cultivated on Japan's limited farmland. This

Table 1.1. Land Use by Country, 1981 (%)

	Cropland	Orchards	Meadows & pastures	Forests	Other	Total
Japan	11.5	1.6	1.6	67.7	17.8	100.0
Britain	28.4	0.3	46.3	8.7	15.2	100.0
Iraq	12.1	0.5	9.2	3.4	74.6	100.0
Paraguay	4.0	0.7	38.5	50.6	6.2	100.0
U.S.A.	20.2	0.2	25.4	30.4	23.8	100.0

Source: Prime Minister's Office, *Kokusai tōkei yōran*, 1984, pp. 52–53.

crop is ideal for utilizing the strong sunshine in summer and the abundant supply of rainfall.

Population

Japan's total population was 121.1 million as of October 1, 1985, ranking seventh in world population. This is half the number of people in the United States, a little less than the number living in Brazil or Indonesia, and twice the number living in France or West Germany.

With four-fifths of the land mountainous and arable land limited, the population density is the highest per unit area under cultivation, that is, the highest number of people per unit area of agricultural land. A comparison of population density per square kilometer of agricultural land is shown in Table 1.2. About 77 % of the people live in cities. Tokyo, the capital, has a population of over 11.7 million within the administrative boundary of the Tokyo metropolitan government. The total population of the greater Tokyo area (within a radius of 30 kilometers) is over 20 million.

Table 1.2. Population Density per Square Kilometer of Agricultural Land, 1980

	Population (1000) (P)	Agricultural land (1000 km²) (A)	P/A
Japan	117,060	54.6	2,144
Brazil	119,099	2,209.5	54
France	53,950	315.3	171
Indonesia	147,490	315.0	468
Philippines	47,900	109.2	439
U.S.A.	226,546	4,281.6	53

Source: Same as Table 1.1, pp. 2–5, 52–54.

Table 1.3. Life Expectancy

Japan			Other Countries		
Year	Male	Female	Country (year)	Male	Female
1921–25	42.7	43.2	Britain (1977–79)	70.2	76.4
1947	50.1	54.0	Ethiopia (1975–80)	37.5	40.6
1960	65.3	70.2	Indonesia (1975–80)	48.7	51.3
1970	69.3	74.7	Sweden (1980)	72.8	78.8
1984	74.5	80.2	U.S.A. (1979)	69.9	77.8

Source: Same as Table 1.1, pp. 27–29; Foreign Press Center 1982, p. 24.

Table 1.4. Trends in Age Distribution (%)

	Age 14 and under	Age 15–64	Age 65 and over
1970	35.4	59.6	4.9
1980	23.6	67.4	9.1
2000 (est.)	17.6	66.8	15.6
2025 (est.)	17.2	61.5	21.3

Source: Foreign Press Center 1982, p. 23; Economic Planning Agency, *Keizai yōran*, 1985, p. 33.

The population increased dramatically from the early nineteenth century until recent times. In the early nineteenth century, the population was about 30 million. After 1868, it steadily increased to 56 million in 1920, and to 103 million in 1970. In recent years, the declining birth rate has caused the population to stabilize. Along with the population increase, the age distribution has changed. The life expectancy has also changed. The life expectancy increased significantly after World War II. Table 1.3 presents trends in life expectancy. The increase in Japan is due to a sharp decline in infant mortality and a decline in the death rate. For these reasons, the age distribution of Japan's population is changing, as shown in Table 1.4. It is estimated that by the beginning of the twenty-first century, Japan will be the country with the highest percentage of its population over the age of 65.

History: Relations with Foreign Countries

Japan's geographic isolation from the Asian continent has served as a natural protection from large-scale invasion or rule by a foreign country until after World War II. Although isolated from the main stage of world history, there was traffic with foreign countries from ancient times. Foreign cultures have had a great influence on Japan throughout its 2000-year history. The history of Japan's foreign relations can be divided into three major periods.

Asian Continent (Prehistoric Period to Sixteenth Century)

The prehistoric period saw the formation and development of the ancient Japanese state. During this period Japan was greatly influenced by the Asian continent, mainly the cultures of China and Korea. Development and widespread use of the rice paddy technique led to agricultural surpluses. Existence of a surplus was a major factor leading to the formation of clans which then resulted in the formation of the ancient Japanese state. Chinese concepts of law and land ownership became the structural basis for Japan being unified under the authority of a single body known as the Yamato court.

The Chinese writing system and Buddhism, accompanied by the architecture and art, entered Japan around the sixth century. These cultural systems were gradually absorbed and a Japanese style was developed in the Nara and Heian periods.

European Countries (Sixteenth to Eighteenth Century)

Japan's first encounter with Europeans occurred in 1543. A Portugese ship was blown ashore onto the island of Tanegashima in southern Japan. The Portugese brought with them firearms. These firearms, which the Japanese called *tanegashima-jū*, caused a revolutionary change in the military strategy during the warring states period. This was a period of warfare and disorder in late medieval Japan.

The contact with European civilization had great significance in the formation of a strong centralized feudal state. It convinced the leaders of Japan that a unified nation was required to combat outside challenge. Existence of countries with large sailing ships and advanced technology in firearms became a strong motivation to unify the country. The rulers, the Tokugawa shōguns, could no longer carry out a domestic policy while ignoring international relations, and in order to maintain the feudal system, Christianity was banned and foreigners refused entry into Japan, except a few Dutch and Chinese merchants. This closed-door policy continued for two and one-half centuries.

A national policy of isolation, extended for so long a time, is unique in world history. Domestically, the long period of isolation and peace, actually continued for almost three centuries, led to economic prosperity. The merchants in Edo (now Tokyo), Osaka, and other castle towns like Kanazawa, Sendai, and Kagoshima benefited from the prosperity, which also encouraged the development of various cultural forms, such as kabuki theater, ukiyo-e (woodblock prints), haiku verse, and bunraku puppet theater. In 1853, Japan's isolation came to an end. Commodore Matthew C. Perry of the United States entered Uraga Bay, south of Yokohama, and opened Japan to foreign trade and relations.

Modern Era (1868–1945)

Commodore Perry's entry into Japan caused changes within the government. In 1868, the Tokugawa feudal regime was destroyed, and the emperor, who had been only a figurehead with political power exercised by the Tokugawa family, was restored as head of state. The capital was moved from Kyoto to Tokyo. The new government leaders made concerted efforts to modernize Japan. In particular, the technology and political systems of advanced countries like England, France, Prussia, and the United States were studied. Japan's advance in technology and warfare was demonstrated in a succession of military victories (the Sino-Japanese War of 1894–95; the Russo-Japanese War of 1904–5; and the First World War). Within a span of forty years, a modern industrial system was developed. From the latter part of the 1920s to 1941, Japan expanded its industrial potential and became a world power.

Japan's defeat in World War II led to the almost complete destruction of the country's economic system. The major industrial centers were leveled by U.S. air raids. The two atomic bombs dropped on the western cities of Hiroshima and Nagasaki and the Russian proclamation of war against Japan made surrender inevitable. Japan surrendered on August 15, 1945.

Postwar Economic Development

Since its surrender, Japan has not only reconstructed its economy from a state of complete destruction, but has also achieved a high rate of economic growth. In addition to the fundamental factor that Japan has enjoyed peace since the end of World War II, there are four factors that have contributed to the recovery and high growth rate: rural land reform, educational reform, urban growth, and economic concentration.

Rural Land Reform

Under the guidance of the Allied occupation forces, Japan instituted large-scale land reforms. Land owned by absentee landlords was distributed (with nominal compensation) among the tenant farmers who worked the soil. Thus today a major portion of the land is owned by farmers who own the land that they farm. Table 1.5 presents data which shows the increase in the percentage of farmers who own their own farms.

The average size of a farm is about 1 hectare (2.5 acres). This area is quite small compared to the farms in other countries. Because of the small size, the farmers have concentrated on increasing productivity. Efforts were made through mechanization and through the use of agricultural chemicals and pesticides. Labor-saving devices resulted in surplus rural labor. This surplus labor was comprised predominantly of young people who migrated en masse to urban areas while their parents remained in the villages as landed farmers.

Table 1.5. Farm Households by Ownership Status

	1941		1960		1970	
	No. (1000)	%	No. (1000)	%	No. (1000)	%
Landed farmers	1,656	30.6	4,552	75.2	4,241	79.4
Landed farmers and tenants	2,216	40.9	1,309	21.6	1,002	18.8
Tenants	1,516	28.0	178	2.9	85	1.6
Total	5,412	100.0	6,057	100.0	5,342	100.0

Note: Total includes small-scale farmers.
Source: Tsuneta-Yano Memorial Society, *Nihon kokusei zue*, 1976, p. 211.

Educational Reform

Large-scale reforms were also implemented in the field of education. Compulsory education was extended from six to nine years, from elementary education to junior high school. The government placed an emphasis on equalizing education nationwide. This equalization policy included financial aid programs to the poorer rural districts. The percentage of students continuing on to senior high school increased steadily to 94% of all junior high graduates in 1983. In the same year, the percentage of high school graduates continuing on to college reached 30.1%. This phenomenon of a highly educated populace, the so-called academic-background society, has become the basis for a standardized and high-quality work force. The sturdy young immigrants from the rural areas, products of the same uniform educational system, adjusted easily to the modern, urban life and availed themselves to the technological innovation.

Rapid Urbanization and Economic Concentration

In the late 1950s, a population flow from the rural to the urban areas began. Predominantly composed of young, single people, the movement occurred every March after graduation at the junior and senior high schools. There was a time when the Tokyo metropolitan government held ceremonies to welcome these young people to Tokyo. Major companies had their representatives welcome them and offer them jobs. As a result, the ratio of urban population to rural population has changed radically. Table 1.6 shows the decrease in rural population and the increase in urban population from 1920 to 1982. Almost half the population today (about 50 million) lives within a 50-kilometer radius of the major metropolitan areas of Tokyo, Osaka, and Nagoya.

Along with the urban migration, economic activities began to con-

Table 1.6. Rural and Urban Populations (1,000)

	Total (T)	Rural	Urban (U)	U/T (%)
1920	55,391	45,371	10,020	18
1930	63,872	48,509	15,364	24
1940	72,540	45,054	27,494	38
1950	83,200	51,996	31,203	38
1960	93,419	33,014	60,405	65
1970	103,674	30,265	73,409	71
1982	118,602	27,590	91,012	77

Source: Shibata 1976; Ministry of Home Affairs, *Chihō zaisei tōkei nempō*, for years tabulated.

centrate within the above three areas. Around 1960, the nature of industry shifted from light manufacturing to heavy goods and to petrochemicals. Energy consumption changed from the use of domestically produced coal to imported oil. Before the 1950s, major energy sources were hydroelectric power and coal, but since then large amounts of crude oil from the Middle East and other areas have been imported.

Large industrial complexes called "Kombinat" were built surrounding the major metropolitan areas. These highly efficient industrial complexes were built on land reclaimed from Tokyo, Osaka, and Ise (Nagoya) bays. Each area saw the building of port facilities, oil terminals, oil refineries, power plants, and steel and chemical plants. Two-thirds of the industrial activities now concentrate in these three areas.

Construction of such large industrial complexes requires a great deal of money capital. A major financial source of this capital was the people's savings. The savings rate in Japan has traditionally been higher than in most countries. According to the statistics by the Bank of Japan (*Kokusai hikaku tōkei*, 1984), in 1982, the savings rate in Japan was 17.7%, compared to West Germany 13.1%, United Kingdom 7.4%, and United States 5.9%. The propensity of the Japanese people to save is often attributed to their diligence, but the following factors are also relevant: the need to save to buy their homes (which are very expensive), for the children's education, and for security in old age.

Savings are collected and distributed by the well-developed financial institutions, including post offices. The major portion of these savings was used for investment in industry: thus expenditures for social security and the public sector for citizens' amenities (housing, public parks, sewerage) were comparatively low. Entrepreneurs bought advantageous land suited for industry and business. Factories and office buildings were constructed, and the most technologically advanced machinery and equipment were installed. The construction and operation of these factories and buildings relied on the young, hardworking labor force which migrated from the rural areas. These young people were used to the hard work on the farms and would work diligently for comparatively low wages. The youthfulness of the education-minded labor force was a prime factor in the constant technical innovations that were made.

The government, both national and local, also invested to improve the industrial environment. By industrial environment, I mean the strengthening of the "industrial base." Construction included harbors, roads, industrial water supply systems, communications, and public transportation. The investment in industry, by private sources and government, resulted in a high rate of growth. Between 1960 and 1969, Japan's GNP (gross national product) grew at an 11.9% annual rate in real terms (i.e., correcting for inflation). Figures for other countries during the same period are as follows: Soviet Union 6.7%; France 5.8%; Italy 5.5%; Canada 5.2%; West Germany 5.0%; United States 4.4%; and the United Kingdom 2.5% (Ōuchi et al. 1971, p. 5). Since the late-1973 oil embargo, the economy has entered a period of stagnation. Yet when compared to other industrial nations, Japan is performing well.

National Income and Labor

Gross National Product and National Income

Table 1.7 presents the gross national product and per capita income of Japan and four other countries. Among the five countries, Japan ranks second in gross national product. In terms of per capita national income, Japan ranks fourth. As the economy grows and the value of the

Table 1.7. Gross National Product and Per Capita National Income

	Gross national product ($ billion)		Per capita national income ($)	
	1971	1982	1972	1983
Japan	230.5	1,063.1	1,744	7,112
France	158.3	541.5	2,395	7,533
U.K.	140.8	485.1	1,967	6,247
U.S.A.	1,077.7	3,073.0	5,226	10,559
W. Germany	215.4	658.9	2,749	8,196

Source: Bank of Japan, *Kokusai hikaku tōkei*, 1984, pp. 5–6.

Table 1.8. Gross Domestic Product by Kind of Economic Activity, 1983

	¥ trillion	%
Agriculture, forestry, and fisheries	9.1	3.3
Mining	1.2	0.4
Construction	21.7	7.9
Manufacturing	83.8	30.5
Electricity, gas, and water	9.8	3.6
Transport and communication	19.1	6.9
Wholesale and retail trade	33.5	12.2
Finance and insurance	15.6	5.7
Real estate	30.8	11.2
Services	49.3	17.9
Public administration	13.1	4.8
Subtotal	287.0	104.4
Import tax	0.9	0.3
Less: interest related to services	13.3	4.8
Statistical discrepancy	0.4	0.1
Total (Gross domestic product)	274.9	100.0

Note: ¥1 trillion equals approximately $4.2 billion.
Source: Tsuneta-Yano Memorial Society, *Nippon: A Charted Survey of Japan 1985/86*, p. 56.

yen rises, Japan's standing in the world economy is likely to improve.

Gross domestic product (GDP) by type of economic activity is shown in Table 1.8. The percentage of the GDP based on agriculture has sharply decreased in recent years: Japan is now the world's largest importer of food. As the agricultural output has decreased, the output of the so-called tertiary industries (service industries, such as wholesale and retail trade) has increased. The high percentage for real estate can be attributed to the rise in urban land prices caused by rapid economic growth and urban concentration. Increase in construction (7.9% of the GDP) is the result of rapid urbanization and the expansion of public facilities, such as highways, ports, and railroads (especially the Shinkansen bullet train).

Industry

Japan's industry processes imported raw materials and manufactures finished goods. Prior to World War II, industry centered on textiles. After the war, industry shifted to heavy industry and high technology where a high degree of processing is required.

Japan has become a leading producer of such items as steel, cement, television sets, passenger cars, and merchant ships. Table 1.9 presents the amount of output for five items listing the leading producer coun-

Table. 1.9. Output of Selected Products by Country, 1981

	Country	Amount produced	World share (%)
Pig iron (million tons)	U.S.S.R.	107.8	22.1
	Japan	79.1	16.2
	U.S.A.	64.7	13.3
	China	34.2	7.0
Cement (million tons)	U.S.S.R.	127.2	14.5
	Japan	84.8	9.7
	China	82.9	9.5
	U.S.A.	66.2	7.6
Passenger cars (thousands)	Japan	6,974	25.2
	U.S.A.	6,253	22.6
	W. Germany	3,590	12.9
	France	2,953	10.7
Electric power (billion kwh)	U.S.A.	2,365.1	28.4
	U.S.S.R.	1,326.0	15.9
	Japan	583.2	7.0
	Canada	377.6	4.5
Synthetic rubber (thousand tons)	U.S.A.	2,248	26.6
	U.S.S.R.	2,000	23.6
	Japan	1,010	11.9
	France	486	5.7

Source: Same as Table 1.7, pp. 56–57.

tries. Major products manufactured in Japan include electronics (computers, integrated circuits), home appliances, precision machinery, plastic, chemical fibers, and ceramics. Japan leads the world in the manufacture and use of industrial robots. The number of robots being used in 1981 was as follows: Japan 67,435; West Germany 11,400; Switzerland 8,050; and the United States 4,100. Introduction of robots is often opposed by labor unions, but in Japan this has not been necessarily the case.

Labor

As of 1984, Japan's total population over 15 years stood at 93.5 million. The labor population was 59.3 million or 63.4% of the over-15 population. In 1950, 45.2% of all workers were employed in agriculture; in 1980 the figure was 9.8%, which is a significant decrease. During the same period, the percentage of workers in wholesale and retail trade increased from 11.2% to 22.8%. In the service industry, the increase was from 9.2% to 18.4%. In manufacturing, the figures are slightly different. From 1950 to 1970 the percentage of workers in manufacturing increased from 15.9% to 26.0%, but dropped to 23.7% in 1980. This decrease was mainly due to the increase in automation during the 1970s.

Wages increased (1.46 times in real terms between 1970 and 1980) along with the growth of the economy. In 1984, the average monthly income of salaried workers in the manufacturing industries stood at ¥292,255 for 180.5 working hours. Although wage comparisons between countries are difficult to make in real terms, wages in Japan are now among the higher in the world.

Japanese industry is characterized by a two-tier system. Large-scale enterprises have a lifetime employment system with the wage scale linked to seniority. Large companies usually hire and train students straight out of high school or university.

Large companies subcontract much of the manufacturing of parts to subcontractors. These companies in turn rely on sub-subcontractors, who in turn may contract out to small-scale family companies. Thus the large company is at the head of a family of companies. The conditions of the workers at the lowest level are usually poorer and more precarious than that of the employees of the parent company. Table 1.10 presents wage differentials based on the size of firm and the age of employee. The parent companies are represented by the large number of employees.

Unions developed on a large scale after World War II. The percentage of unionization differs greatly according to the size of the enterprise. Labor union membership in 1984 was 12.5 million which represented a unionization rate of 29.1%. The labor union movement was very radical following the war and was critical of the companies' profit-making activities. However, recently the so-called enterprise

Table 1.10. Wage Differentials Between Younger and Older Workers by Size of Firm, June 1983 (¥1000)

| Number of | Age group | | |
employees	20–24	30–34	50–54
10–99	136	193	184
100–999	141	209	243
1000 and over	154	254	341

Note: Monthly regular earning excludes bonus and allowances.
Source: Ministry of Labor, *Rōdō tōkei yōran*, 1985, pp. 100–101.

or company union, which cooperates with the companies' productivity improvement movement, prevails.

The Results of High Economic Growth

Improvement in Quality of Life

In the past 20 years, Japan's living standards have risen rapidly. Household income and expenditure increased, as shown in Table 1.11. People no longer have to worry about such basic needs as food, clothing, or durable goods. Evidence of this rise can be seen in the numbers of microwave ovens, air conditioners, stereos, and color television sets per household. Between 1970 and 1982, the number of microwave ovens per 100 households increased from 2.1 to 39.9; air conditioners from 5.9 to 42.2; stereos from 31.2 to 61.5. In 1980, there were 114 refrigerators, 141 color television sets, and 113 cameras per 100 households.

According to the annual National Livelihood Survey (conducted by the Prime Minister's Office), over 90 % of the respondents answered "middle class" to the question "How would you rate your standard of living?" This response has remained the same for the last ten years.
Improved Transportation and Communication Japan has developed a highly advanced and efficient public transportation system. Its symbol is the bullet train, the Shinkansen, which runs at a maximum speed of 210 to 230 kilometers per hour (130 to 140 mph). Rail transport plays an important role in the urban commute. During morning rush hour, commuter trains run at intervals of two minutes and ten seconds (Chūō line in Tokyo). The daily passenger volume at Tokyo's Shinjuku station (a major junction between the national railroad, private lines, and subways) is over 2 million, equivalent to the total population of Singapore or Costa Rica.

Automobile and truck transport has also increased. The number of motor vehicles in Japan rose from 1.4 million in 1960 to 43.6 million in 1984. As for inland freight transportation, motor vehicles constituted 45.8% (coastal shipping 47.6%; railways 6.5%) of the total (42.2 billion ton-kilometers) in 1983. The country has built more than 4,000 kilometers of expressways; these expressways play an important role in the nation's economic activities. Privately owned cars have increased drastically and are now causing serious traffic congestion problems in the urban areas.

Since Japan is surrounded by the sea, marine transport is very important to its economy. In 1983, imports amounted to 547 million tons

Table 1.11. Monthly Household Income and Expenditure of Average
Worker (¥1,000)

Income

	Total	Regular income	Other	Disposable income (X)
1969	97.7	61.4	36.3	89.9
1975	236.2	149.5	86.7	215.5
1983	405.5	263.2	142.3	344.1

Expenditure

	Total	Consumption		Non-Consumption		Propensity to
		Subtotal (Y)	Food	Subtotal	Income tax	consume Y/X
1969	80.4	72.6	23.8	7.8	4.2	80.8
1975	186.7	166.0	49.8	20.6	10.8	77.0
1983	333.6	272.2	72.1	61.4	35.3	79.1

Note: Average family in 1983 was 3.76 people. Income tax includes in-
come-related local taxes.
Source: Economic Planning Agency, *Keizai yōran*, 1985, pp. 276–77.

(mainly raw materials, such as crude oil, iron ore, and timber). Export
tonnage was 83 million tons (mainly manufactured goods, such as
automobiles, steel, radio, television sets, tape recorders, and machinery).

Communications have improved markedly. In 1955, there were only
3 million telephones in Japan. In 1983 the number had increased to 64
million (53.5 phones per 100 people). All of the exchanges are auto-
mated and international direct-dial telephone links are being expanded.
There is also active involvement in such modern technologies as fiber
optics, satellite communications, and CATV.

Leisure and Culture   The economic growth has resulted in an increase
in household income and a decrease in working hours. Expenditures
for leisure activities, culture, and education have shown a marked
increase as seen in the non-consumption expenditure figures in Table
1.11.

Leisure activity increases can be seen by tourist activities and utili-
zation of sports facilities. In 1980, 3.9 million Japanese traveled abroad
(to the U.S.A. 0.9 million; Taiwan 0.6 million; France 0.4 million).
In the same year, the 1,365 golf courses were used by 51 million people.
The country's 3,678 swimming pools were used by 310 million people.
Television viewing of spectator sports (e.g., baseball, sumo, soccer)
has also increased. The music industry is also flourishing with the
increase in tape recorders and stereo systems.

Interest in educational materials is shown by the number of bookstores and newsstands. These are 12,000 bookstores and numerous newspaper stands, usually clustered around train stations. About 3 million copies of magazines and 1 billion copies of books are sold at these bookstores and newsstands yearly.

New Social Problems

Although the high economic growth has greatly improved the daily lives of the citizens, new problems have arisen, which must be solved in the future. These include housing, lack of social capital, care for the elderly, and environmental pollution.

Housing and Land Since World War II, the price of land has risen sharply, especially in metropolitan areas. In residential areas of Tokyo (about one hour by train from the downtown central business districts) urban land easily costs ¥300,000 to ¥500,000 per square meter (this is equivalent to $125 to $200 per square foot). There is no law regulating subdivision of land, and thus the majority of the people living in urban areas are mini-landowners. For example, in the ward (*ku*) districts of Tokyo where 8.3 million people live, 43% of the 820,000 private landowners own less than 100 square meters of land each, approximately one fortieth of an acre. Houses are also very expensive, the equivalent of 7 to 10 times an average worker's annual income. High costs result in more people moving to the suburbs, creating commuting problems that grow worse every year.

Social Capital With most government expenditures used for industrial facilities, spending for public amenities, such as parks, libraries, and sewage plants has been minimal (see Table 1.12). Spending for

Table. 1.12. Public Parks in Major Cities

	Year	No. of parks	Total area (1,000m²) A	Population (1,000) P	Area per citizen (A/P=m²)
Tokyo	1982	3,779	21,177	11,634	1.8
Birmingham	1980	238	32,053	1,030	31.1
Detroit	1981	311	21,654	1,192	18.2
Kyoto	1982	541	4,075	1,477	2.8
Greater London	1978		169,750	6,918	24.5
Osaka	1982	679	6,516	2,635	2.5
Paris	1979	44	28,320	2,104	13.5
Yokohama	1982	1,059	5,490	2,806	1.9

Source: Tokyo Metropolitan Government, August 1983.

such projects was especially insufficient in the metropolitan areas, where almost a half of the nation's population lives. As long as the population is predominantly young, a city can maintain its vitality in spite of poor housing and a lack of public amenities. However, Japan's population is aging (see Table 1.4).

Aging Society As its citizens age, life in Japan becomes more difficult. Commuting in crowded trains for two to three hours to a full work day can be exhausting. Trains or subways are reached by steep stairs. Standing in trains for long periods of time is strenuous. All these are negative factors for the elderly worker.

Companies face a different problem. Where the age structure of a company's work force is in the shape of a pyramid (fewer elderly workers and more young workers), a company can use a lifetime employment with escalating wage scales based on seniority. As a large number of employees age and their wages rise accordingly, the total amount for salaries becomes very large: the company becomes stagnant and less efficient. Young employees lose hope for future promotion and company morale suffers.

Other Social Problems Unemployment in 1983 was 1.6 million persons, an unemployment rate at 2.6%. These figures are lower than countries such as the U.S. 9.5%, United Kingdom 12.3%, and West Germany 9.1% in the same period. However, Japan's unemployment rate does not include retired people who seek work or women working part time who wish to become full-time employees. The lifetime employment system in large companies makes reemployment very difficult for the worker who is laid off during a time of recession.

Japan's divorce rate is relatively low. In 1983 there were 1.51 cases per 1000 persons in Japan. In the United States there were 5.1 cases and in Canada there were 2.86 cases (1982 figures). The number of single-parent families and unmarried mothers is small but has slowly and steadily increased since 1963, and the future of the family seems unpredictable.

The urban violence rate is very low. Tokyo is said to be one of the world's safest cities: one can walk at night without fear of attack. In 1980, there were 1.6 murders per 100,000 persons (United States 10.0, Sweden 4.7, West Germany 4.4 in that year). However, juvenile delinquency is on the increase. Incidents of violence in schools, especially during the graduation period, have been given wide publicity. Drug abuse is not prevalent, but stimulant drug offenses have doubled in the past five years.

Environmental Pollution Rapid expansion of the industry has caused serious environmental pollution problems. Public awareness of pollution began during the late 1960s with the outbreak of mercury poisoning (Minamata disease) and cadmium poisoning (Itai-itai byō) cases, which showed the severity of the environmental health problem. Mercury poisoning centered in the fishermen's villages in Kumamoto and Niigata. Over 1,900 people have been officially declared victims of the poisoning and about 5,500 persons are seeking official recognition as victims. A similar situation exists for cadmium poisoning. Near the industrial complexes constructed near the metropolitan areas of Tokyo, Nagoya, and Osaka (e.g., Yokkaichi, Kawasaki, and Chiba), many old people and children are suffering from asthma caused by sulfur dioxide and other harmful chemicals emitted by the factories.

By the end of 1970, many pollution control laws were enacted and the acute pollution problems have improved. However, chronic pollution (such as noise and vibration around airports, highways, or railroads, noxious odors around restaurants or small factories, nitrogen oxide emission by automobiles, and water pollution by detergents) affects both the urban and rural areas alike.

Foreign Economic Relations

Trade

Despite its large high-quality labor force, Japan is very limited in resources. It must earn its income by processing imported raw materials and exporting them to foreign countries in the form of precision machines, electronic equipment, and cameras. The economy is heavily dependent on foreign trade.

From 1960 to 1984, the country's exports increased from $4.1 billion to $170.1 billion; imports increased from $4.5 billion to $136.5 billion. Japan now ranks as the world's third largest trading country in terms of both imports and exports, after the United States and West Germany.

Prior to World War II, the main industry was light manufacturing, and the main import items raw cotton, wool, and porcelain. After the war, the heavy and electronic industries became the mainstay. Japan has become the largest importer of crude oil. Export items are the products of heavy industry. Table 1.13 shows a breakdown of exports and imports in 1984. The categories indicate that Japan imports raw materials and exports manufactured products.

The United States is Japan's biggest trading partner. In 1984, exports to the United States account for 35.2% of Japan's exports; and imports from the United States account for 19.7% of Japan's imports. Export

Table 1.13. Exports and Imports by Commodity Groups, 1984

Exports			Imports		
	¥ trillion	%		¥ trillion	%
Machinery	15.7	39.0	Petroleum	10.8	33.3
Automobiles	7.1	17.5	Liquefied gas	2.3	7.0
Iron & steel	3.3	8.2	Machinery	2.0	6.3
Optical			Coal	1.3	3.9
instruments	1.9	4.6	Fish & fish products	1.0	3.0
Ships	1.7	4.3	Lumber	0.9	2.9
Textile products	1.6	4.0	Iron ore	0.8	2.3
Manufactures	.9	2.2			
of metals					
Total (including others)	40.3	100.0	Total (including others)	32.3	100.0

Source: Same as Table 1.8, p. 85.

Table 1.14. Japan's Foreign Trade Value by Country, 1984 ($ billion)

	Exports	%	Imports	%
U.S.A.	59.9	35.2	26.9	19.7
Saudi Arabia	5.6	3.3	14.7	10.8
Indonesia	3.1	1.8	11.2	8.2
Australia	5.2	3.0	7.3	5.3
S. Korea	7.2	4.2	4.2	3.1
W. Germany	6.6	3.9	2.7	2.0
Canada	4.3	2.5	4.9	3.6
Total (includes others)	170.1	100.0	136.5	100.0

Source: Same as Table 1.8, pp. 91–92.

items include automobiles, electrical machinery, iron and steel, optical instruments, television sets, video tape recorders, cameras, and watches. Import items include maize, coal, lumber, soybeans, and aircraft. Export and import figures with various countries are presented in Table 1.14.

International Balance of Payments

Japan has maintained a surplus in its trade balance for over two decades. This surplus is generally recycled abroad through invisible trade and investment of long-term capital (see Table 1.15).

Japan's gold and foreign exchange reserves at the end of 1984 were $25,702 billion. Gold accounted for only 3.9% or $935 million, which

Table 1.15 Balance of Payments, 1984 ($ billion)

	Receipts	Payments	Balance
I. Current transactions	211.0	176.0	35.0
Foreign trade	168.3	123.9	44.4
Invisible trade	42.2	50.0	−7.8
Transportation	12.9	16.0	−3.1
Travel	1.0	4.6	−3.6
Investment income	18.8	14.5	4.2
Others	9.6	14.9	−5.3
Transfer payments	0.6	2.1	−1.5
II. Capital transactions			−54.5
Long-term			−49.8
Short-term			−4.7
Errors & omissions			4.3
III. Overall balance (I–III)			−15.2

Source: Same as Table 1.8, p. 100.

is smaller than other industrial countries; e.g., United States $10,194 billion, West Germany $3,675 billion, and France $3.16 billion.

Problems in Public Finance Today and in the Future

During the past century or so, Japan has developed highly centralized political and administrative systems in its effort to modernize the country. Its public finance has played a great role in laying the foundation for the country's economic activities as a whole. After World War II, the role of the central government became even greater in order to rebuild the country's economy from a state of complete disruption. In the postwar years, for private companies it was indispensable to maintain direct contact with the government for guidance and protection. Accordingly, many big corporations moved or established their head offices in the central business districts of Marunouchi and Nihonbashi in Tokyo, adjacent to Kasumigaseki and Nagatachō, the areas where government offices were located. Tokyo has thus become not only the center of politics but also of business.

The administrative power of the central government remains strong. What the national government does, especially in budget formation, is still of primary concern to the local government officers. This is symbolized in the word *chinjō*. Toward the end of each calendar year, when the Ministry of Finance starts concluding the following fiscal year's budget draft, a great number of local representatives, such as governors, mayors, members of local assemblies, and business leaders, gather around the ministry building to lobby. In late December, at the final stage of budget formation, the number of these lobbyists from all over Japan is said to exceed 100,000. Because of this annual event, *chinjō*, which originally meant to "petition or appeal," now refers to such lobbying and soliciting activities.

It seems that those centralized systems have so far worked well in steering the ship of state. What then, are the problems that the public finance of Japan faces at this point?

As described in the following chapters, Japan was one of the countries which were most seriously affected by the oil crisis of late 1973. It brought about a serious depression which had caused a sharp decrease in tax revenues, especially corporate income tax revenue, and increase in expenditures necessary to pull the economy out of recession. Consequently, the budget deficit snowballed. To cover the deficit, the government began issuing bonds, and the bond dependence ratio rose annually and the remainder of deficit-covering (or deficit-financing) bonds doubled and tripled (see chapter 8). Given the proof that this measure is outdated and ineffective, the government now has to search for some other solutions.

The current goal is to stop the issuance of deficit-covering bonds by reducing expenditure and/or increasing tax revenues. There is no objection in cutting down expenditures as a whole. However, there is yet no consensus on what to do with such ever-increasing items as defense, foreign aid, agricultural subsidy, and national railway subsidy.

In order to increase tax revenues, the government is considering the introduction of a general consumption tax (similar to value-added tax in European countries). But many workers, claiming that their tax burden is already heavy and the tax system unfair, strongly oppose the proposed new tax.

The performance of the Japanese economy has so far been considerably better than that of other advanced economies. Its trade balance has been favorable, with its exports still increasing. As a result, however, the problem of trade friction is becoming more and more serious. The government, realizing the necessity of taking effective steps in opening the domestic market and increasing its purchasing power, has formulated such big projects as the construction of the Tokyo Bay Bridge and New Osaka International Airport. But where would the money for such large-scale projects come from?

What can we do with the public finance system to solve these problems? To add to this, new problems, perhaps far more serious than the present ones, are lying in the near future.

As the birth rate is decreasing and life expectancy is increasing, the Japanese society is aging rapidly. We can foresee a labor shortage and spiralling in social security expenditure for care of the aged in the near future. How are we to reduce the heavy financial burden of the future young generation? Is it possible to increase expenditures to provide them with a healthy and cultural environment and at the same time, reduce their tax burden to maintain their purchasing power?

—reduction of Japan's financial deficit
—decrease in necessary expenditures and increase in tax revenues
—strengthen local finance and thus ensure local autonomy
—reduction of trade friction to contribute to the world economy
—improve urban living conditions and encourage a larger birth rate
to support the coming aged society

Such approaches will be necessary to solve the issues we face today and will face in the future of Japan's public finance.

2 | The Public Sector in the National Economy

Makoto Takahashi

Growth of the Public Sector

As described in detail in Chapter 1, Japan's economy was severely damaged by World War II but recovered dramatically in the postwar period. Catching up with the standards of Western industrialized economies was a postwar goal, a goal which was achieved. The economy was marked by "high economic growth," and Japan's position in the world economy expanded to represent about 9.5% of the world gross national product (GNP). Table 2.1 presents a comparison of Japan's share in the world GNP with the United States, the Soviet Union, China, and the European Community. The steady increase in Japan's economic activities has had a great impact on the world economy. Although rapid growth is unlikely to continue, Japan's role in the world economy will not necessarily decrease; its role is likely to increase in the future.

Much has been written in foreign countries about "Japan Incorporated." This label symbolizes the unity between government and private enterprises but is too general to describe the economy. A more

Table 2.1. Percentage of World GNP by Country, 1955–79

Country Year	1955	1960	1970	1978	1979
Japan	2.2	2.9	6.0	10.0	9.5
U.S.A.	36.3	33.7	30.2	21.8	21.9
E. C.	17.5	17.5	19.3	20.2	22.1
U.S.S.R.	13.9	15.2	15.9	13.0	11.0
China	4.4	4.7	4.9	4.6	4.4
(Total in $ billion)	(1,100)	(1,500)	(3,250)	(9,660)	(10,870)

Sources: U.S. Government 1971; U.S. Government 1978–81.

accurate picture can be drawn from an analysis of the status of the public sector in real economic terms. In examining the role of the public sector within the economy and changes in the public sector during the high-growth period along with those likely in a transition to a "moderate growth" economy, this chapter will provide a general survey of public finance and its position in the national economy.

A Historical Survey of the Public Sector

Prior to World War II, Japan was the only Asian country whose economy was modernized. But the economy was devastated by Japan's reckless conduct during World War II, and defeat resulted in the occupation of the country by the Allied Forces. During the Occupation,

Table 2.2. GNP and Fiscal Sizes, 1885–1980

(1885–1940 ￥1 million, 1947– ￥100 million)

Year	GNP (A)	Central government general account expenditure	Local government expenditure	Central and local governments net expenditure (B)	$\frac{(B)}{(A)} \times 100$ (%)
1885	806	61	30	89	11.0
90	1,056	82	40	119	11.3
95	1,552	85	55	136	8.8
1900	2,414	292	128	412	17.1
05	3,084	420	131	543	17.6
10	3,925	569	280	837	21.7
15	4,991	583	295	862	17.3
20	15,896	1,359	879	2,170	13.7
25	16,265	1,524	1,300	2,694	16.6
30	13,850	1,557	1,647	3,033	21.9
35	16,734	2,206	2,118	4,057	24.2
40	39,396	5,860	2,788	7,823	19.9
(World War II)					
47	13,090	2,058	905	2,473	18.9
50	39,460	6,332	5,099	9,185	23.3
55	88,646	10,407	11,369	16,957	19.1
60	162,070	17,431	19,249	28,631	17.7
65	336,425	37,230	43,651	63,011	18.7
70	752,382	81,876	98,149	143,154	19.0
75	1,519,491	208,608	256,545	375,446	24.7
80	2,393,414	436,814	457,808	672,379	28.1

Source: Takeda 1983, p. 36.

postwar reforms forced Japan to embark on a new political and economic course. The lack of consistency in the governmental policy makes it difficult to generalize about economic trends before, during, and after World War II. Furthermore, the statistics during the period immediately preceding World War II are not reliable.

A quantitative approach has been chosen to examine the historical relationship between Japan's public sector and the national economy. Although such quantification may be insufficient, valuable insights as to historical trends may be gained.

Table 2.2 presents the gross national product and the fiscal sizes of the central and local governments from 1885 to 1980, omitting the war years. The last two columns list net government expenditure (central and local) and the ratio between the net government expenditure and the GNP. Note that the net expenditure for central and local governments is less than the combined total of central government and local government expenditures. This is because part of the central government expenditure is allocated to local governments. The local governments in turn dispense the money. This system will be described in detail in chapters 9 and 10.

It has been said that the economy grew by about 3% annually in real terms. Table 2.2 shows that nominal GNP had increased by 49 times during the 55 years from 1885 to 1940. During the same period, central and local government size (net expenditure) expanded by eighty-eight fold. These two ratios indicate the increasing role of the public sector in the national economy. The fiscal size of the public sector did not undergo growth at a fixed rate. The early twentieth century marked a turning point. It can be said that fiscal size increased after the economy "took off" (i.e., showed large increases in GNP). Prior to 1900 the maximum percentage of net expenditure to GNP was 11.3%. Since 1900, the percentage value of net expenditure to GNP has averaged about 20%. A minimum value of 13.7% occurred in 1920, and a maximum value of 28.1% was reached in 1980. From 1900 to World War II the ratio of fiscal size to GNP was around 17% with the exceptions of 1920 (13.7%) and 1935 (24.2%). The overall trend during this period was a stable ratio with a slight increase over the years.

The great increase in military expenditure during World War II expanded the fiscal size. It took the nation a full decade to recover from the wartime chaos and its aftereffects. From 1955, the country enjoyed a high economic growth rate for 20 years: Fiscal size increased steadily during this period, and the ratio of net government expenditure to GNP remained stable at around 20%. The sharp increase after 1970 will be discussed in detail below.

Comparison of Fiscal Size with Other Countries

Three characteristics of Japan's fiscal size distinguish it from other industrialized countries. First, in many developed countries the Great Depression of the 1930s and World War II triggered the "displacement effect." This phenomenon refers to the drastic expansion of the public sector. In Japan, this phenomenon did not take place explicitly. A partial explanation is the decrease in military expenditure following World War II.

Second, after the war, other developed countries saw a stable and gradual increase in the ratio of fiscal size to net expenditure. In contrast, Japan's ratio of fiscal size to GNP remained stable until the early 1970s. Stability of this ratio is due in part to the high growth of Japan's economy.

Finally, in many industrial countries the public expenditure was concentrated in the central government. Japan dispersed its fiscal expenditure among local governments. This deconcentration of government expenditures to local institutions was a result of postwar reforms.

The Size of Government: An International Comparison

The role of the public sector has expanded in recent years. As Japan's role in international commerce increases, detailed knowledge of the public sector has become vital to ensure the allocation of resources in the most humane and efficient manner possible and to inform other nations of the nature of Japan's economy. The nations of the world are becoming increasingly interdependent, as are their national economies. Thus each nation must understand the economies of other nations.

There are three measures one might use in comparing the sizes of public sectors of other industrialized countries:
(1) the ratio of general government expenditure to national income;
(2) the ratio of fiscal burden to national income; and
(3) the ratio of number of government employees to total population.
Table 2.3 presents a comparison of these ratios for six industrialized nations.

The first method of measuring the size of the public sector is to use either GNP or national income to represent the total size of the national economy. Government expenditure in terms of national accounts of economy is used as a measure of fiscal size. National accounts of economy is represented by the general expenditures of the central and local governments plus social security fund expenditures.

In terms of the first measure, Japan and the United States are com-

Table 2.3. Government Sizes in Industrialized Countries

| | Ratio of general government expenditure to national income (%) | Fiscal burden | | | Number of government employees per 1000 persons (population) |
		Tax burden ratio (%)	Social security contribution ratio (%)	Fiscal burden ratio (%)	
Japan (1980)	40.8	23.4	9.3	32.7	44.9
U.S.A. (1978)	41.7	28.9	9.6	38.5	80.7
U.K. (1979)	57.4	39.3	9.7	49.0	105.4
W. Germany (1979)	57.0	32.6	19.6	52.2	82.6
France (1979)	58.8	29.3	25.3	54.6	67.4
Sweden (1979)	76.0	46.1	19.0	64.1	—

Sources: Economic Planning Agency, *Kokumin keizai keisan nempō*, 1980; OECD 1981.

parable, while the ratio for European countries is much higher, i.e., the Japanese government is "relatively small" in comparison to those in European countries.

The second measure, comparing the ratio of national fiscal burden (tax and social security contribution) to national income, again indicates Japan as having a "small" government. As seen in Table 2.3, Japan's fiscal burden ratio is slightly lower than that of the United States. In European countries the fiscal burden ratios are much higher, Sweden's being the highest with 64.1 %. The lower fiscal burden ratio is related to the greater use of public bonds in financing government expenditures.

The third measure, the ratio of national and local government employees to the national population, has also been calculated for Table 2.3. For every 1,000 people, the government employees of the five industrialized countries are far more numerous than Japan. The United Kingdom's 105.4 is more than twice Japan's 44.9.

These ratios indicate that the Japanese government is "smaller" than those of other industrialized countries. Although "small" at the present time, Japan's government will not remain so too long; there is every indication that it is likely to become a "big" government.

Factors Contributing to an Increase in Fiscal Size

The history of Japan's public sector has been summarized and its fiscal size compared with other industrialized nations. While Japan experienced an unprecedented, rapid economic growth of 20 years (from the middle of the 1950s to the oil crisis of 1973) the fiscal size as a percentage of gross national product has been maintained at a level under 20%. Fiscal size as a percentage of national income has held steady at a little over 20%. These two ratios have remained stable over two decades. When using the various measures of fiscal expenditure, fiscal burden, or number of employees, the Japanese government has remained small in comparison to other developed countries (Table 2.3).

One may well ask how Japan maintained a small government during this period. The government budget and the private sector economy experienced high growth rates. Although the government expenditures increased, the budget remained stable with respect to the total national economy. As a policy, the Japanese government did not plan to be small. Expansion of the private sector resulted in automatic increases in tax revenue (due to the so-called bracket creep) during this high growth period. As tax revenues increased, the government initiated tax reductions. Government policy encouraged household savings and established a framework to promote private investment. Tax reductions and individual savings used to promote private investment are the major reasons the government remained small for this period.

While the private sector initiated the economic growth, the government played a secondary role by providing funds to the private sector, primarily behind the scenes. Private-sector activity emphasized self-development and thus contributed to high economic growth. The government's role did not require large-scale expenditures, and the government remained small. In this regard, the small government is a heritage from the period of high economic growth, a heritage that is gradually being consumed.

The first oil crisis (1973) led to an increase in the government's role. For example, the ratio of government expenditure to national income has been increasing: 30.9% in 1974, 38.2% in 1978, and 40.8% in 1980. Significantly, the ratio has increased by 15 percentage points in the past decade. If this trend continues, Japan will soon join the European countries and will have a big government.

A second factor which allowed Japan to maintain a small government was the age distribution of the population. Postwar society was characterized by the small ratio of aged citizens with respect to the overall population. The increase in number of elderly persons and the subsequent increase in social security expenditures were major factors that led to the expansion of the public sector in Western countries. As explained in the previous chapter, the present-day birth rate and life expectancy indicate that Japan is transforming into an aging society at a rate far exceeding that of Western countries. The experience of Western nations shows that the rapid aging of a society results in the expansion of government expenditure.

The large number of young people migrating to metropolitan areas from the countryside has supported the high rate of economic growth. The relatively low rate of unemployment, crime, and divorce, and the small number of single-parent families contribute to a small share in the budget for social welfare. However, the number of young migrants is decreasing, and social problems may become more serious in the future. Japan is entering a period of maturity: in terms of demography and economic growth, it can be said that Japan's public sector is approaching the state of the Western European countries.

Structure and Characteristics of the Public Sector

Dual Structure

The organization of the public sector is very complex. Besides the public sector in the limited context of central and local government expenditures and the social security fund which have been discussed, it also includes the activities of the public corporations. In other words, the public sector has a dual structure.

Figure 2.1 presents a simplified diagram for the organization of the

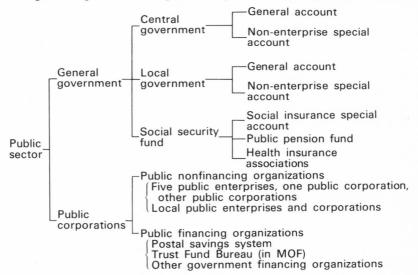

Fig. 2.1. Organization of the Public Sector
Source: Economic Planning Agency, *Keizai hakusho*, 1983, p. 212.

public sector. The first major division is that between the government and public corporations. Public corporations can be divided into two categories: financing organizations and nonfinancing organizations. Nonfinancing organizations are supervised by either the central or the local government. The nonfinancing public corporations supervised by the central government were the Japanese National Railways, Nippon Telegraph and Telephone Public Corporation, and the Japan Tobacco and Salt Public Corporation (employees numbered 396,000, 331,000, and 39,000, respectively, in 1982); the latter two were privatized in 1985. Five enterprises that are supervised by the central government are: the Mint Bureau; Printing Bureau; Postal Services; National Forest Service; and Alcohol Monopoly. Chapter 6 describes these organizations in detail.

Locally supervised nonfinancing organizations described in detail in chapter 9 include local public enterprises (such as city transportation, water supply works, sewerage systems, city hospitals) and "third sector corporations." Third sector corporations refer to semi-public and semi-private organizations (e.g., Housing Supply Corporation, Regional Development Corporation).

A significant feature of Japan's public sector is its public financing institutions. A large-scale postal savings system was implemented during the Meiji era. Presently, about 30% of personal savings are deposited as postal savings which are handled through post offices and managed by the central government. Postal Life Insurance and Postal Annuity are enterprises that also collect additional voluntary savings. Funds collected by these means are either invested in or used to finance public corporations. The Fiscal Investment and Loan Program (FILP) is described in detail in chapter 6.

When Japan is referred to as an "enterprise state," one is talking about the extensive scale and breadth of activities of the public sector. These public-sector activities are not included in the category of general government expenditure. From the government's large role in the monetary market, one can describe Japan as a large-scale enterprise state, as well as a banking state. In terms of the general government budget, Japan's government is still small but heading toward a larger government. But considering its characteristics as an enterprise state and a banking state, Japan can be referred to as "Japan Incorporated," with government activity in its totality playing a large role.

Structural Comparison of Government Expenditure

A comparison of government expenditures with those of other industrialized nations will highlight certain aspects of Japan's public

Table 2.4. Government Expenditures in Industrialized Countries (%)

	Final consumption expenditure		Special security transfer		Capital formation		Others		Total	
	A	B	A	B	A	B	A	B	A	B
Japan (1980)	12.4	30.4	12.8	31.4	7.7	18.9	7.9	19.3	40.8	100
U.S.A. (1978)	22.4	53.7	13.0	31.1	2.0	4.9	4.3	10.3	41.7	100
U.K. (1978)	26.0	46.7	14.9	26.8	3.7	6.6	11.1	19.9	55.7	100
West Germany (1979)	25.5	44.7	19.7	34.6	4.5	7.9	7.3	12.8	57.0	100
France (1979)	19.3	32.8	29.3	49.8	3.8	6.5	6.4	10.9	58.5	100
Sweden (1979)	35.5	46.7	21.8	28.7	5.4	7.1	13.3	17.5	76.0	100

Note: A = ratio of category to national income; B = ratio of category to total expenditure.
Sources: Same as Table 2.3.

sector. Table 2.4 divides government expenditures into four categories: (1) final consumption, (2) social security transfer, (3) capital formation, and (4) others. The ratio of each item to national income and to total expenditure is presented.

From the figures in Table 2.4 we can make the following observations: First, Japan's final consumption expenditure (which includes government workers' wages plus expenditure for consumption of goods) is much smaller than that of other countries. This is primarily due to the smaller number of government employees and the small expenditure for national defense (defense spending occupies about 1% of the gross national product).

Second, the ratio of social security transfer in Japan is at a comparable level with that of the United States and the United Kingdom. However, when compared to West Germany, France, and Sweden, Japan's ratio is much lower. Expenditures for social security transfer are likely to increase as the proportion of aged citizens increases.

Third, the ratio of public investment, whether measured with respect to national income or total expenditure, is much larger in Japan than in other countries. The size of this category is a significant characteristic of public expenditure. Historically, Japan spent less for social capital per capita than other developed countries. During Japan's period of high economic growth, private capital formation could not satisfy the capital requirements of industry, and thus public financing was used to aid the high economic growth. Although social capital expenditure increased as a percentage of total expenditure, Japan's standards of public housing, sewerage, public libraries, and park areas in cities are much lower when compared with other developed countries.

Intergovernmental Fiscal Relations

The central and local governments of 47 prefectures and over 3,000 municipalities are the two pillars that comprise the public sector.* These two levels of government are closely linked by the apportionment of taxes, intergovernmental fiscal transfers, and grants-in-aid. Detailed description and analysis of the fiscal relations between the two governments are presented in chapters 9 and 10. A few observations concerning the fiscal interrelationships will be made here.

Among the developed nations, Japan has the largest ratio of local government expenditure to total expenditure in the public sector. Local government expenditure is broad and extensive. In comparison to Western countries, Japan's local governments play a dual role: as a local government and as an agency of the central government. The large size of local government expenditure should not be interpreted to mean strong local autonomy.

Relations between the central and local governments are based on a large-scale apportionment of taxes. Local government expenditures occupy two-thirds of the total government expenditure, while local taxes occupy only one-third of the total tax revenue. Therefore, tax revenues are transferred on a large scale from the central government to local governments. The amount of tax revenue reapportioned to local governments represents more than one-half of the total tax revenue. This transfer of tax revenue is the means by which local governments maintain their budgets. In overall terms, tax revenues concentrate at the national level while expenditures concentrate at the local level.

Transfer of the tax revenues is accomplished with a high degree of coordination between the central and local governments. This coordination results in the fiscal transfer from high-income urban areas to low-income rural areas. Thus there are no great regional differences

---

* The 47 prefectural governments consist of Tokyo (*to*), Hokkaidō (*dō*), Osaka and Kyoto (*fu*), and 43 prefectures (*ken*). There are 3255 municipal governments, consisting of 646 cities (*shi*) and 2609 towns (*chō*) and villages (*son*) as of March 1984.

in terms of local public services. Regional differences in the local tax burden are also small. Standardized local public services and local tax rates are characteristic of Japan's public system.

Fiscal Imbalance in the Public Sector

Japan's fiscal expenditures have increased rapidly since the first oil crisis. The following is a brief overview of public-sector expenditure in the decade since then. Table 2.5 presents government expenditure and other national burden accounts as a percentage of national income from 1970 through 1981.

The ratio of government expenditure to national income has increased by 18.7% from 1970 to 1981. What items expanded to account for such a large increase? Social security transfer represents the greatest increase with a total increase of 7.9 percentage points. The next largest increase was an increase of 4.0 percentage points in the public bond interest burden. Of the remaining items, final consumption has increased by 3.5 percentage points and public investment by 2.0 percentage points. A study of government expenditure in relation to the fiscal burden rate and social security transfers will disclose an economic problem that exists today.

Between 1970 and 1974 (the year after the oil crisis), government expenditure as a percentage of national income and the similar ratio for fiscal burden rate remained about the same. The period following the oil crisis saw gradual increases in the fiscal burden rate ratio. In 1973 the fiscal burden rate ratio stood at 27.6%. By 1981, this ratio had increased by 6.7 percentage points to 34.3%. From 1974 to 1981, the government expenditure ratio increased at an even greater rate. In 1973 government expenditure stood at 26.9% of the national income,

Table 2.5. Government Expenditure and National Burden, 1970–81
(Ratio to National Income) (%)

Year	Government expenditure	Fiscal burden rate	Social security transfers	Public bond interest cost	Final consumption	Public investment	Others
1970	24.0	24.8	5.8	0.7	9.3	5.7	2.5
1973	26.9	27.6	6.5	1.1	10.1	6.4	2.8
1976	34.1	27.5	10.6	2.0	12.2	6.4	2.9
1979	39.5	31.4	12.4	2.4	12.3	7.9	4.5
1980	40.9	32.8	12.9	4.1	12.5	7.7	3.7
1981	42.7	34.3	13.7	4.7	12.8	7.7	3.8

Note: Fiscal burden rate is tax rate and social security contribution.
Source: Economy Planning Agency, *Keizai hakusho*, 1983, p. 359.

but by 1981, it had risen 15.8 percentage points to 42.7% of the national income. The widening gap between the two ratios represents a fiscal imbalance in the public sector which has been covered mainly by public bonds.

The fiscal deficit in the public sector has increased drastically from the first oil crisis. The present value for the ratio is high in relation to other countries. The deficit in the central government's general account is the major factor in the fiscal deficit. Fiscal deficits are covered by a large amount of public bonds, and dependency upon public-bond financing is increasing. After 1975, deficit-covering bonds have been issued every year. As chapter 8 deals with the public bonds in detail, only three observations will be made here.

Within the general account, revenue from the issuance of public bonds has been increasing. In the FY 1984 budget, the general account revenue is listed as 25% and the amount of deficit-covering bonds is 12.8%. As the issuing of public bonds has increased, the rate of interest on public bonds has been rising. The cost of public bonds occupied 10.1% of the general account expenditure in 1975. In 1985, this cost has risen to 17.5% of the FY 1984 budget. The ratio of the government's long-term debt as a percentage of GNP was 34.5% in 1975. This ratio quickly rose to 47.7% in 1984. Management of the government's long-term liabilities has now become a major problem.

Although the Japanese economy has performed well by international standards, the fiscal deficit remains a difficult policy problem that must be solved. The government has become aware of this problem and has addressed the issue since 1980. As part of a fiscal reform movement, the government has been trying to keep expenditures down. The current goal is to stop the issuance of deficit-covering bonds. However, the government has thus far not been as successful as it had hoped to be.

3 The Development and Present State of Public Finance

Yukio Noguchi

The purpose of this chapter is to describe the development of Japanese public finance and to review its present and future problems. In view of the great discontinuity caused by World War II, only the postwar period is covered.[1] Although much data in this chapter include those of local as well as the central government, most of the discussion concerns the latter because of its key role in policy formation.

With respect to the nature and role of public finance, the postwar period can be divided into the following three phases:

1. The reconstruction period: From 1945 through the early 1950s. This period overlaps with the Occupation period.

2. The rapid-growth period: From the early 1950s through the mid-1970s. For convenience, I define the beginning and the end of this period as 1952 (the year in which Japan's independence was regained) and 1973 (the year of the first oil crisis), respectively.

3. Oil crises and thereafter: Since the mid-1970s up to the present. The first four sections of this chapter cover these periods in chronological order. The final section discusses the present problems and the future prospects.

The Reconstruction Period

Immediately after World War II, the Japanese economy needed to reconstruct its industries, and public finance played an important and straightforward role in this process. In FY 1946, almost 20% of the national budget was allocated to industry-related purposes, among which the most important was the subsidy for the reconstruction of commercial banks, a vital sector in a capitalist economy.

In 1947, the Priority Production Policy was initiated. Under this policy the reconstruction of strategic industries (e.g., coal, electric power, and iron and steel) was given top priority. To implement this policy, the public sector played key roles through the following measures. A subsidy was provided by the national budget which covered the differences between the regulated product prices and the actual costs. Since the difference amounted to as high as 30 to 40 % of the total cost in the above industries, the amount of the subsidy was enormous, almost one-quarter of the total budget in FY 1947.

A second measure was the establishment of the Reconstruction Finance Bank in 1947 as an independent organization entirely owned by the government. The bank provided a significant portion of the fund for the basic industries. The source of the fund was a government subsidy and the revenue from bonds that were purchased by the central bank, the Bank of Japan, through currency creation.

Together with the deficit of the national budget general account, this inevitably caused hyperinflation in the economy whose productivity was still very low. The rate of increase in consumer prices was as high as 80 % per annum in FY 1949. Reconstruction of basic industries was made possible by forced savings caused by the hyperinflation. In this sense, the basic role of public finance during this period followed Marxist doctrine: to serve capitalist interests by providing resources for big enterprises through money gained from exploiting the public.

The nature of public finance changed drastically in 1949 when the Dodge Plan was introduced. In accordance with the policy recommendation by American banker Joseph Dodge, the Allied Forces compelled the Japanese government to terminate subsidies to industry and to balance the budget. The balancing requirement was quite strict in that not only the general account but also special accounts, government-affiliated institutions, and local governments were included. For this reason, this policy was called the super balancing policy. Loans from the Reconstruction Finance Bank were also terminated.

The immediate objective of this policy was to bring inflation under control by terminating deficit financing. But this policy also had a long-run effect on the basic structure of the Japanese economy; the macroeconomic saving-investment balance was changed from one in which the public sector shows a deficit to one in which it shows a surplus. As a result, it became possible to allocate household savings almost entirely for investments by private corporations. Specifically, provision of funds from the public sector to the leading industries was terminated, and the private sector took over the financing role. As is argued later, this became the basic macroeconomic framework of the rapid-growth era.

Another important event was the basic reform of the tax system in FY 1950 according to recommendations by a mission headed by Carl Shoup, professor of Columbia University. The Japanese tax system during the prewar period was one which depended heavily on indirect taxes. The Shoup reform tried to transform the tax system to one in which direct taxes, especially the income tax, are the major taxes. Regarding the structure of the income tax, an almost ideal form of comprehensive taxation was proposed. The mission also recommended establishing the autonomy of local public finance. In order to realize this goal, local taxes were improved.

It is not easy to evaluate whether the Shoup reform has in fact formed the basic structure of the postwar Japanese tax system. Some recommendations, such as the wealth tax and the capital gain tax (on profits from sales of securities), were abolished a few years after they were implemented. Proposals such as the introduction of the value-added tax were not adopted at all. Also, some reforms were modified significantly by subsequent amendments which aimed at promoting capital accumulation. This is especially true for the corporate income tax. However, the implications of the Shoup reform were quite profound, especially in that the income tax did become the most important tax. In this sense, the reform established the basis of the Japanese tax system in the postwar period.

The Rapid-Growth Era

After completing the reconstruction phase, the Japanese economy embarked upon a remarkable long-run growth process from the early 1950s. An unprecedented economic growth was enjoyed during the 1950s and 1960s. The average real rate of economic growth during this period amounted to as high as 10% per annum, which is why this period is usually called the rapid-growth era. In this section, the role of public finance during this period is reviewed.

Since the Dodge Plan turned the national budget to a balanced budget in FY 1949, the general account of the national budget pursued a balanced budget policy and did not rely upon bond revenue for many years, in spite of the fact that the Public Finance Law allowed bond issuance. In FY 1965, the balanced budget policy was finally abandoned, and long-term bonds were issued to supplement tax revenues. During the rapid-growth era, however, bond revenue was only a marginal source of revenue: The average bond dependence ratio (the ratio of bond revenue to total revenue) was about 10% between 1965 and 1974.

In terms of macroeconomic saving-investment balance, the balance changed significantly over the previous period. Excess savings of the general government, which were negative before the Dodge Plan, became positive. It thus became possible to use excess savings of the household sector almost entirely for capital formation in the corporate sector. This kind of macroeconomic environment was the essential basis for the investment-led economic growth during this period. If the public sector had continued to show deficits, the crowding out of investments would have occurred, and, as a result, the remarkable growth might not have materialized.

Not only was the budget balanced, but the size of the public sector was kept small during this period, both in terms of public expenditures and tax burdens. The ratio of national and local taxes to national income remained at stable levels of about 18 to 19%. Note that the progressive structure of the personal income tax would have caused the relative burden to increase automatically if the tax structure had been fixed in the face of economic growth. During the rapid-growth period, the income tax law was amended almost every year in order to prevent this phenomenon from occurring: A tax reduction of about 2 to 5% of the total tax revenue was instituted in most years until FY 1974.

We have seen that subsidies to leading industries were terminated by the Dodge Plan. During the rapid-growth era, the basic function of the national budget was to provide subsidies to low-productivity sectors or to rural regions in order to compensate for the distortions brought about by rapid economic growth.[2] This conclusion can be confirmed by the fact that no subsidies were given to the leading industries from the national budget and that all industry-related subsidies were given to such low-productivity sectors as agriculture and small-scale firms. The national budget contributed to economic growth indirectly by occupying a small part of the economy, thereby leaving resources to be used by the leading industries.

In a broader sense, the public sector contributed to the growth of the leading industries in the following two respects. One was through the government-operated financing system. In the above-mentioned macroeconomic environment, excess savings of the household sector were channeled to the corporate sector through financial intermediation. An important characteristic of this system was that the providing of funds to private industry was performed not only by private financial institutions, such as banks, but also by public financial institutions. These public financial institutions included the Japan Development Bank (JDB), which was established in 1951 as successor to the Reconstruction Finance Bank, and the Export Bank of Japan, which was established in 1950. In the early stages of rapid economic growth, almost 30% of the funds supplied to industry came from public financial institutions. In the four basic industries—electric power, shipping, coal, and iron and steel—the share was as high as 40%.

Funds for government-affiliated financial institutions were supplied through a system called the Fiscal Investment and Loan Program (FILP). Although the FILP is a fairly complicated program, its basic function is to provide financing through the Trust Fund Bureau to various government-affiliated agencies. The main sources of the Trust Fund Bureau are postal savings and reserve funds of state-operated pensions. Since government bonds were not issued from the general account for many years before 1965, these funds were not used for purchasing government bonds. Hence it was possible to allocate the funds directly to government-affiliated agencies. In this sense, the FILP was a result of the balanced budget policy of the general account budget. On the other hand, some of the functions that could have been performed by the general account were executed by the FILP. In this sense, the FILP contributed to the continuation of the balanced budget policy of the general account (see chapter 6).

Another measure through which the public sector contributed to economic growth was tax policy, especially that of the corporate income tax. The Ministry of Finance states that the loss of tax revenue due to special tax treatment was 8.2% of the corporate income tax revenue in FY 1965 and 7.0% in FY 1970. These figures are not large when compared with tax expenditures of the U.S. federal budget, which amount to as much as one-third of total U.S. federal receipts. However, there are differences in definition. Since the Ministry of Finance treats the actual tax laws as the basis and included only those provisions allowed in separate laws as special tax measures, the result becomes substantially different from official estimates if a different definition is adopted.

In this regard, an important factor is tax-free reserves. In the corporate income tax system, accumulation of certain kinds of reserves can be deducted from the tax base. For example, a firm can accumulate a tax-free fund up to a certain fraction of the amount needed to pay lump-sum retirement benefits for its employees. Thus, if the necessary amount increases due to an increase in the number of employees, the difference from the previous year can be deducted from the tax base. There are several other tax-free reserves, such as reserves for irrecoverable debts and for bonus payments.

Among these provisions, some are prescribed in the tax law, and some are admitted by separate laws. The estimate by the Ministry of Finance mentioned above includes only tax revenue losses for special laws on the grounds that the former do not fall under a special treatment category. However, there is no essential difference between the two (in fact, the former were prescribed by separate laws until FY 1963).

If all of these provisions are taken into account, the amount of revenue loss was as large as 19.6% of the corporate income tax in FY 1970 (during the mid-1970s, the ratio was above 20%). Thus, during the rapid-growth era, tax burdens of firms were reduced significantly by various tax provisions. It must be noted that this in turn contributed to enhancing economic growth. Moreover, since the tax advantage was greater for a fast-expanding firm, the provisions encouraged further growth.

Embarking upon a Welfare Era

As mentioned above, the basic function of the national budget during the rapid-growth era was to provide subsidies to low-productivity sectors of the economy. This function is closely related to the insufficiency of social security benefits. Throughout most of the rapid-growth period, the social security system was small. The state-operated Employees' Pension covered only employees. Farmers and the self-employed were not covered by state-operated pensions until 1961 when the National Pension was established. Even after that, the benefits were insufficient for sustaining retirement living. In the case of the National Pension, full pension benefits were not provided because people had not paid contributions for the required number of years. Even in terms of the model benefit, the benefit that a recipient satisfying eligibility conditions can expect, the old-age benefit of the Employees' Pension was only about 20% of the average salary. As for the medical insurance program, the cost covered by the program was only 50% in the case of the self-employed. It was necessary to supplement these low social security benefits by such piecemeal programs as subsidies to low-productivity sectors. In general, piecemeal programs require less fiscal resources than general social security programs because the number of recipients is limited. In fact, this was the main reason why the relative size of government in the economy remained small during this period.

A dramatic change occurred in the early 1970s, the final stage of the rapid-growth era. The most significant change was in state-operated pension programs. By a change made in 1973, the replacement ratio of the model benefit of the Employees' Pension was raised to 43%. An indexation provision for inflation was also introduced. Medical insurance programs were also improved substantially. New programs, such as free medical care for the aged and subsidies for expensive medical treatment, were introduced. In addition, insurance coverage for the self-employed was raised from 50 to 70 %.

A number of other social security programs were improved or newly introduced during this period. In fact, FY 1973 was called the first year of the welfare era because many new programs were introduced. As a result of these changes, the share of social security expenditures in the national budget rose from 14.1 % in FY 1970 to 19.3 % in FY 1975. There were several reasons why the social security system was improved so dramatically during this period. One was the growing awareness of the quality of life, reflecting the fact that Japan had reached a stage at which it could allocate resources to areas not directly related to increases in productivity. Another reason can be found in changes in local government politics. In the late 1960s, non-conservatives— in most cases, the Socialist-Communist coalitions—succeeded in gaining political power in many local governments. Their political slogan was anti-growth and anti-corporation, and emphasized improvements in welfare. They actively introduced welfare programs, and there was a tendency for similar programs to be adopted by neighboring local governments due to the electorates' demands. After a program had spread among a number of local governments, pressures arose demanding that the central government adopt the program as a policy financed by national tax revenues. A typical example of a program that was adopted in this way was free medical care for the aged.

Note also that fiscal conditions, as represented by automatic increases (bracket creep) in tax revenues, were exceptionally favorable during this period. Thus new programs were adopted without introducing new taxes. New social security programs were introduced by local governments because of similar increases in local tax revenues. In this sense, the essential factor that caused great changes was fiscal affluence. From the point of view of public finance, the above changes in the social security system had two consequences: increases in government expenditures and in government deficits.

The Oil Crises, the Fiscal Crisis, and the Emergence of Big Government

The state of the world economy during the 1970s may be described by the word "turmoil." The period began with the collapse of the Bretton Woods regime in the international currency system, followed by a worldwide inflation. In 1973, the first oil crisis occurred and caused serious difficulties in the world economy. Japan was one of the countries most seriously affected by these events. During this period, the public finance system was forced to undergo several major changes. The most apparent change was the significant increase in the budget deficit. We must note in addition that an important irreversible change had occurred in Japanese public finance: the increased size of government in the economy. This section will first review the process and the cause of the growth in the deficit and then consider the implications of the growth of government.

The bond dependence ratio of the national budget general account was moderate during the period of rapid growth, but a fundamental change occurred in the supplementary budget of FY 1975. Tax revenues, especially corporate income tax revenue, dropped sharply due to the depression caused by the oil crisis of 1973. As a result, it became necessary to increase bond issuance significantly. In the supplementary budget of FY 1975, the bond dependence ratio rose from the initial budget level of 9.4 to 25.3%. Until recently, the ratio never fell to a level below 25%. This high bond dependence ratio situation is usually called the fiscal crisis. Because the Public Finance Law limits bond issues to the amount of public works expenditures, and because deficits have continued to exceed this ceiling since FY 1975, it has been necessary to enact a special law every year in order to legalize the issuance of bonds exceeding the legal ceiling. For this reason, the bonds are usually called deficit-covering bonds.

The direct cause of the increase in the deficit in FY 1975 was a fall in tax revenues, as mentioned above. However, from a longer point of view, the true cause of the deficit can be found in expenditures. In fact, the ratio of tax revenues to national income, which fell during FY 1975–77, soon returned to the pre-oil-crisis level and has been significantly higher in recent years than in the 1960s. During the rapid-growth era, the ratio of tax revenues to national income was stable at a level of 18–19%. The ratio rose to about 24% in FY 1984. This implies that the increase in expenditures is the cause of the deficit rather than the decrease in tax revenues.

As for increases in expenditures during this period, some regard the expansionary fiscal policies undertaken to cope with the depression created by the oil crisis as the main cause of the deficit. This view is incorrect. First, it was in FY 1977, two years after the deficit had increased, that an expansionary fiscal policy was undertaken. Second, although the bond dependence ratio rose from 29.4% in FY 1976 to 32.9% in FY 1977, the change was marginal compared to the magnitude of the dependence ratio itself. The increase in the deficit was, therefore, not a result of a Keynesian-type expansionary policy.

The major change in expenditures was the continuous increase in social security expenditures. This change was caused by the large improvements in social security programs in the early 1970s. Once new social security programs are introduced or payment levels are upgraded, outlays usually grow automatically as the general income level grows and as the number of recipients increases. In this sense, the present deficit is a structural one. In terms of general account expenditures, debt-servicing costs also increased significantly. But this increase is based on increases in other expenditures in the past. Thus, in order to see the intrinsic causes for change, debt-servicing costs should be disregarded.

In spite of the fact that the structural change in social security occurred in the early 1970s, the deficit did not grow until FY 1975 because tax revenues also increased during this period. In other words, the rise in tax revenues in FY 1973–74 had an effect of "concealing" the potential fiscal gap temporarily. The depression in 1975 made this gap visible. In this sense, the oil crisis of 1973 was not the most essential factor for the structural changes as is usually argued.

What was the implication of the above changes on macroeconomic conditions? During the rapid-growth era, the investments of the general government were about equal to its savings. The structure changed significantly as a result of the above developments; in the general government sector, savings became smaller than investments, the gap being about 4% of GDP. This meant that the general government had become a net demander of funds. Such a condition had a strong impact on the supply and demand condition of funds. In 1977 and 1978, the government absorbed almost one-half the excess savings of the household sector (in recent years, the share of the government has been about one-third).

At the same time, a significant change had occurred in the private sector. (Note that public corporations are included in the "private sector" defined here.) On the average, the private sector showed neither surplus nor deficit during the rapid-growth era. After the oil crisis of 1973, an excess saving of about 4 to 5% of GDP has resulted. The major reason for this change was a fall in corporate investments. (It should be noted that although the tendency was accelerated by the 1973 oil crisis, the trend had already begun during the early 1970s).

Therefore, increased deficits of the general government sector have been absorbed by increases in savings in the private sector. In this sense, the increases in government deficits have caused no serious macroeconomic problems. If one regards Japan's huge external surplus as one of the causes of international economic friction, it can be argued that the public-sector deficit should be increased further, because that would reduce the external surplus. (Recall a basic macroeconomic identity that excess savings in the private sector are equal to the sum of the government deficit and the current external surplus.)

The above observation does not mean that the budget deficit is not a serious problem, especially from a political or administrative point of view. In fact, under a huge budget deficit, public expenditures cannot be significantly increased even if it is desirable from the macroeconomic view of resource allocation. For this reason, reducing the budget deficit has been regarded as an important task during the past decade.

Let us now consider the problem of the growth of government. Peacock and Wiseman (1967) have argued that significant public sector growth occurs only in time of war because people will not accept tax increases unless extraordinary events such as war occur. They reached this conclusion from analyses of U.K. data during the period 1890–1967. However, the experience of the OECD countries, including Japan, in the past decades refutes this hypothesis. In Japan, the relative size of government has increased substantially in the last ten years. The share of general government expenditures to GDP, which was below 20% until 1970, has steadily increased during the 1970s and is now about 35%. The general account expenditure of the national budget has increased its share of the GDP from about 10 to 18%.

The growth of government in the European countries was caused mainly by increases in transfer payments (see, e.g., OECD 1978). The same phenomenon has occurred in Japan. While government consumption and investment do not exhibit clear trends in terms of ratios to GDP (except for the increase in government consumption caused by the inflation of 1973–75), that of transfer payments has increased remarkably during the past ten years. Therefore, public sector growth has been brought about by a creation of (or at least an attempt to create) a welfare state. This trend is important because it is completely different from the Marxist thesis that state expansion will occur from increased military expenditures and subsidies to monopolistic industries.

The growth of government has increased fiscal burdens. The ratio of total tax revenues (the sum of national and local tax revenues) to national income which was about 18% in FY 1965 rose to 23.8% in FY 1983. If social security contributions are included, the increase in government receipts is even more dramatic: The share in national income has risen from 23.2% in FY 1965 to 34.3% in FY 1983. Recall that tax burdens were quite stable during the 1960s. Thus the increase in tax burden is a relatively recent phenomenon.

The increase in tax burden was brought about by an increase in direct taxes, especially income taxes. This result can be verified by the following figures. While the ratio of indirect taxes to national income in recent years has been about the same as in the 1960s, that of direct taxes has increased a great deal during the past decade—from 9.3% in FY 1965 to 14.4% in FY 1983. Among the national taxes, income taxes have increased the most sharply. In FY 1965, the share of income taxes to national income was about 3.6%, whereas in FY 1983, it had risen to 6.1%.

Note that the increase in income taxes is not a result of explicit revisions in the income tax law. Rather, it is the result of the automatic increase (bracket creep). During the rapid-growth era, the income tax law was amended almost every year in order to prevent this mechanism from operating. The trend changed completely since the first oil crisis. Adjustments in the income tax law were not undertaken for a full seven years from FY 1977 through FY 1984.

In recent years, public opinion concerning the role of the government has changed significantly. The number favoring small government has become predominant, especially among business people. This change is probably caused by the fear that further increases in fiscal burdens will fall on the business community in the form of increases in the corporate income tax. This concern is a background for the fiscal reconstruction movement discussed below.

Fiscal Reconstruction and Future Prospects

Since the increase in the budget deficit in FY 1975, deficit reduction, usually called fiscal reconstruction, has become one of the most important objectives of economic policy. The current economic plan, "The Outlook and Guidelines of the Economy in the 1980s," which was formulated in August 1983, designates deficit reduction as one of the main policy targets to be realized by 1989.

The initial strategy of the government was to reduce the deficit by introducing a new tax. A general consumption tax, which is similar to the value-added taxes in European countries, was proposed in 1977. However, this attempt failed, due to a setback for the Liberal Democratic party (LDP), the government party, in the national election of 1979 when the introduction of the tax was the greatest issue. Since then, introduction of a new tax has become a political taboo. Thus, the government was forced to change the basic strategy for reducing expenditures.

The first step was to give deficit reduction the utmost priority. Since FY 1980, the amount of bond issue reduction has been determined at the beginning of the budget preparation process before any other budgetary decisions are made. The next step was the strengthening of the upper limit imposed on budget requests. Since FY 1982, the principle of zero growth requests has been imposed. The third step was the establishment of the Ad Hoc Council on Administrative Reform in March 1981. The task of this council was to review all government activities and to make recommendations necessary for rationalizing the government system. Before it terminated its function in March 1983, the council made several sets of recommendations, including reforms of the social security system and privatization of such public corporations as the Japanese National Railways and the Nippon Telegraph and Telephone Public Corporation.

As a result of these policies, the growth rate of expenditures has fallen significantly since FY 1982. The rate of increase of general expenditures, which is the total budget minus debt-servicing costs and disbursements to local governments, fell to 1.8% in FY 1982, 0% in FY 1983, and then to -0.1% in FY 1984. It is true that the fall in the nominal economic growth rate has contributed to lowering the expenditure growth rate. However, the growth rate of general expenditures has been lower than the nominal economic growth rate in recent years. Issuance of bonds also declined steadily since FY 1980. The bond dependence ratio, which was as high as almost 40% in the initial FY 1979 budget, has been reduced to 22.2% in FY 1985. The above reduction does not mean, however, that the fiscal crisis has been overcome or that it can be overcome in the near future. On the contrary, there are possibilities that the situation will be aggravated in the future.

In spite of the recent growth, the relative size of the government is still small when compared to European countries, due mainly to the relatively low level of social security expenditures. In FY 1984, social-security transfers in Japan were about 14.9% of its national income. The corresponding figures for European countries are above 20%. This is not a result of insufficient payment levels. In fact, as a result of the large changes in the 1970s, the Japanese social security system has become one of the best in the world. The low level of social security expenditures is because the percentage of aged people is still small and the state-operated pension system has not yet matured. In this sense, the potential effect of the improvements in the social security programs has not yet been fully realized.

In the coming decades, however, these conditions will change dramatically. As a result, social security expenditures will increase further. This will increase overall government expenditures because the share of social security expenditures in the total budget is significant.

According to a report by the Council of Economic Affairs in 1982, social security transfers as measured by their ratio to national income are estimated to increase from 12.8% in 1980 to 24.7% in 2000 and to 36.9% in 2025 (Economic Planning Agency 1982). Most of the increase is due to the growth of state-operated pension payments: Their share in national income will rise from 4.3 to 19.4% during the period between 1980 and 2025. Increase in outlays must be accompanied by increase in burdens. Social security contributions, which were 9.3% of national income in FY 1980 will rise to 14.6% in 2000 and further to 24.1% in 2025.

These projections may overestimate the magnitude of the problem, since they are based on the assumption that the present system will continue into the future. If the burden exceeds a certain level, pressures will arise to reform the system. In fact, a fairly radical reform has been undertaken in the public pensions in 1985: The Employees' Pension and the National Pension have been combined into a new system of the National Pension. Also, independent pension rights have been bestowed on women. However, cutting existing benefits is extremely difficult because of vested interests. Thus, it would be meaningful to consider the implications of the above estimates on future budget balances.

First, the relative size of government will become about the same as that of the present European countries, both with respect to revenues and expenditures. Also, the gap between revenues and expenditures will grow in the future. This gap must be closed by tax increases, expenditure cuts, bond issues, or their combinations.

Budget deficits in Japan have not caused serious economic problems so far because of the large savings of the household sector. However, there is a possibility that savings might fall in the future, due to an aging population and improvements in state-operated pension benefits. These changes in economic conditions will make the public-sector deficit a serious economic problem. The necessity of reducing the deficit will become urgent, not only for political or administrative reasons but also for macroeconomic reasons. The introduction of a new tax, such as a general consumption tax, will become necessary. It is uncertain, however, whether such a reform can be actually imposed in view of the considerable political difficulties.

Notes

1. For a description of prewar Japanese public finance, see, for example, Ōshima 1965.

2. For further discussions, see Noguchi 1982b.

4 National Finance Administration

Takashi Katō

This chapter presents an overview of the administration of national finance. The legal bases for this administration are discussed in the first section. Budgetary processes are described in the second section. The budgetary process is divided into the following items: contents of the budget; classification of budget items; formulation, approval, and execution of the budget. The third section is devoted to special accounts and government-affiliated agencies. A final section discusses the audit system.

National Finance Administration: The Basic System

Constitutional Provisions

The constitution of Japan provides for the administration of national finance in Chapter VII, entitled Finance. Article 73, clause 5 provides that the Cabinet shall prepare and submit the budget to the Diet. Articles 83 to 91 provide that the Diet shall deliberate and pass legislation for the budget (revenue/expenditure), impose and collect taxes, bear liabilities, and attend to other important financial matters concerning national finances, which should not be performed without Diet determination. These functions are in accordance with principles of parliamentary democracy which has taken form over a long period of history. Article 60 provides the House of Representatives the right to prior deliberation on a budget bill. Also provided is the settlement of expenditure and revenue by an annual audit by a Board of Audit. This board is an independent body and the board's audit is submitted by the Cabinet to the Diet.

This budgetary process is subject to certain conditions contained in Articles 83 to 91. Three of these conditions are as follows:

1. All property of the Imperial Household shall belong to the state,

and all expenses of the Imperial Household shall be appropriated by the Diet in the budget;

2. No public money or other property shall be expended or appropriated for the use of any religious institution or association or for any charitable, benevolent, or educational enterprises in the private sector not under the control of the public authorities;

3. At regular intervals and at least annually, the Cabinet shall report on the state of national finances to the Diet and to the people.

Legal Structure for Finances

Based on the Constitution, many laws have been passed for the execution and administration of national finances. These laws can roughly be classified as follows: Tax laws which provide the power to tax and to collect revenues for use by the national government; and financial administration laws which provide management of national revenue including tax and coordination of national expenditure.

Among the more important financial administration laws are the following: Public Finance Law; Accounts Law; National Property Law; National Goods Management Law; Law Concerning Management of National Credits; Board of Audit Law; and the Law Concerning Government Bonds. The Public Finance Law provides the basic system for the budget and the settlement of accounts. The Accounts Law provides the management of procedures for receipts and disbursements, for contracts, and for a system of accounts. The National Property Law provides general rules for management or disposal of national real estate, some movables, and other properties. The National Goods Management Law provides the basic rules of acquisition, keeping, submission for public use, and disposal of goods owned by the state. The Law Concerning Management of National Credits provides the organization and procedures for the management of national credits for money. The Board of Audit Law and the Law Concerning Government Bonds will be discussed in later sections. These basic laws play central roles in the legal structure for finances with a wide range of subordinate, complementary laws, or laws making exceptions.

General Rules of Finance and Accounts

Chapter 1 (General Provisions of Finance) of the Public Finance Law provides general rules for finance and accounting. These rules include provisions for the fiscal year, unified accounts, unified revenues and expenditures, overall budget (gross-totaled budget), and various accounting definitions. Specifically, these provisions are as follows:

1. Fiscal Year Provisions:

The fiscal year begins on April 1 and ends on March 31 of the following calendar year;

A fiscal year is the term of validity of a budget;

Fiscal year independence is a guiding principle (expenses in each fiscal year must be defrayed by revenues in the same fiscal year);

2. Unified Accounting: all national revenues and expenditures shall form a unified account and be under a unified accounting system;

3. Unified Revenue and Expenditure:

All revenues or expenditures in each account are to be treated as one unified group of revenues or expenditures;

An individual revenue should not pay for an individual expenditure;

4. A Gross-totaled Budget: All revenues and expenditures are to be included in the budget. This principle comes from the same source as the above three principles and they form the principle of unified treasury transaction provided for in the Accounts Law.

Definitions of receipt/disbursement or revenue/expenditure are as follows:

budget: a plan of cash receipt/disbursement in a fiscal year;

receipts: cash receipts which are to finance payment and cover the various demands of the state;

disbursement: payments in cash to satisfy and cover the various state demands;

revenue: all receipts in a fiscal year;

expenditure: all disbursements in a fiscal year.

Note that with respect to receipts and disbursements there is no concept of term. When expressed as revenue or expenditure, the time period is a fiscal year.

Government Bond Systems

Provisions for government bonds are made in articles 4 and 5 of the Public Finance Law, the Law Concerning Government Bonds, and the Special Account for Government Bonds Consolidation Fund. The three major principles that form the basis for the issuance of government bonds are as follows: (1) the principle of sound financial policy; (2) the principle of construction bonds; and (3) the principle of government-bond underwriting in the market.

The sound financial policy principle means that tax revenue is given priority as the source of revenue for national expenditure, but government bond issuance is not prohibited. The size of the budget should be "proper" in the light of the national economy, and thus this principle might be labelled "the principle of an optimum-sized budget." The construction-bond principle means that government bonds are to be issued only as a financial source for such capital expenditures as public works, investments, and advancements.

Market underwriting for government bonds means that government bonds should not be issued based on money printing by the central bank. The issue prices, interest rates, maturity, and other matters concerning bond issues are determined by the minister of finance. Redemption or consolidation of government bonds occurs by three kinds of transfer:

1) The fixed rate transfer (1.6% of the bonds outstanding as of the beginning of the preceding fiscal year, this transfer is in disuse at present);

2) The transfer of over half (all at present) of the surplus in the settlement of the general account; and

3) The budgetary transfer in case of necessity.

Bonds are consolidated in the course of sixty years. This time period reflects the life of public works assets. Refunding bonds are issued to obtain the money for redemption of bonds.

Since FY 1975 supplementary budget deficit-covering bonds have been issued. These bonds finance current expenditures rather than capital expenditures. Deficit-covering bonds are based on annual legislation and have been issued to finance huge deficits in the national budget. Construction bonds and deficit-covering bonds are the same in terms of issue and maturity. However, the fiscal reform movement promotes a goal of ceasing the issuance of deficit-covering bonds by FY 1990. (See chapter 8.)

Outline of the Budget System

Determination of the budget is one of the major tasks of the Diet. This task is performed in addition to the drafting and passing of national legislation. This section describes the following items in the budget process: budget contents; budget classifications; budget formulation; budget deliberation by the Diet; budget execution; and settlement of accounts.

Budget Contents

The term "budget" has various meanings. Generally, budget refers to the expenditure budget of the general account. The Public Finance Law provides that a budget consists of the following: general budget provisions; revenue and expenditure budget; continued expense; approved carry-over expense; and contract authorization.

General Budget Provisions General Budget Provisions provide for the following matters:

1) limits to the amount of government bonds or borrowing;

2) the content of public works expenditures financed by bonds or borrowing;

3) limits to the amount of government bonds undertaken by the Bank of Japan (BOJ) (only refunding bonds at present) or borrowings from BOJ (none at present);

4) maximum amounts of treasury bills or temporary borrowing;

5) limits to the amounts of contract authorization in cases of urgent necessity (e.g., restoration from calamity or damages); and

6) other matters necessary for budget execution.

In addition, general budget provisions contain summary regulations pertaining to the revenue and expenditure budget, continued expense, and contract authorization.

Revenue and Expenditure Budget The revenue and expenditure budget is the main part of the budget; thus it is often called the budget, using the term in a narrow sense. This budget can be divided into the revenue budget and the expenditure budget. The revenue budget compiles estimates for all receipts for the fiscal year. Likewise, the expenditure budget lists estimates for all kinds of disbursements for the fiscal year. The revenue budget shows the estimate of total national receipts, such as from tax collection by laws, but it does not mean that the state will collect the estimated amounts of revenue. Expenditures are somewhat different. Expenditures are permitted only when they are listed in the expenditure budget, and the estimated expenditures are basically the upper limits of expenditure for each disbursement.

The revenue and expenditure budget is divided by organization (i.e., ministry, agency) unit related to receipts and disbursements; under each organization unit there are further subdivisions according to nature and purpose. These divisions are made to delineate organizational responsibility for budget execution and to aid in the supervision of budget execution. For example, a division of the revenue budget is as follows: department, Ministry of Finance; part, tax and stamp revenues; title, taxes; item, corporation tax. For a division of the expenditure, an example is as follows: department, Ministry of Construction; organization, ministry proper; item, expenses for road improvement. These examples are the general categories. Each item of revenue and expenditure estimate is further divided into sub-item or sub-sub-item.

The item is the unit for determination by the Diet. For FY 1984 budget about 500 items comprised the list.

Continued Expense Continued expense contains items for which the state makes payments over a period of several fiscal years, the maximum period being five years. These payments are for projects in construction, manufacturing, or other enterprises. Prior Diet approval is required for a continued-expense item, and the Diet specifies the total amount of the expense and the annual allotments.

Approved Carry-over Expense Some expenses in the expenditure budget require disbursement in different fiscal years. This occurs when complete disbursement within the fiscal year is not possible due to the nature of the expense or the circumstances occurring after the formation of the budget. Prior Diet approval is necessary for these carry-over expenses.

Contract Authorization Contract authorization is the Diet approval for the national government to bear certain liabilities. These liabilities are separate and distinct from any liabilities decreed by laws and within regulations. Limits for contract authorization are placed by the extent of amount of the expenditure budget or within the extent of the total amount of the continued expense.

Reserve (for miscellaneous expenses) Under the Public Finance Law, the reserve is not included in the contents of the budget but is a part of the revenue and expenditure budget and is approved by the Diet. The purpose of the reserve is to meet unforeseen deficits in the budget.

The budget is one legislative form of the Diet determination, whereas law is another.

Budget Classification

Three Budget Groupings All of the revenue and expenditure of the state are, as a rule, divided into groups. The general account budget is the principal budget. However, there are 38 special account budgets and 12 government-affiliated agency budgets as of FY 1985. The special account and government-affiliated agency budgets will be referred to in later sections.

(Regular) Budget and Provisional Budget The budget is usually formed and approved before the beginning of each fiscal year. However, events such as the dissolution of the House of Representatives or delays in the Diet's deliberations on the budget may result in failure to approve a budget. To ensure the existence of a budget, the provisional budget system has been devised. The provisional budget is presented for a period from the beginning of a fiscal year until the time the budget is passed. This provisional budget is nullified and absorbed into the budget when the budget is passed.

Initial Budget and Supplementary Budget As a rule, the budget formulation process in the government starts just after the beginning of the previous fiscal year and ends at the end of the calendar year or the beginning of the following year. After budget formulation, additions or changes may occur in the initial budget due to changes in the international situation or in domestic social or economic conditions. In such cases, a supplementary budget is formulated.

Formulation of the Budget

The constitution provides that the Cabinet shall prepare a budget and present it to the Diet. The Public Finance Law provides that the minister of finance shall examine the reports of the estimate of expenditure that are presented by the ministers of the respective ministries. After making adjustments, the minister of finance presents the provisional estimates in order to get the decision of the Cabinet. (See Fig. 4.1.)

The basis for the budget formulation process is the report of estimate (budget request) prepared by each ministry. (Hereafter, the report of estimate will be referred to as ROE.) The ROE is standardized in order to make the process of budget formulation simple and efficient. Standards for the ROE are established by the Ministry of Finance. These standards are presented to the Cabinet for approval. Upon Cabinet approval the ROE standards are sent to each ministry. This notice of the ROE standards is usually sent to the ministries during the last ten days of July.

In each ministry, the preparation of the ROE begins in April and May. Each bureau within a ministry makes a draft of their ROE and presents it to the division in charge of coordinating the budget (e.g., the Accounting Division of the Minister's Secretariat). Each division examines the draft and adjusts it in the light of the Ministry of Finance standards. The divisions prepare their respective ROE for their ministry and the consolidated reports are presented to the Ministry of Finance by the end of August.

All ministry ROEs are received by the Budget Bureau, Ministry of Finance. Deputy budget examiners in the Budget Bureau examine the ROEs and schedule hearings. This examination and hearing process begins in September. Detailed explanations are requested from related divisions of respective ministries where necessary. The hearing process may involve the examination of relevant documents, discussion, and justification for the various expenses. The Budget Bureau divides expenses into current administrative expenses and important expenses related to debatable policies. In October and November the various expenses are screened on three levels: budget examiners, deputy director-general, and director-general. The Budget Bureau presents a draft

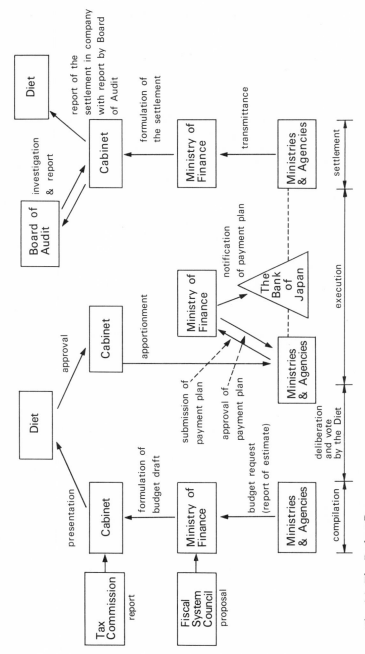

Fig. 4.1. The Budget Process

Source: Ministry of Finance, *The Budget in Brief Japan.*

budget to the minister of finance for review and modification. This review occurs between late November and the beginning of December. The review includes consultation with other ministries, including the Finance Ministry, and the Economic Planning Agency prepares the "economic outlook and the basic attitudes for economic management," which includes the main economic indicators for the next fiscal year.

While the budget review proceeds, other advisory bodies present recommendations regarding fiscal administration. These advisory bodies include the following: the Tax Commission (advisory body to the prime minister); the Fiscal System Council (advisory body to the minister of finance); and the Government Bond Issue Advisory Group (advisory body to the director-general of the Finance Bureau). These bodies present suggestions for tax, budget and government bonds, government-guaranteed bonds, or borrowing. The Cabinet also determines the general principles upon which the budget will be formulated for the following fiscal year's budget.

Toward the end of the calendar year, the Ministry of Finance shows its draft, called the MOF draft, to the respective ministries. In this draft is included the necessary funds for the negotiation for additional appropriations. (In the FY 1985 budget, total expenditure is ¥52,499.6 billion. This necessary fund totaled ¥160 billion with ¥80 billion pending for official negotiations and ¥80 billion unallocated for public works.) This fund is allocated through negotiation for additional appropriations between the Ministry of Finance and the respective ministries. Even after additional appropriations, the total amount of expenditure is the same as that in the MOF draft. The negotiations are conducted on a level-by-level basis. For example, ministry division directors negotiate with deputy budget examiners; directors-general with budget examiners; vice ministers with deputy directors of the Budget Bureau; and each minister of a ministry with the minister of finance. Matters which cannot be settled by ministerial negotiation are decided by the decision of three key officials of the government party: the secretary-general of the party; the executive board chairman; and the policy commission chairman. The ministers concerned, the minister of finance, and the director-general and deputy director of the Budget Bureau also attend the meeting where these matters are decided. The recommendation of the three party officials is subject to approval by the prime minister if necessary. After the various adjustment stages, the provisional estimate is decided by the Cabinet toward the end of the calendar year.

The government party's role in the budget formulation should be discussed. The respective ministries prepare the ROEs after hearing the opinions of the related divisions in the policy commission of the government party. The Ministry of Finance also exchanges opinions with the policy commission. General principles of budget formulation are established by the government party prior to the government formulating the budget. The party's principles are transmitted to the government.

The Ministry of Finance examines each ministry's ROE and prepares the MOF draft. The MOF draft forms the basis for the provisional estimate of the government. This government estimate results after negotiations for additional appropriations between the ministries, the government party, and the Ministry of Finance.

It is quite rare that the budget draft of the government is amended during the process of Diet deliberation. This lack of change results from the system of the parliamentary cabinet. There is so much prior consultation between the government and the government party that by the time of Diet deliberations a consensus has been reached.

The Revenue Budget, the main part of which is tax income, is drafted by the Ministry of Finance based on the economic outlook made by the government after the exchange of opinions regarding the tax system between the Tax Bureau of the Ministry of Finance and the government party and the Tax Commission.

Diet Budget Deliberation

After approval by the Cabinet, the Ministry of Finance prepares the budget, prints the budget book, and submits the budget to the Diet. The budget submission usually occurs toward the end of January.

Diet deliberation on the budget starts in the House of Representatives. After submission to the House, the minister of finance speaks to the House concerning the following matters: (1) principles used in budget formulation; (2) characteristics of the budget and the tax plan; (3) principles of fiscal management; and (4) any special situations regarding fiscal management. On the same day, the same speech is made to the House of Councilors.

The Budget Committee of the House of Representatives deliberates on the budget and makes a recommendation to the full House. The House of Representatives then votes on the budget and passes it on to the House of Councilors, usually in the beginning of March.

The House of Councilors Budget Committee, or related committees that have been commissioned, deliberates. Following a procedure similar to the lower House, the budget is approved by the full House of Councilors around the beginning of the fiscal year, i.e., April 1.

If the House of Councilors decides budget questions that are different from the House of Representatives, the issue is referred to a joint committee of both Houses. In the event that the joint committee cannot agree, the decision of the House of Representatives is the decision of the Diet. In the event that the House of Councilors does not take final action within 30 days after receipt (not including periods of recess), the decision of the House of Representatives is the decision of the Diet.

When the budget contains items for which legislative action is necessary, the government submits bills related to the budget at the time of or immediately following budget submission. These bills are deliberated upon in the various committees concerned in both Houses.

Budget Execution

The expenditure budget is executed mainly according to purpose or by apportionment.

Execution by Purpose Heads of the respective ministries and agencies have the overall responsibility for execution of the expenditure budget. As previously stated, the expenditure budget is divided according to departments, organizations, and items. Each item has an explanation of its purpose and content. Some expense items may be transferred among the appropriations allocated to a specific organization or among respective items under an organization unit. Heads of the respective ministries and agencies cannot use the appropriation of the expenditure budget for purposes other than those provided for in the respective items. For items that are transferred, approval of the minister of finance is required with the prior approval of the Diet. After budget formation, the Cabinet apportions the budget with the various items being divided into sub-items. The heads of ministries or agencies may transfer amounts between sub-items within an item with the approval of the minister of finance.

Execution by Apportionment Heads of the ministries and agencies cannot disburse more than the amount of the apportioned budget. For public-work expenditures and Ministry-of-Finance-designated expenditure, each head, based on the allocated budget, prepares plans for executing his obligations and forwards them to the minister of finance for approval. Obligations mean contracts and other acts which result in disbursement by the government. Heads of the respective ministries and agencies, according to the apportioned budget, prepare quarterly disbursement plans which include necessary amounts of disbursement for each personnel in charge. These plans are then forwarded to the minister of finance for approval. Disbursements are made in accordance with the plans for disbursements. As a rule, they are executed by issuing checks drawn on the Bank of Japan.

Settlement of Accounts

The settlement of revenues and expenditures is made by the minister of finance. This settlement is based on the detailed statement of the reports sent by the heads of the ministries and agencies. The Cabinet passes on the plan for settlement and submits it to the Board of Audit, usually by the end of November of the following fiscal year. The Board of Audit audits the settlement and prepares a report of audit and forwards the results of the examination to the Cabinet. The Cabinet then presents the audited settlement and the report of audit from the Board of Audit to the Diet. This presentation is usually in December. The Diet then submits the reports to the audit committees of both Houses for deliberation.

When there is a surplus in the settlement of accounts, the surplus is transferred to the revenue for the following fiscal year. However, when a shortage of revenue is foreseen before the end of the fiscal year, the deficit can be met by the supplementary budget. If the shortage becomes apparent just before or after the end of the fiscal year, the deficit is financed by transfer of the deficit amount from the settlement adjustment fund to the general account.

Special Accounts and Government-Affiliated Agencies

The Special Accounts

The special account is the part in the national account where a specific revenue meets a specific expenditure. These special accounts are accounted for separately from the general revenue and expenditure to achieve a specific administrative intent. A special account is established by a law authorizing its establishment. Thus a special account is an exception from the viewpoint that the whole financial operation should be surveyable and sound in the overall philosophy of the national finance system.

Thirty-eight special accounts existed at the end of FY 1984. The Public Finance Law states that special accounts be provided under the following three circumstances: (1) a specific state undertaking; (2) state possession and operation of a specific fund; (3) separate accounts from the general revenue and expenditure established by appropriating the specific revenue for the specific expenditure.

Usually special accounts are classified into five groups as shown in Table 4.1. A special account is established when necessary to separate the account from the general revenue and expenditure. Thus a special account is independent from the general account. But much overlap

Table 4.1. Special Accounts (1984)

I. National Undertakings (11)
   Government Undertakings (6)   Public Works (4)
     Mint Bureau   Harbor Improvement
     Printing Bureau   Airport Improvement
     National Forest Service   Road Improvement
     Specific Land Improvement   Flood Control
     Postal Services   Other
     Alcohol Monopoly   Postal Savings

II. Insurances (11)
   Welfare Insurance
   Seamen's Insurance
   National Pensions
   Agricultural Mutual Aid Reinsurance
   Forest Insurance
   Fishing Boat Reinsurance and Fishery Mutual Aid Insurance
   Export Insurance
   Reinsurance of Compensation for Motorcar Accidents
   Postal Life Insurance and Postal Annuity
   Laborer's Insurance
   Earthquake Reinsurance

III. Management (8)
   Foreign Exchange
   National Schools
   National Hospitals
   Foodstuff Control
   Special Measures for Establishment of Landed Farms[1]
   Motorcar Inspection and Registration
   Patent
   Registration[2]

IV. Public Investment and Loans (3)
   Trust Fund Bureau
   Industrial Investment
   Finance for Urban Development

V. Consolidated Funds (5)
   Promotion of Electric Power Resources Development
   Government Bonds Consolidation Fund
   National Property Special Consolidation Fund
   Allotment of Local Allocation Tax and Local Transfer Taxes
   Coal Mining and Petroleum or Alternative Energy to Petroleum Industry

[1] To be changed to Special Measures for Reinforcement of Agricultural Management Condition in FY 1985.

[2] To be established in FY 1985. Machinery Installation Credit Insurance and Opium Special Accounts abolished in FY 1985.

exists between the revenue and expenditure of the general account and the special accounts (e.g., transfers from the general account which are revenues for a special account). In addition, there is much money-flow among those of special accounts. To determine the real size of the state budget, we have to subtract the overlapping amounts between the general account and a special account, or between two special accounts, from the gross total budget. The amounts remaining after subtracting these overlaps from the budget and from the settlement of accounts are called the net total budget and the net total of the settlement of accounts, respectively. For example, in the fiscal 1985 budget, the general account budget amounted to ¥52,499.6 billion; the total revenue of special accounts ¥125,743.7 billion; the total expenditure of special accounts ¥119,530.6 billion; the net total of revenue ¥102,952.4 billion; and the net total expenditure ¥97,102.9 billion.

Government-Affiliated Agencies

A government-affiliated agency is an agency for which the budget and settlement of account are subject to deliberation and approval of the Diet in a way similar to those of the state. All of the government-affiliated agencies are special corporations totally invested by the government. As of April 1985, there were 12 government-affiliated agencies as follows: one public corporation (Japanese National Railways; prior to April 1985, the Japan Tobacco and Salt Corporation and Nippon Telegraph and Telephone were public corporations but they have been converted into private corporations); 9 finance corporations (People's Finance; Housing Loan; Agriculture, Forestry and Fisheries Finance; Small Business Finance; Hokkaidō-Tōhoku Development Corporation; Japan Finance Corporation for Municipal Enterprises; Small Business Credit Insurance; Environmental Sanitation Business Financing; and Okinawa Development Finance; in January 1985, the Medical Care Facilities Financing Corporation was absorbed into the Social Welfare and Medical Care Enterprise); and 2 special banks (Japan Development Bank and the Export-Import Bank of Japan).

A special corporation is a corporation which has been established by a specific law. Ninety-eight (including the 12 government-affiliated agencies) existed as of April 1985. In the documents for reference which accompanied the FY 1985 budget, there are documents showing financial conditions for 56 of the government-invested corporations, in which the government has invested heavily. Many of these corporations are objects of the Fiscal Investment and Loan Program.

The government-affiliated agencies are established separately from the state to raise efficiency through independent organization, personnel, and business management. Since the activities of these agencies are related to public benefits, they are regulated by law, the Diet, and the government. The contents of an agency budget, somewhat different from those of the general and special accounts of the state, are provided according to the characteristics of each agency. The accounting system of these agencies is on an accrual basis. The nine financing corporations are regulated by the Law Concerning the Budget and the Settlement of Accounts of the Financing Corporations.

The Audit System

Fixation of the Settlement of Revenue and Expenditure

The amounts in the settlement of revenue and expenditure are fixed when the accounting book is closed on July 31 of the following fiscal year. Settlement of revenue and expenditure is fixed when the Cabinet decides to send the Board of Audit the draft made by the minister of finance. This transmittal usually occurs in December in the following fiscal year. The finance minister's draft is based on the reports sent from the heads of the respective ministries and agencies. But the settlement is not finished at this stage; it is still subject to audit by the Board of Audit.

Legal Status and Organization of the Board of Audit

The constitution establishes the Board of Audit as an independent organization. The Board of Audit is composed of the Audit Commission and the General Executive Bureau. A commissioner is appointed by the Cabinet and approved by the Diet. The Board of Audit Law provides that a commissioner cannot be dismissed against his will during his seven-year term except in cases of incapacity by mental or corporeal injury.

The Audit Commission consists of three commissioners, each of whom has an equal vote. The president of the Board of Audit is elected by mutual vote by the three commissioners and is appointed by the Cabinet. The Audit Commission is not a fact-finding body. It makes decisions on important matters related to the audit: e.g., the report of audit; enactment of Board of Audit rules; or establishing compensation for irregularities by personnel in charge of accounting or budget execution.

The General Executive Bureau takes charge of the general affairs and audit works under the direction and supervision of the Audit Commission. This bureau consisted of 1,229 persons in 1985. The personnel of the General Executive Bureau fall under the provisions of the National Officials Law, as do general personnel in other ministries. Appointment, dismissal, promotion, and transfer are decided by the president of the Board of Audit, based on the decisions of the Audit Commission. In addition to the status security of the commissioners, the independence with regard to personnel management, the power to enact the Board of Audit rules mentioned above, and some exceptions concerning the examination of the provisional estimate of the expenditure (the same as that of the Diet and the court) guarantee the independence of the organization provided for in the constitution.

The Power of Audit

The audit power of the board encompasses not only the research and report but also the confirmation of the settlement of revenue and expenditure. When, as a result of the audit, violations of law, the budget, or other improper facts are found, the Board of Audit mentions the irregularities in the report of audit. Audit of the settlement is based on the detailed statement of the settlement of revenue and the reports on the settlement of expenditure of the respective ministries and agencies. The audit of the settlement submitted by the Cabinet includes the following: (1) Attested documents on each item submitted by the heads of the respective ministries and agencies; (2) Results of the field audit by the board itself; and (3) the report of receipts and disbursements of cash submitted by the Bank of Japan. In addition, the board also takes charge of auditing at all times and regulates the accounting, checking to see that the accounting is in order and correcting when necessary. The board has both the powers of prior audit and post audit.

In the accounts labeled "matters for necessary audit," accounts of the state and the accounts of corporations in which the state has invested more than half of the capital are included. For accounts of the state, receipts and disbursements of cash, acquisitions and disposal of goods, national properties, and national credits are included. Furthermore, the board may audit, at the board's discretion or at the request of the Cabinet, the accounts of bodies that are granted subsidies, bounties, or such financial assistance as loans from the state, or a government corporation. These additional audits are called "matters for optional audit."

As for the method of audit, there are documentary audits and field audits. The board may request audited bodies to submit accounting books, documents, or reports, or ask questions on facts and request an appearance. It may ask the ministries, public bodies, and other persons for the submission or examination of documents.

Deliberation on the Settlement

The Board of Audit audits and confirms the settlement sent by the Cabinet, based on accompanying documents. It then prepares the report of audit with the approval of the Audit Commission. The board sends the settlement and the report of audit to the Cabinet, which then submits them to the Diet for deliberation. Confirmation of the settlement by the board of audit is the declarative act. This confirmation does not void, totally or partially, the settlement even if parts of the settlement are found to be illegal or improper.

Deliberation in the Diet is done by the Audit Committee. The Board of Audit may explain the report of audit by the appearance of a commissioner or by documents, if the board deems it necessary. The Diet Audit Committee reports the result of its deliberation on the floor. When deliberation ends, the House passes a resolution on the report. This deliberation and resolution on the settlement are merely the deliberation of facts and publication of opinions on the report. It does not reflect the decision of the Diet. Even if the Diet decides that the settlement is illegal or improper, it has no effect on the settlement itself.

5 | The General Account Budget

Seiji Furuta and Ichirō Kanō

The general account budget is the basic account of the nation. When one speaks of a budget, more often than not it means the general account budget, i.e., the general account of revenue and expenditures. The expenditure side of the general account consists of the major programs of the government, such as social security, education and science, national defense, public works, economic cooperation, and measures for small businesses. In this sense, the general account budget directly reflects government policies, i.e., represents the skeletal framework of the nation stripped of its embellishments and disguises of various ideologies.

This chapter deals with the general account budget in terms of the functions or targets being served. (For a discussion of the compilation of the budget and its deliberation in the Diet, see chapter 4.) Expenditures for each program are placed in the single items that best depict the program's major function. (See Table 5.1.)

Social Security

Social security is, needless to say, offered through governmental organizations to guarantee the fundamental necessities of life. This includes assistance to the socially weak; social insurance for various economic difficulties due to illness, aging, and unemployment; and other public welfare services. Social security functions as a kind of public insurance for all of the individuals with heavy burdens due to various causes, and at the same time redistributes personal incomes.

The social security budget recently exceeded ¥9 trillion (Table 5.2). It represented about 18% of the total expenditure of the general account. Social security expenditure is divided into five items: public assistance, social welfare, social insurance, public-health services, and

Table 5.1. General Account Budget by Major Expenditure Programs
(¥ billion)

	1954	1964	1974	1984
1. Social security	[11.2]	[13.2]	[16.9]	[18.4]
	111.9	430.7	2,890.7	9,321.1
2. Education and science	[11.3]	[12.7]	[11.5]	[9.6]
	113.1	413.6	1,963.3	4,866.5
3. Government bonds	[4.0]	[1.4]	[5.0]	[18.1]
	40.2	45.5	862.2	9,155.1
4. Pensions and others	[7.8]	[4.6]	[3.4]	[3.7]
	78.4	151.3	584.3	1,885.9
5. Local finance	[12.6]	[19.1]	[19.8]	[17.9]
	—	621.4	—	9,069.3
(Local allocation tax)	(125.6)	—	(3,382.3)	(8,886.4)
6. National defense	[13.3]	[9.3]	[6.4]	[5.8]
	132.6	300.7	1,093.0	2,934.6
7. Public works	[15.3]	[19.5]	[16.6]	[12.9]
	152.8	635.8	2,840.7	6,520.0
(general public works)				(6,313.9)
8. Economic cooperation	[1.8]	[0.3]	[1.0]	[1.1]
	17.5	10.7	166.0	543.9
9. Small-scale business	—	[0.5]	[0.6]	[0.4]
	—	16.6	102.1	229.2
10. Energy measures	—	—	—	[1.2]
	—	—	—	603.1
11. Foodstuff control	[1.7]	[4.0]	[4.2]	[1.6]
	17.2	128.9	713.2	813.2
12. Miscellaneous	[20.2]	[14.5]	[12.9]	[8.6]
	201.4	470.4	2,209.6	4,335.3
13. Reserves for public works	—	—	—	—
14. Reserves	[0.8]	[0.9]	[1.5]	[0.7]
	8.0	30.0	260.0	350.0
Total	[100.0]	[100.0]	[100.0]	[100.0]
	999.6	3,255.4	17,099.4	50,627.2

Note: The figures in brackets are the share of the total. The item 11 in 1954 represents expenditures for agricultural insurance.

Source: Expenditures are based on initial budget figures. Ministry of Finance, *The Budget in Brief Japan*, for years tabulated.

measures for the unemployed. Among these, the ratio of social insurance to social security is the highest and continues to increase. The social welfare ratio is also increasing, while those of the other items are decreasing. This is because as the nation becomes more affluent,

Table 5.2. Social Security (General Account) (¥ billion, %)

	1964		1974		1984	
Public assistance	91.8	21.3	443.0	15.3	1,139.4	12.2
Social welfare	37.2	8.7	431.2	14.9	1,999.2	21.5
Social insurance	163.6	38.0	1,659.6	57.4	5,347.9	57.4
Public health service	78.5	18.2	217.9	7.6	467.0	5.0
Measures for the unemployed	59.5	13.8	139.1	4.8	367.5	3.9
Total	430.6	100.0	2,890.8	100.0	9,321.0	100.0

Note: Expenditures are based on initial budget figures.
Source: Same as Table 5.1.

people want more comprehensive insurances and a higher quality of welfare services, rather than the programs for the poor that were provided in the past.

Public Assistance

Public assistance is provided for in the constitution and is divided into seven categories: subsistence, housing, education, medical care, maternity, occupation, and funeral services. Local governments provide office work for the above, using grants transferred from the general account. Both assistance for subsistence and medical care carry the largest weight among the seven categories. The minimum living standard for public assistance is determined annually by the minister of health and welfare, taking both consumption and price trends into consideration. (In 1984, the standard was ¥152,960 per month for a family of four, a couple with two children.)

Social Welfare

Based on related measures such as for children, the physically handicapped, the mentally retarded, and the aged, four basic activities are covered by the social welfare system: (1) free medical care for the aged, administration of old people's homes, improvement of employment opportunities for the aged, and financial support to local activities assisting the aged, (2) income maintenance of various kinds, rehabilitation of the old and sick, home-help services, and special allowance payments for the handicapped, (3) income assistance for the children of poor families and for single-parent families, and (4) measures for several kinds of intractable diseases.

Social Insurance

Social insurance, the core of social security, is a public institution of mutual assistance supported by the receipts of compulsory contributions. These can be classified into four categories: medical-care insurance, public pensions, unemployment insurance, and workers' accident compensation insurance. The program was instituted before World War II, but it was not until 1961 that it became compulsory.

Medical-care insurance should, in principle, be operated on the insurance premiums paid by employees and employers. However, some insurance is assisted by the government, depending on the financial statuses of the various programs. For instance, both Health Insurance and Day Laborers' Insurance suffer from accumulated deficits, thus both receive substantial subsidies transferred from the government every year. Also, National Health Insurance, whose recipients are mostly the aged and people in a low-income category, is heavily subsidized by the government. The recent amounts of transfer were about ¥0.5 trillion to Health Insurance, and ¥2 trillion to National Health Insurance, the latter of which was a quarter of the total social security expense.

Medical-care expenses have doubled every five years since 1961, the year that all citizens joined the system. This has seriously affected the financing of other insurances: Their premiums have had to be raised, placing a greater burden on the people. Furthermore, it has been pointed out that this also leads to social waste in terms of resource allocation. Thus, the very concept of public insurance is now under discussion as to how the burden should be borne.

The Employees' Pension and the National Pension are the two major types of public pension schemes. The former is for employees of businesses, with about 25 million subscribers, and is financed by the employees (40%), the businesses (40%), and the government (20%). The latter is for non-employees and is composed of about 27 million subscribers. Of the latter, the government pays one-third of the expenses of contributory pension, the operating costs (¥0.8 trillion), and the expenses of the non-contributory pension (¥1 trillion).

Before mutual-aid associations were established in 1958, there was a pension scheme for civil and military personnel. In this old pension, a public employee who retired due to injury or illness or who died during a work period was paid a pension. Since 1959, the scheme was replaced by the associations, and there have been no new recipients since. Most of the old pension is now composed of aid to war-bereaved families of the unrepatriated.

Health and Sanitation

Central government expenses are primarily for the cure of intractable diseases, medical facilities for remote areas, and the training of nurses. All other aspects of public health and sanitation are covered by local governments using grants-in-aid.

Employment

The employment policy, originally to improve the conditions of the unemployed, has enlarged its scope in three directions: (1) the prevention of unemployment and the increase in opportunities for employment; (2) the improvement of the standard of living of the unemployed; and (3) a policy for the jobless to find employment. The last consists of two policies: one for the jobless in general, and the other for the aged, the handicapped, and specific regions or industries.

The core of the anti-unemployment policy is Employment Insurance, which developed out of the former unemployment insurance in 1975, in order to meet the serious unemployment situation caused by the first oil crisis in 1973. The present insurance has raised the rate of allowance (60 to 80 % of daily wages) and, for the benefit of old people, extended the duration of benefits in proportion to age. In the same year, Employment Adjustment Funds were established to cover part of the salaries of the unemployed. In order to promote their employment, the ratio of employment of the aged and the handicapped has been set by the government. Businesses also are assisted by the government in various ways. The Employer Security Fund, for instance, provides a training program for those changing their line of specialization.

Education and Science

No one would deny that education is the primary foundation for the recent industrial and cultural developments of the nation. And today's industrial success is also supported by the remarkable development of science and technology. Thus, the promotion of education and science is considered to be absolutely necessary in order to enhance the national welfare. (See Table 5.3.)

Education

The education budget is about 9 % of the general account; one of the largest items is compulsory education grants. Half of the salary of all teachers and school staff and of expenses for teaching materials used in compulsory education is, according to the law, borne by the national treasury. Futhermore, costs for public school facilities are appropriated for in the education budget. Also included in the budget are the ex-

Table 5.3. Education and Science (General Account) (¥ billion, %)

	1964		1974		1984	
Compulsory education expenses	204.7	49.5	921.2	46.9	2,302.6	47.3
Expenses of public school facilities	18.1	4.4	156.9	8.0	427.3	8.8
School education assistance	25.1	6.1	146.4	7.5	567.9	11.7
Transfer to the National Schools Special Account	114.5	27.7	448.1	22.8	1,071.7	22.0
Scholarship loans for students	8.6	2.0	28.7	1.5	86.2	1.8
Promotion of science and technology	42.6	10.3	261.9	13.3	410.8	8.4
Total	413.6	100.0	1,963.3	100.0	4,866.5	100.0

Note: Expenditures are based on initial budget figures.
Source: Same as Table 5.1.

penses for free textbooks (started in 1963), tuition aids to children of low-income families, education in remote rural areas, night schools, correspondence courses, education for the handicapped, school lunches, school health plans, and kindergarten education.

There are 93 national universities, 35 national colleges, advanced training schools, graduate schools, and schools attached to the universities. These expenses are financed by the Special Account for National Schools, which, in turn, is supported by transfers from the general account revenues of university hospitals and issued debt, as well as tuition. Not only for public schools, but also for private schools, there are various kinds of assistance: for the improvement of education and research facilities and for the operating costs of private universities. Long-term low-interest loans are also provided through the Japan Private School Promotion Foundation. Scholarship loans are awarded by the Japan Scholarship Foundation to cover part of the school expenses of students. Since 1944, more than 3 million students have been granted this kind of loan. There are some expenses for social and physical education, too.

Promotion of Science and Technology

This budget is allocated to basic research of space and ocean, and large-scale computers and technology. The funds are used, for instance, to develop a system of large rockets for communication or weather satellites by the National Space Development Agency of Japan, and ocean development by the Ocean Science Technology Center. Others are recycling of resources, economic applications of ultra-advanced lasers, multiproduct production, new measurement and control systems, new production method of fundamental chemicals, mining methods of manganese mass, high-speed computation systems for science and technology, development of new generation computers, and Antarctic observation.

Public Works

Among the important roles of the public administration, there are improvements of social capital or social infrastructures used for the public and industry. Providing the social capital has a long history as seen in embankment works of old times. Unlike the daily public services, it can be undertaken as social investment providing long-run benefits so that it is financed by the national debt as an exception of the Public Finance Law. Most of the expenditures for social capital formation are classified as public works expenses. However, the expenditures for school facilities are grouped as education and science.

Public works, the next largest item in the social security budget, covers a wide variety of activities, changing their focus in accordance with the needs of the public. Until 1955, most works were for river and forestry improvements and disaster relief. Between 1955 and 1965, expenses for road improvements increased to 30 or 40% of the total of public works. This has, of course, facilitated the rapid economic growth of the nation. Since that period, the weight has been shifted to a large extent to a steady though slow improvement of living conditions, such as sewage systems and housing programs. (See Table 5.4.)

Housing

The three fundamental factors in our lives are food, clothing, and housing. Due to the scarcity of land and a heavy population density, Japan's standard of housing is rather low. Immediately after the war, in order to cope with the absolute shortage of housing, public housing construction was rapidly undertaken by local governments and the Japan Housing Corporation. At present, there are programs administered by local governments for low-income housing as well as by the Housing Loan Corporation for privately owned housing.

Table 5.4. Public Works (General Account) (¥ billion, %)

	1964		1974		1984	
General public works						
Erosion and flood control	102.0	16.1	445.2	15.7	1,098.5	16.8
Road improvement	274.8	43.2	1,030.1	36.3	1,873.0	28.7
Port, harbor, and airport improvement	46.7	7.3	239.6	8.4	519.8	8.0
Housing	30.0	4.7	245.5	8.6	766.4	11.7
Public amenities	8.8	1.4	275.0	9.7	980.3	15.0
Improvement of conditions for agricultural production	77.2	12.1	347.6	12.2	891.9	13.7
Forest roads and water supply for industrial use, etc.	32.8	5.2	72.1	2.5	173.2	2.7
Reserve for adjustment	0.7	0.1	13.8	0.5	10.9	0.2
Subtotal	573.0	90.1	2,668.8	93.9	6,313.9	(96.8)
Disaster reconstruction	62.7	9.9	171.9	6.1	206.1	3.2
Total	635.7	100.0	2,840.7	100.0	6,520.0	100.0

Note: Expenditures are based on initial budget figures.
Source: Same as Table 5.1.

Public Amenities

Among the core of improvements in public amenities, there is the sewage system. It has long been said that the sewage system, as well as the other kinds of social capital of the nation, is behind the standard of developed nations. For this reason, sewage improvement has been emphasized since 1965. The target has been set at about 44% of all homes to be installed with flush toilets by the end of 1985 (estimates at the end of 1980, about 30%). Furthermore, there are additional public investments in city parks, water supplies, and industrial waste facilities.

Roads

Roads are generally regarded as an indispensable social capital for the public and industry, and are recognized as a necessity in almost every public opinion poll. There are four types of roads: 1) freeways for automobiles, 2) national roads, 3) prefectural roads, and 4) local community roads. Most of the freeways are not free, however, being planned to become free after the whole payment for the construction costs is made. A plan of the nation's roads improvement was begun in 1954 with the First Roads Improvement Program of five years. Thus, the paved-road ratio increased from 3.1% in 1960 to 47.6% in 1980. Specifically, the ratio of both the national and prefectural roads has gone to 84.9% from 11.9% of those days. The expenses for road construction other than freeways are financed as earmarked revenue sources by the gasoline tax and the petroleum gas tax.

Ports, Harbors, and Airports

The nation enjoys extremely long coastlines and many good ports and harbors. These serve as a major social capital for international trade of the nation. There are 1,085 harbors (1980) administered by various municipalities. About ¥250 billion is transferred each year from the general account to the Special Account for Harbor Improvement. There is also a growing demand for more efficient air transportation because of the advent of larger and faster airplanes. Thus, more weight has been placed recently on airport improvements. The New Tokyo Airport at Narita is administered by the New Tokyo International Airport Authority and other major airports by each municipality. The Special Account for Airport Improvement is financed by transfers from the general account, a part of which comes from the aviation fuel tax and the airport user charge.

Prevention of and Recovery from Disaster

The nation is often struck by such disasters as typhoons and earthquakes, and prevention measures and recovery preparations are needed for the national welfare. For this purpose, improvements in forestry, rivers, and coastline have been promoted by five-year plans. The forestry conservation program consists mainly of replantation of abandoned forests and planting forests for flood control, water preservation, and landslide prevention. The flood control program consists of constructing various types of dams, such as river embankments, sand arrestations, and multipurpose dams. The coastal improvement program consists mainly of constructing coast banks and other related facilities.

Improvement of Basic Conditions for Agriculture

This item of the budget is to facilitate productivity, selective growth of the produce, and structural changes in agriculture, directed toward developing and improving farmland and collective production. This is a part of the total agricultural policy whose aim is toward adapting Japan's agricultural structure to demand changes and at improving self-sustenance rates of food in the nation. The major activities are directed to irrigation, farmland improvement, farm road improvement, prevention of farm disasters, and the development of farmland. Others are, for instance, forest road improvements, national afforestation, assistances for private afforestation, improvements of industrial waterways, pumping-up underground water for industrial use, and developing fishing grounds for the fishery.

Energy

Since the first oil crisis of 1973, the importance of natural resources and energy has commanded national recognition. In terms of natural resources and energy, the nation is almost entirely dependent on foreign sources. Therefore, to secure a stable supply of both natural resources and energy in the long run is a "life or death" problem for the nation. As for energy measures, focus is placed on the development of substitute energy, technology for energy-saving, and exploitation of petroleum resources. There is, for instance, the development of atomic energy being done by the Japan Atomic Energy Research Institute and the Power Reactor and Nuclear Fuel Development Corporation. Research on solar energy, terrestrial heat, coal energy, and hydrogen energy is also being pursued. As for energy conservation, developments of the reutilization system of abandoned heat, magneto hydrodynamics power (MHP) generation, and highly efficient gas turbines are all being studied. Also, trials of exploitation of petroleum resources are now being undertaken by the Petroleum Public Corporation.

Foodstuff Control

This item includes expenses of transfers to the Foodstuff Special Account. The Foodstuff Account was started in 1921 to resolve, by indirectly controlling rice prices, the social unrest caused by the rapid hike in rice prices. During the war, as a part of the regulation due to the war economy, direct control of rice prices was introduced, a policy that continues to the present day. During and after the war, the purpose was to assure adequate supplies of rice and wheat. Since around 1965, however, price control serves to protect the agriculture of the nation, which is obviously fragile compared to the industrial sector. The Foodstuff Account buys rice at higher prices and sells it at lower prices; the difference, i.e., the deficit, is covered by the general account. This problem has been reviewed critically as one of the inefficiencies of the government sector. Higher incomes have brought about changes in eating habits, and recently the demand for rice has been declining sharply. The highest per capita consumption was 118.3 kg in 1962, and it went as low as 79.8 kg in 1979. The total demand for rice decreased from 13 million tons in 1962 to 11 million tons in 1979. Until 1965, rice production was below the domestic demand; overproduction began after 1967, causing a problem in surplus supplies of old rice. Improvements in soil and seed, and the annual hike in rice prices were the direct causes of the surplus rice supplies. Then, programs for production adjustment and for rice surplus management, expending ￥1 trillion each, resulted in temporarily restoring the balance of demand and supply. However, the surplus rice problem persisted. Since 1978, a ten-year plan for the reutilization of rice fields, assisting and promoting the planting of other kinds of crops has been in operation.

Economic Cooperation

Today, no one denies the fact that one of the major problems of the international political economy is what is called the North-South problem. With international cooperation among the advanced nations, the economic cooperation for developing nations has continued in order to resolve the problem. Especially after the first oil crisis, the economic difficulties of the non-oil-producing developing nations were so great that the request for economic assistance has been very urgent. At the Third UN Conference of Trade and Development (UNCTAD) in 1972, a resolution was passed that the assistance target by each industrial nation should be about 1% of GNP, of which 0.7% of GNP should be regarded as Official Development Aid (ODA) till the mid-1970s. In 1979, the net expenditure amounted to around U.S.$7.5 billion, 0.75% of GNP of the nation. Japan, with this amount, ranks fourth, following the United States, the United Kingdom, and West Germany. Also, Japan's ODA in 1979 was about U.S.$2.6 billion, 0.26% of GNP, which also places it fourth.

As the national economy continues to grow, the nation must bear more responsibility for making a contribution toward the international economy and society. This budget is, thus, treated as an exception, despite the recent stringent situation of the general account budget. Moreover, since 1981, the mid-term target has been set to double the ODA in five years. More than 40% of the ODA funds comes from the general account. The rest is financed by the fund of Fiscal Investment and Loan Program and national bonds. These are directed to international agencies for development investment and to yen-based loans. The yen-based loans are offered by the Overseas Economic Cooperation Fund and the Export-Import Bank of Japan.

National Defense

Considerable efforts have been made to improve the nation's defense power within the framework of the constitution. The intent is that the nation shall contribute to stabilizing the international order, and to maintain the nation's peace and independence. For this purpose, the nation's principle for defense is to abide by the Japan-U.S. Security Treaty and to improve the efficiency of defense within the range of self-defense. After 1977, a defense improvement program was advanced, based on the general principle of the defense plan, which was decided at a Cabinet and defense meeting in 1976. Also, a resolution was made to limit the total amount of annual defense budget to 1% of GNP. As a consequence, the ratio of defense budget to GNP is still significantly lower than that of any other major nation.

Modernization of Small Businesses

In Japan, the ratio of small-scale businesses (as a rule, businesses with capitals under ¥100 million and under 300 employees) is 99.4% in terms of the number of whole businesses, of employees, 81.1% (1978), of production shipment, 53.2%, and of industrial product export, 34.8% (1979). Thus, it might be well said that small businesses play an important role in the economy and that their growth implies a basis for activation of the national economy. Today, business circumstances, such as the slow economy, financial difficulties, and increases in costs, are not necessarily favorable to businesses. Therefore, financial assistance provided by government organizations has helped small businesses adjust themselves with their own strength to economic and social changes.

These are divided into two parts: giving useful instruction to, promoting modernization of, and reorganizing the small businesses, and loans by the governmental financial institutions. The former includes expenses for training programs of the businesses, economic aid to chambers of commerce and industry leading to the better management of businesses, and expenses for reorganizing businesses. As for the latter, the long-term low-interest loans are provided by the People's Finance Corporation, the Small Business Finance Corporation, and the Shoko Chukin Bank (Central Co-operative Bank for Commerce and Industry) utilizing the Fiscal Investment and Loan Program Fund. Other measures are for supplementary credit insurance of the businesses, retired persons, and the mutual assistance in case of bankruptcy and its prevention. Transfers of this kind from the general account are made for loan funds and interest-aids available to the government-affiliated financial institutions.

Local Finance

The local allocation tax is transferred from the national government to most of the local governments without specifying its use. Each locality has a different economic background, making differences in the amount of tax revenues among each of them. If a certain level of public service is expected by the public in each locality, it is often the case that some local governments lack the revenue to meet the standard need of the services. This gap is then filled with national grants, which are called local finance expenses. The local allocation tax consists of 32% of the total amount of personal and corporate income taxes and the liquor tax revenues. Each local government has its own grants ratio to the total budget, according to its standard need and its amount of tax revenue. There is also an extra allocation grant from the nation to specific regions, such as Okinawa, to render financial assistance. After the first oil crisis, the total revenue of the three major taxes has gone down drastically, while inflation has raised the local service expenses. Thus, the deficit of almost all local financing has become very significant during the period. To solve this issue, the special account takes the loan fund from the general account and, in turn, transfers it to the deficit communities. See chapters 9 and 10 for details on local finance.

Government Bonds

From 1948 on, there was no bond issue due to the principle of the Public Finance Law. A new bond issue, however, was started in 1965 to make up for a decline in tax revenues. Thereafter, based on Article 4(1) of the Public Finance Law, construction bonds have been issued. Moreover, since 1975 a special bond, which is often called the deficit-covering bond has been issued to cover the expenses of current services. Thus, the outstanding bond debt of the general account has grown larger each year to reach more than ¥120 trillion in 1984. The bond account has, therefore, grown enormously to deal with the above amount. It is well known that this causes considerable inflexibility in the budgeting of the general account and is a source of much criticism. (See chapter 8.)

6 | The Government Credit Program and Public Enterprises

Hiromitsu Ishi

In addition to its fiscal activities, such as tax collection, borrowing, and public spending, the government also finances loans in credit programs and manages the public enterprises. This chapter analyzes the so-called off-budget scope of government activities. In the first three sections, the basic function of the government credit program is discussed in historical perspective. The fourth section describes the present organization of non-financial public corporations and enterprises.

The Fiscal Investment and Loan Program (FILP): An Overview

Purpose and Scope

The fundamental role of the government is to collect taxes, borrow money, and provide public goods and services. Apart from these activities, the government operates the financial functions of capital investments and loans, mainly at the national level. For example, postal savings, public pension funds, and insurance funds are all important financial sources besides tax revenues, and they can be used to make loans and to invest in government enterprises for the promotion of specific policy objectives.

To foster investment and loan money, the government has constructed a credit program called the Fiscal Investment and Loan Program (FILP). The FILP provides a comprehensive instrument for government investment and loans, financed by the special sources mentioned above. This program is not a budget, but the FILP is considered as important as the general budget. Therefore, each year the FILP is compiled and presented to the Diet in the same period as the regular budgets (i.e., the general and special accounts, government-affiiliated budgets).[1] The FILP provides financing for the investments of government enterprises (including some local governments). It also makes loans to selected categories of private business that are regarded as having special importance for the purpose of development and social policy or to fund projects that cannot find adequate financing in the private sector. Most government loans to private enterprises are administered through a variety of special banks or finance corporations.[2]

Figure 6.1 is a graphic presentation of the FILP and its sources and

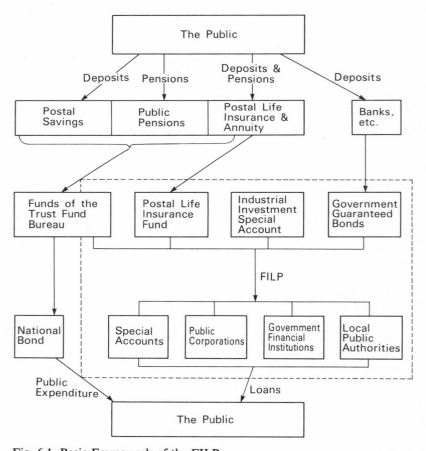

Fig. 6.1. Basic Framework of the FILP
Note: The area enclosed by the dotted line indicates the scope of the FILP.

uses. The major sources raised from the public are postal savings, public pensions, and postal life insurance. These sources combined with the financing by bonds are placed in the following four funds.

(1) Funds of the Trust Fund Bureau: postal savings and public pensions (e.g., National Pension, Employees' Pension), which are collected from the private sector and reserved in related special accounts, are deposited in this fund.

(2) Postal Life Insurance Fund: Postal life insurance and postal annuity also form a reserved fund, which is channeled through special accounts.

(3) Industrial Investment Special Account: The investments, not the loans of the FILP, are made through this special account to which the general account of the government transfers the funds.

(4) Government Guaranteed Bonds and Borrowings: Domestic bonds are issued by some government enterprises and public corporations to raise money from private financial institutions. The payment of both principal and interest are guaranteed by the government.

Once the funds are collected from the private sector in various forms, the FILP dispenses them through four channels to the public, mainly in the form of loans. As indicated in Figure 6.1 they are: (1) special accounts (e.g., National Forest Service Special Account, National School Special Account), (2) public corporation (The Japanese National Railways), (3) government financial institutions (see the list in Table 6.3), and (4) local public authorities.

What is important in Figure 6.1 is the limited scope of the FILP in the areas surrounded by the dotted line. A portion of funds of the Trust Bureau Fund is devoted to the purchase of national bonds directly from the general account,[3] and the flow of this fund is out of the FILP. This allocation of funds has expanded recently, reflecting the difficulty of selling large amounts of national bonds in the financial markets.

Tables 6.1 and 6.2 indicate the size of the FILP relative to the general account and the GNP for 30 years. In 1953, the FILP was 33.4% of the size of the general account and 4.5% of the GNP. Its percentage relative to the general account rose to nearly 50% in 1972, immediately before the outbreak of the first oil crisis. Thereafter, this percentage began to diminish, mainly because funds from the Trust Fund Bureau were used to purchase substantial amounts of national bonds, not to make loans or investments through public corporations and government financial institutions. However, the present level remains higher than in 1953. The size of the FILP as a percentage of GNP continued to increase over a long period and reached a high of 7.7% in 1982.

Table 6.1. The FILP Compared with the General
Account Budget (¥ billion; %)

Year	General account budget	FILP	FILP as percentage of G.A. budget
1953	965.5	322.8	33.4
1960	1,569.7	606.9	38.7
1965	3,658.1	1,620.6	44.3
1970	7,949.7	3,579.9	45.0
1972	11,467.6	5,635.0	49.1
1974	17,099.4	7,923.4	46.3
1976	24,296.0	10,619.0	43.7
1978	34,295.0	14,887.6	43.4
1980	42,588.8	18,179.9	42.7
1982	49,680.8	20,288.8	40.8
1984	50,627.2	21,106.6	41.7

Note: Budget and FILP figures are for the original budget and the initial plan.
Source: Ministry of Finance, *The Budget in Brief Japan* for years tabulated.

Table 6.2. The FILP Compared with GNP (¥ billion; %)

Year	GNP	FILP	FILP as% of GNP
1953	7,526.4	337.4	4.5
1960	16,207.0	625.1	3.9
1965	33,550.2	1,776.4	5.3
1970	75,091.6	3,799.0	5.1
1972	96,424.0	6,037.8	6.3
1974	138,044.6	9,037.8	6.5
1976	172,090.0	11,217.9	6.6
1978	206,762.5	14,020.7	6.8
1980	240,847.0	18,103.6	7.5
1982	267,350.9	20,603.7	7.7
1983	279,500.0	20,718.6	7.4

Note: Figures for GNP and FILP are actual amounts except for 1983, which shows estimates for GNP and planned expenditures for the FILP.
Source: Same as Table 6.1.

Obviously, the importance of the FILP has increased relative to the size of the national economy.

Sources

Let us investigate the movement of each source in the FILP. Figure 6.2 presents figures for the different sources for selected years in terms of percent distribution. There are two phenomena worth noting: one is the continuous increase in the size of the Trust Fund Bureau; the other is the sharp decline in the share of the Industrial Investment Special Account. When the FILP was established (1953), the share of the Trust Fund Bureau was less than 50%. This share steadily increased up to 84.1% in 1980 and thereafter declined to 76.5% in 1983,

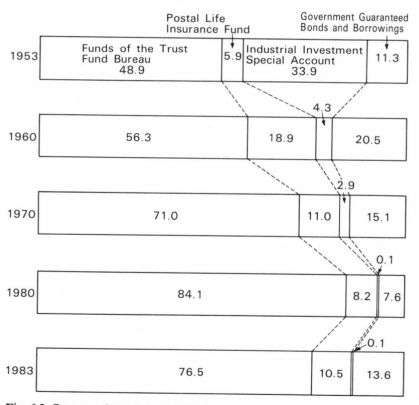

Fig. 6.2. Sources of Funds in the FILP
Source: Ministry of Finance, *Zaisei kin'yū tōkei geppō.*

mainly reflecting the expanded purchases of national bonds. In contrast, the role of collecting funds of the Industrial Investment Special Account (IISA) decreased in importance. Its relative size declined from 33.9% in 1953 to nearly nil in 1983. The Postal Life Insurance Fund and the Government Guaranteed Bonds and Borrowings now share a substantial portion of the total fund, although the relative importance of the two funds has varied from year to year.

FILP funds must be allocated to revenue-producing projects through government financial institutions. Because FILP funds are financed from sources on which interest must be paid, say, postal savings accounts, the FILP is required by law to make loans on a profitable basis. This requirement is different from the principles of government expenditures that are financed by tax revenues. However, funds in the FILP can be employed in less profitable areas to accomplish special policy objectives (e.g., housing, urban renewal, regional development), supported by interest subsidies from tax sources.

In addition, long-term (i.e., over five years) financing and loans are annually included in the FILP. The shorter-term loans are not part of the FILP, although there are a number of short-term capital investments and loans in both the general government and several special accounts.

Uses

Funds collected from various sources are used for loans and investments to the private sector. This is the use side of the FILP, which is operated by special agencies relevant to the FILP. These special agencies are often called the Fiscal Investment and Loan agencies (FIL agencies) which now total 48 in number. In Figure 6.1, they were classified into four groups on the use side of FILP, but Figure 6.3 shows the movement of fund allocations by the FIL agencies in more detailed groupings. In contrast to Figure 6.1, the scope of public corporations is only limited to the Japanese National Railways. The remainder (e.g., *kōdan*, *jigyōdan*) are included in "Other public corporations." Special companies (e.g., Japan Air Lines Co., Ltd.) are listed as "Others," as are foundations (*kikin*) and associations (*kyōkai*).

Three points are worth noting in Figure 6.3. First, government financial institutions have maintained the largest share among fund recipients, and their share has increased since 1953. In recent years more than 50% of the funds in the FILP is channeled through these agencies. Second, the sharp rise of the share for other public corporations can be observed from the 1960s to the 1970s, reflecting the establishment of many new *kōdan* and *jigyōdan* during this period. Third, the fund

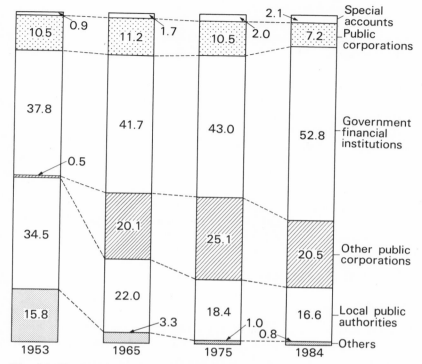

Fig. 6.3. The Fund Allocation of the FIL Agencies (%)
Source: Same as Fig. 6.2.

allocation to local public authorities has gradually decreased although it was ranked second largest in 1953.

What are the specific objectives of the allocation of FILP funds? According to an official classification of the Ministry of Finance (MOF),[4] the objectives are grouped into 12 categories with special reference to specific policy targets:

(1) housing;
(2) public amenities;
(3) social welfare;
(4) education;
(5) small-scale industry;
(6) agriculture, forestry, and fishing;
(7) national land preservation;
(8) roads;

(9) transportation and telecommunications;

(10) regional development;

(11) key industries; and

(12) international trade and cooperation.

The following four objectives are often employed as a broader classification:

(I) Areas that improve the standards of life (1–6);

(II) Areas that preserve the nation's infrastructure (7–10);

(III) Industrial development (11); and

(IV) Foreign trade (12).

Percentage distributions in 1984 for the four categories were as follows: I, 69.7%; II, 21.2%; III, 3.0%; and IV, 6.1%. Category I has increased from 38.2% in 1953 to the present level of 69.7%. Categories II and III have decreased in importance since 1953. In particular, industrial development has fallen from 29.1% in 1953 to 3.0% in 1984. Category IV has remained about at the same percentage level for the last two decades.

Historical Background of the FILP

Prewar Period

The FILP was established in 1953, the year after Japan regained its independence. The idea of the FILP as established was unprecedented, but its historical basis dates from the Meiji era, from the postal savings system in 1875.[5] The Postal Bureau of the Ministry of Home Affairs operated a system enabling the general public to deposit money in savings accounts at post offices.[6] This scheme was part of a government campaign to raise funds and stimulate the economy. The savings collected at the post offices were controlled by the Ministry of Finance in the Yokinbu.[7] The Yokinbu, which is the predecessor to the FILP, was merely one of the government's special accounts.

Before the twentieth century, postal savings were used only to secure national bonds. In 1907, the functions of the Yokinbu were expanded to include: loans to the general and special accounts, collateral for local bonds and for special bank bonds. The Yokinbu continued to increase in size, particularly around the time of the two world wars when the fund grew enormously. Using these expanded funds, the government began to make grants and loans to munitions companies and key industries, such as iron and steel.

Of special interest is the sharp increase in postal savings during the

1930s. Small savers (e.g., farmers, workers, and owners of small enterprises) tended to put their money into postal savings accounts for two reasons. They feared defaults by private banks in the great depression after the panic of 1927. The other reason was the patriotic appeal to co-operate with wartime national policies. The increase in postal savings occurred in spite of interest rates lower than the private sector.

In 1944, government pension funds were added to postal savings in the government fund. These new funds were from employee pension funds which were established to provide old age, disability, and death insurance for workers.

Apart from postal savings and pensions, another important development was the emergence of special banks. These banks were charged with promoting economic development and include the following: Kangyō Bank of Japan (1897); Hokkaidō Development Bank (1899); and Industrial Bank of Japan (1902). Of the three, the Industrial Bank of Japan played the largest role.

The Industrial Bank was franchised by the special law of March 1900. Its major purpose was to meet the strong demand for long-term capital needed by joint-stock companies. This demand was related to the proliferation of joint-stock companies around the time of the Russo-Japanese War (1904–5). The Industrial Bank generated revenues by selling its government-guaranteed bonds at home and abroad and played an important role in the financing of Japan's industrial development.

Similarly, other special banks had the same purpose and function as the Industrial Bank. For example, the 1906 bond issue of the Kangyō Bank was purchased by the Yokinbu, and special loans were made to help the less-developed Tōhoku area when a bad harvest caused financial difficulties.

Postwar Reforms

During the American occupation (1945–52), a variety of postwar reforms were instituted in politicial, economic, and social spheres by the Supreme Commander for the Allied Powers (SCAP). Government investment and loan programs were subject to crucial changes.[8]

Most important to economic recovery was the Reconstruction Finance Bank (RFB). The RFB was established as a department within the Industrial Bank and in the following year became an independent special legal entity. The major task of the RFB was to make loans to industries essential for economic reconstruction[9]—coal, fertilizers, electric power, iron and steel—using funds obtained by selling RFB bonds to the Bank of Japan (BOJ). Strong inflationary pressure was built up by the extensive money creation, and it resulted in a tremendous price hike which was labeled the "RFB inflation."[10]

Inflation was finally halted as part of the Dodge Plan reforms, which were adopted by Joseph M. Dodge, an advisor to the SCAP, in 1949.[11] The Dodge Plan prohibited the RFB from issuing bonds, and three years later the RFB was dissolved. In 1952, the RFB was absorbed by the Japan Development Bank (JDB). The Industrial Bank, from which the RFB emerged, was transformed into an ordinary long-term credit bank for the industry at the request of the SCAP in 1948. The nature and functions of the Industrial Bank and the RFB were quite controversial among the American advisors to the SCAP.

During the occupation period, U.S. aid was also very important. Until 1949, when Dodge first came to Japan, the United States provided Japan with about $1.2 billion worth of commodities purchased in America with Government and Relief in Occupied Area (GARIOA) and Economic Rehabilitation in Occupied Area (EROA) funds. These commodities were sold by the Japanese government and the yen proceeds were deposited in the Foreign Trade Fund Special Account.

Dodge renewed this special account for the U.S. Aid Counterpart Fund in 1949, mainly because the U.S. government wanted to know how its aid was used and how its money was being spent. Dodge and the SCAP were irritated upon learning that the Japanese government used this aid to finance the RFB and thus induce inflation. This counterpart fund was maintained until 1953 and thereafter was renamed the Industrial Investment Special Account. This account is now a part of the FILP (see Figure 6.1) and is supplied with direct appropriations from the general account.

The SCAP instituted several financial innovations. Among these was the creation of the Export Bank of Japan and the JDB in 1950 and 1951.[12] The SCAP recognized the importance of providing long-term credit to exporters of heavy industrial equipment for export expansion. This meant that banks would contribute to Japan's earning more foreign currency. Dodge agreed to establish a special bank to promote Japan's exports subject to the following restrictions: it should not compete with private banks, and the government was to supply the capital instead of issuing bonds or borrowing. Based upon these ideas, the Export Bank of Japan Law was passed by the Diet in 1950, and the Export Bank of Japan began business with an authorized capital of ¥15 billion, which was provided by both the general account and the U.S. Aid Counterpart Fund. Although Dodge wanted a private-dominated bank, the law specified that the president of the bank was to be appointed by the prime minister and that the bank was to operate under the supervision of the Ministry of Finance. When the Occupation ended in 1952, the government renamed the bank the Export-Import Bank of Japan (JEIB).

The JDB was created in 1951 to supply long-term, low-interest loans for domestic economic reconstruction and industrial development. In the initial planning stages, the Japanese government had ambitious plans for the bank,[13] but the SCAP considered the idea as a renamed RFB and a renewal of an inflationary policy. When established, the JDB was not allowed to issue bonds, borrow funds, or grant loans to cover a borrower's current expenses. Furthermore, the entire initial capitalization of ¥10 billion was to come from the Counterpart Fund. At the outset, the SCAP thought that the old RFB or the old Industrial Bank could not be revived, but the JDB expanded rapidly from this modest start. In fact, it enlarged its capital beyond the small amount from the Counterpart Fund that the SCAP had authorized.

While the various postwar reforms proceeded, the Yokinbu began to be revised. The MOF had complained about the restrictions on the uses of the Yokinbu and wanted the restrictions removed. Dodge approved the government's desire to open up the Yokinbu completely to government use. In 1951, the Yokinbu was abolished and replaced with a new special account called the Trust Fund Bureau. This account combined postal savings, several pension funds, and other trust funds. The use of such funds was broadened to cover loans to special legal entities and to allow use of the funds as collateral for bond issues.

Regarding reform of trust funds, attention should be paid to the increase of special legal entities.[14] Since the trust funds were available to special legal entities, those that already existed began to make use of the funds immediately. At the same time, many new entities were established to meet the country's urgent needs, e.g., electric power, regional development, housing, and financing of small and medium enterprises. In response to these needs, government financial institutions have been established since 1950. These institutions now include two government banks and ten public finance corporations as listed in Table 6.3.

Several other financial institutions (i.e., the People's Finance Corporation (PF), Housing Loan Corporation (HL), Agriculture, Forestry and Fisheries Finance Corporation (AFF), and Small Business Finance Corporation (SBF)) were also created around the time of the reform in trust funds in 1951. Similarly, such public corporations and agencies

Table 6.3. Government Financial Institutions

Name	Year of establish- ment	Control	Number of employees in 1981
Government banks (2)			
Export-Import Bank of Japan (JEIB)	1950	MOF	489
Japan Development Bank (JDB)	1951	MOF	1,090
Public finance corporations (10)			
People's Finance Corp. (PF)	1949	MOF	4,781
Housing Loan Corp. (HL)	1950	MOF	1,156
Agriculture, Forestry and Fisheries Finance Corp. (AFF)	1953	MOF, MAF	951
Small Business Finance Corp. (SBF)	1953	MOF, MITI	1,768
Hokkaidō-Tōhoku Development Corp. (HTD)	1956	HDA, MOF NLA	300
Japan Finance Corp. for Municipal Enterprises (JFM)	1957	MOF, MHA	89
Small Business Credit Insurance Corp. (SBC)	1958	MOF, MITI	396
Medical Care Facilities Financing Corp. (MCF)	1960	MOF, MOW	183
Environmental Sanitation Business Financing Corp. (ESB)	1967	MOF, MOW	61
Okinawa Development Finance Corp. (ODF)	1972	MOF, ODA	236
Others			
Overseas Economic Cooperation Fund (OEC)	1961	EPA	1,956
Post offices (PO)	1876	MOP	23,122*

Notes: 1. Year given is of actual establishment, not Diet authorization.

2. Abbreviations: MOF: Ministry of Finance; MAF: Ministry of Agriculture, Forestry and Fisheries; MITI: Ministry of International Trade and Industry; HDA: Hokkaidō Development Agency; NLA: National Land Agency; MHA: Ministry of Home Affairs, MOW: Ministry of Health and Welfare; ODA: Okinawa Development Agency; EPA: Economic Planning Agency; MOP: Ministry of Posts and Telecommunications.

3. The asterisk indicates the number of post offices in March, 1981.

as the Nippon Telegraph and Telephone Public Corporation and the Electric Power Development Co. were established as a result of the flexible use of trust funds.

Recent Issues of the FILP

Cooperative or Competitive

In principle, the government credit program has favored "strategic" or "target" private industries over others. The FIL agencies, in particular the JDB, have played a key part in aiding selected industries to expand. The JDB loans to selected borrowers were designed to support investments judged to be more in the public interest than others. Government lending, especially from major FIL agencies such as the JDB, PF, and SBF, usually provide indications to commercial banks as to which industries or enterprises are designated for preferential treatment. As a result of these loans, it becomes easier for the favored borrowers to seek further loans from private financial institutions, and thus the loans serve as a guarantee for private financing.

For instance, the role of the JDB is a good example of a typical government credit program. Its role is to foster industrial development and economic and social progress while conforming to the concept of a selective industrial development policy. The past performance of the JDB's lendings is seen in Figure 6.4. For 20 years starting from 1955, the two principal customers were the ocean shipping and the electric utilities industries (the latter as a part of the category "resource and energy"). Together with urban and regional development (e.g., warehouses, shopping centers, truck terminals), these four categories received over three-quarters of all the JDB's loans.

Since 1972 (not shown in Figure 6.4), the emphasis in the JDB lending program has shifted notably. The quality of life (including pollution prevention) has become an important concern. Thus, urban and regional development, and the quality of life dominated the JDB lending in the 1970s. The share represented by energy loans (for oil refining and storage, energy conservation projects, nuclear power) increased after a long decline, mainly reflecting the oil crisis. Simply speaking, the bulk of the post-1972 lending program was for infrastructure and improvements in the quality of life.

Government credit programs have played an important role in achieving special policy objectives, but their function should be thought of as complementary to private financial activities. Both private and government financings have been cooperative, rather than competitive.

In spite of the success of the government credit program in the process of economic growth and development, its recent performance has begun to be criticized by private financial institutions. Government financial institutions find it difficult to diminish the size and scope of

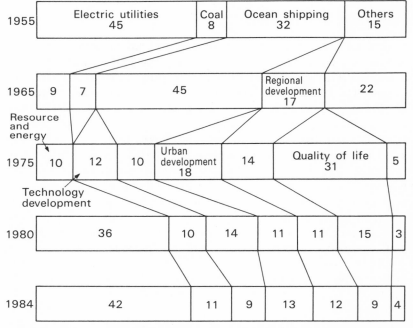

Fig. 6.4. Loans by Categories: The Case of the Japan Development Bank (%)
Source: Japan Development Bank, *Annual Report.*

loans and investments in response to the decrease in demand in the nation's economy. Since the mid-1970s, government financing seems to have become competitive, rather than cooperative and complementary, with private financial institutions.

Inefficiencies?

It is difficult to measure the efficiency of the government credit programs. Some doubts have been raised with respect to the efficiency of the FIL agencies, doubts which are related to the rapid expansion of government share in financial markets. In the private sector, profitability is the criterion of efficiency generally recognized. This criterion cannot be applied to the FIL agencies, mainly because the objectives they pursue lead them to operate in areas that the private sector has not considered profitable. Thus, their activities are not comparable with those of private financial institutions. No measure seems to be accurate, but it may be possible to observe indirectly the recent inefficiencies in government financial institutions.

Observation can be made of efficiency in relation to the size of the funds obtained from the general account. Following this approach, Table 6.4 shows which of the FIL agencies depend on financial aid in terms of borrowings and subsidies from the general account. These amounts indicate the sharp increase since 1975 in every agency.

Particular attention should be paid to the following three agencies, the PF, the HL, and the AFF. The PF provides general assistance to

Table 6.4. Borrowings and Subsidies from the General Account (¥ billion)

	1965	1970	1975	1980	1984
JEIB (1)			3.6		
(2)					
JDB (1)					
(2)					
PF (1)			15.7	18.4	
(2)		0.1	0.8	1.6	12.5
HL (1)					
(2)	0.7	7.1	55.0	195.9	286.3
AFF (1)					
(2)	0.9	12.8	25.1	86.2	135.0
SBF (1)					
(2)				0.9	9.6
HTD (1)					
(2)					
JFM (1)					
(2)		0.3	1.4	8.0	15.0
SBC (1)					
(2)					
MCF (1)					
(2)		0.6	1.2	4.2	3.2
ESB (1)					
(2)		1.1	0.6	7.1	6.8
ODF (1)					
(2)			1.3	8.2	11.9

Note: (1) Borrowings, (2) subsidies.
Source: Ministry of Finance, *Zaisei kin'yū tōkei geppō*.

the private sector, and in recent years the borrowings and subsidies from the general account have increased, indicating the enlargement of inefficient operations. Likewise, for the HL and the AFF, the amount of subsidies from the general account which are in the form of interest subsidies sharply increased. The HL has to make loans to individual borrowers on preferential terms at an interest rate of 5.5%. The AFF also provides assistance to the agriculture sector at interest rates sen-

Table 6.5. Amounts of Carry-forward and Disuse in Government Financial Institutions (¥ billion)

		1976	1978	1980	1982	1983
JEIB	(1)	991.9	1,344.4	862.7	1,063.0	870.0
	(2)	150.0	195.0	180.0		155.0
	(3)		498.4	29.0		
JDB	(1)	760.8	992.4	973.4	849.0	
	(2)	60.0	165.0	35.0		
	(3)		60.0			
HL	(1)	1,360.5	2,374.2	3,060.3	3,526.8	3,660.7
	(2)					
	(3)		176.0	0.7	1.6	1.3
AFF	(1)	462.0	550.8	641.5	542.0	527.5
	(2)					
	(3)		60.0		28.0	
SBF	(1)	1,270.5	1,550.9	1,805.4	1,595.6	1,648.5
	(2)					
	(3)		90.5		11.5	11.5
HTD	(1)	121.8	146.3	143.6	124.1	105.4
	(2)					
	(3)		30.5	28.0	20.0	25.0
MCF	(1)	74.0	108.5	82.8	89.4	72.8
	(2)					
	(3)		16.0	13.1	11.0	20.0
ESB	(1)	180.7	233.5	254.0	208.0	185.0
	(2)					
	(3)		25.0	7.7	58.0	49.5
ODF	(1)	88.7	110.0	118.9	101.0	95.0
	(2)					
	(3)		11.0	0.2	13.5	13.9

Note: (1) Actual amount of lendings; (2) carry-forward to next year; and (3) amount unused.

Source: Same as Table 6.4.

sibly below market rates. Recent trends of such financial aid can lead to criticism of the efficiency of the operations of the government financial agencies. In order to decrease the gap between market rates, the government lending rate might have to be increased.

Another indicator of efficiency is the amount of carry-forward as unused funds at the end of fiscal year, shown in Table 6.5.[15] Nine financial agencies out of 12 have unused funds. Of special importance is the sudden emergence of these trends since 1976. Before 1975, no amounts were recorded in the "unused funds" category at the end of the fiscal year. As compared with actual lendings, these unused funds in the JEIB and the JDB are large enough to be worth noting. Sometimes other agencies also show figures similar to those of the JEIB and the JDB; e.g., the Environmental Sanitation Business Financing Corporation (ESB) in 1982, and the Hokkaidō-Tōhoku Development Corporation (HTD) in 1978 and 1980.

In a competitive environment with the government sector, private financial institutions often complain about the inefficient performance of government agencies. These private institutions advocate withdrawal of the government from areas that are considered the dominion of the private sector.

Special Problems Concerning Postal Savings

In the past several years, postal savings have posed serious problems to the functioning of financial markets and monetary policy in Japan. Broadly speaking, there are two points worth mentioning here. The first is the marked increase in the postal savings share in the total amount of personal savings. Indeed, their percentage distribution rose up to about 30% in 1982, compared with 16% in 1965. This is explained as follows: "The outstanding balance of postal savings exceeded 60 trillion yen, about three times the deposits held by Banque National de Paris, the largest bank in the world."[16]

As a result of the sharp rise, postal savings are beginning to compete with private financial institutions. Why have postal savings increased so rapidly in recent years? The postal savings system as a government institution has a number of advantages over its private counterparts. For instance, there are more than 23,000 post offices throughout the country to collect money from individual savers; private financial institutions have branch offices totaling 13,500.[17] Furthermore, interest on postal savings is completely tax exempt, although the total amount invested cannot exceed the legal limit of ¥3 million.[18] Likewise, the post office can offer depositors an attractive service called Teigaku Chokin, a deposit account that can be canceled any time after six months and kept up to ten years at gradually increasing rates of interest on a compound basis.

A second problem posed by the size of postal savings is the difficulty in the efficient operation of monetary policy. What results is divided authority with respect to the establishment of interest rates. Generally speaking, changes in lending rates charged by private financial institutions are related to changes in the official discount rate charged by the Bank of Japan. The interest rates charged by private institutions are legally controlled by the Policy Board of the Bank of Japan. However, postal savings interest rates are formally fixed by the Cabinet upon the recommendation of the Ministry of Posts and Telecommunications (MOPT).

Problems result because of this two-tier determination of the structure of interest rates. In order to protect its depositors' income, the MOPT has often been reluctant to reduce postal savings interest rates. During periods of declining interest rates, the cuts in postal savings rates have come after the rate changes decreed by the Bank of Japan. In general, the Bank of Japan cannot take the initiative of cutting discount rates until the MOPT approves the reduction of postal savings interest rates. Thus the lack of coordination between the Bank of Japan Policy Board and the MOPT results in the inefficient operation of monetary policy.

Nonfinancial Public Enterprises

Overview

For "off-budget" government activities, public enterprise performance must be examined. In general, the sphere of government activities has expanded to include social and economic policy. In many cases, these functions are entrusted to independent organizations rather than to administrative agencies in the general government. These independent organizations are simply called public enterprises or corporations. They are established when efficiency in management is expected, independent management being more efficient than direct government administration. Public enterprises are less under the special supervision of the government since they have public responsibilities, but they are generally given the autonomy and flexibility to conduct their businesses independently.

Broadly speaking, public enterprises are classified into two types, financial and nonfinancial. The FIL agencies that have been discussed earlier under government credit programs are all classified as financial public enterprises. This section will discuss nonfinancial enterprises.

Scope

It is difficult to demarcate the line between private and public enterprises. Arbitrary decisions must be made to clarify the borderline between the two. Using the concept of national income accounts, the classification of nonfinancial public enterprises can be outlined as follows:

I. Special accounts of the government (as of January 1984)
   Business Special Accounts
   (1) Mint Bureau
   (2) Printing Bureau
   (3) National Forest Service
   (4) Postal Services
   (5) Alchohol Monopoly
   Management Special Accounts
   (1) Foodstuff control
II. Public corporations (*Kōsha*):
   (1) Japanese National Railways
   (2) Japan Tobacco and Salt Public Corporation*
   (3) Nippon Telegraph and Telephone Public Corporation*
   (* (2) and (3) were converted into the private sector.)
III. Other public corporations
   Kōdan:
   (1) Water Resources Development Corporation
   (2) Agricultural Land Development Public Corporation
   (3) Forest Development Corporation
   (4) Japan National Oil Corporation
   (5) Maritime Credit Corporation
   (6) New Tokyo International Airport Authority
   (7) Japan Highway Public Corporation
   (8) Japan Railway Construction Public Corporation
   (9) Japan Regional Development Corporation
   (10) Housing and Urban Development Corporation
   (11) Metropolitan Expressway Public Corporation
   (12) Hanshin Expressway Public Corporation
   (13) Honshū-Shikoku Bridge Authority
   Eidan:
   (1) Teito Rapid Transit Authority

Jigyōdan:
(1) Livestock Industry Promotion Corporation
(2) Japan Raw Silk and Sugar Price Stabilization Agency
Others:
(1) Electric Power Development Company
(2) Japan Atomic Energy Resource Institute
In addition to the above, local governments have their own independent organizations. In some cases, local government agencies are directly in charge of providing water supply and transportation. In other cases, they form public enterprises which are established to perform specific functions (e.g., Land Development Corporation and Local Road Public Corporation).

National public enterprises are divided into four categories. Particular attention should be paid to the following three points. First, the five items included in Business Special Accounts of the government are usually called national enterprises which are directly managed by the national government. These enterprises are given flexibility in their financial management including the right of collective bargaining in labor-management relations. Second, public corporations comprise three cases of public corporations, two of which were converted into private enterprises in April 1985. The monopoly sale of tobacco and salt, the railways, and telephones were originally under the direct control of the government. After World War II, public corporations were established as independent entities to carry out these activities. Their budgets were subject to the approval of the Diet, and settled accounts were submitted to the Diet.

Third, the other public corporations are the *kōdan*, *eidan*, and *jigyōdan*. The title of the corporations indicate the extent of budgetary control and supervision from the government, the flexibility of financial management, and personnel. *Kōdan* include 13 corporations that carry out public works such as the construction of roads and airports, the development of water resources, and forestry. The main financial sources are capital investment and loans from the national government. *Eidan* applies only to corporations that perform public-service activities in mass transit. *Jigyōdan* include 16 corporations of which only 2 are included in the above list of public enterprises, reflecting the non-commercial or less public character of *jigyōdan* activities. They are smaller in size than the *kōdan* and their commercial nature is weak. The major role of the *jigyōdan* is to achieve specific policy programs, such as price stabilization and the promotion of agricultural products. *Jigyōdan* capital is financed in part by the national government as well as by private sources.

Recent Reform Trends

During the period of rapid economic growth (1960s–1970s), the number and size of public corporations and enterprises sharply increased. The rapid accumulation of fiscal deficits since the oil embargoes of 1973 and 1979 resulted in efforts to cut public expenditure. These economy measures led to administrative and fiscal reform by the government, and the contraction of public corporations and enterprises became one of the main targets for this purpose.

The importance of public corporations and enterprises has diminished in certain areas, due to changes in social and economic conditions. A decrease in activity by public corporations occurred where these public entities coexist with a private enterprise, as the case of private financial institutions. In finance, the private sector is developing and maturing sufficiently so that it can fulfill the needs of the public. Therefore, the pressure to abolish and reorganize the public corporations and enterprises has increased.

The Ad Hoc Council on Administrative Reform was established in 1981 to study the overall performance of government activities. Some plans for reorganizing public corporations and enterprises have been formulated. Some consolidations were pursued to achieve rationalization of management and to increase efficiency. For example, the Japan Housing Corporation and the New Town Development Corporation were merged into one corporation, the Housing and Urban Development Corporation. Among recent reform trends, three major public corporations have become the targets for promoting administrative reform: (1) reconstruction of the Japanese National Railways (JNR); and (2) conversion to private management of the Nippon Telegraph and Telephone Public Corporation (NTT) and the Japan Tobacco and Salt Public Corporation (JTS).

The JNR is a typical case of a public corporation whose capital investment was entirely financed by the national government. Major portions of revenue must be derived from passengers' fares, but the JNR has suffered huge deficits for a long period. Since 1964, the JNR has been subsidized by the general account in order to maintain its mass transit operation. The pressure to reform the JNR management has increased, and a number of reorganization plans have been examined by the Ad Hoc Council on Administrative Reform. One proposal is to reduce the total number of employees and to discontinue or change the type of transportation on unprofitable local lines. Basic reconstruction plans are also being considered to reestablish sound management: Included are such ideas as dividing JNR into regional divisions or conversion of JNR to private management (as in the cases of NTT and JTS).

Notes

1. The general account, financed by taxes and public debt, spends both in purchases of goods and services and in transfers. It also contains the transfers of substantial funds to other budgets. The special account is established when the government needs to administer and manage certain funds in relation to specific projects. Depending upon the purpose of its functions, each account has its own financial sources, such as transfers from the general account, profits from public enterprises administered under the special account, interest revenue from loans, or contributions for social insurance. For an outline of the Japanese budget system, see Ministry of Finance, *Quarterly Bulletin of Financial Statistics* 1982, pp. 47–48 and chapter 4 in this book.

2. If the scope of government financial institutions is restricted to two banks and ten public finance corporations, they have no interlinkage with other public enterprises. Financial funds are mainly channeled through funds of the Trust Bureau Fund to public enterprises with no relation to government financial institutions. On this point, however, there is the exception of the Finance Corp. of Local Public Enterprise (FLP), which is charged with making loans to public enterprises of local governments.

3. The issue of national bonds mainly relies upon the subscription of syndicate groups which are organized by private financial institutions.

4. See Ministry of Finance, *The Budget in Brief Japan*, 1983, pp. 52–53.

5. See Johnson 1978, ch. 8.

6. Later in 1881, the Postal Bureau was transferred to the newly established Ministry of Agriculture and Commerce. In 1885, the bureau itself became the Ministry of Communications (the predecessor of the present Ministry of Posts and Telecommunications).

7. *Yokinbu* in this context means post office deposits account.

8. For a comprehensive discussion, see Patrick 1970, Patrick and Rosovsky 1976, ch. 1, and Yamamura 1967.

9. On the basis of the "weighted (priority) production policy" (*keisha seisan hōshiki*), several basic industries were chosen loans intensively for the purpose of concentrating the recovery efforts in capital investments.

10. The consumers' price level, computed on the basis of 1934–36 prices, was 48 times higher in 1946, 191 times higher in 1947, and 230 times higher in 1950.

11. The most famous policy he took was the balanced budget to cover all budgets in the government sector. For a comprehensive discussion concerning the Dodge Plan, see Yamamura 1967, ch. 2.

12. See Johnson 1978, pp. 93–95.

13. Finance Minister Ikeda Hayato proposed that the funds for the new bank should come from the *Yokinbu*, direct appropriations, counterpart funds, and recovered funds from the RFC. In addition, it was said that the new bank should have the authority to issue its own bonds.

14. The term "special legal entities" is similar to public corporations, used in the section on non-financial public enterprises below.

15. Of course, an unused amount might be the result of economizing the initially allotted funds. In this sense, it means the efficient indicator to the used fund. Given the current state of bureaucratic functioning, however, it would be difficult to anticipate the effect of efficient use of funds.

16. Federation of Bankers Associations of Japan 1982, p. 9.

17. This figure covers the total number of branch offices in all banks and mutual loan and savings banks.

18. For a more expanded discussion, see Ishi 1983.

7 | The National Taxation System

Torao Aoki

This chapter discusses Japan's system of taxation. Following a brief description of the classification of taxes and other salient features, the history of national taxation is given. Income tax for individuals and corporation tax are described, and inheritance and gift taxes are discussed. Consumption taxes and customs duties are then outlined, followed by an account of the national administration of taxation.

Taxes can be divided into two types according to their collecting sources: there are national taxes levied by the national government, and local taxes levied by prefectural and municipal governments. In recent years, the revenue from national taxes has been almost twice that of local taxes.

The two large categories of taxes, direct and indirect, are determined by how and to whom they are levied. Direct taxes are those levied directly on individuals or corporations, while indirect taxes are a sort of consumption tax not directly levied but included in the prices of commodities or charged as fees. Revenues from direct taxes are far greater than those from indirect taxes. In 1982, direct taxes represented almost three-quarters of total tax revenue (Table 7.1). In local taxes, a main part (85%) of the revenue came from direct taxes. In national taxes, revenues today are also largely from direct taxes, although

Table 7.1. Components of Direct and Indirect Taxes, 1982

(¥ billion)

	Direct tax	Indirect tax	Total
National	22,644	9,359	32,003
Local	15,773	2,856	18,629
Total	38,418 (75.9%)	12,214 (24.1%)	50,632 (100.0%)

Source: Ministry of Home Affairs, *Chihōzei ni kansuru sankō keisū shiryō*, 1985, pp. 14–15.

103

Table 7.2. Components of National Taxes (%)

	1934–36	1950	1970	1980	1985
Direct taxes	34.8	55.0	66.1	71.1	73.4
of which:					
Income tax	11.4	38.6	31.2	38.1	39.2
Corporation tax	9.5	14.7	33.0	31.5	31.8
Inheritance tax	2.4	0.5	1.8	1.6	2.4
Indirect taxes	65.2	45.0	33.9	28.9	26.6
of which:					
Liquor tax	17.6	18.5	7.9	5.0	5.0
Sugar tax	6.7	0.1	0.6	0.2	0.1
Gasoline tax	—	1.3	6.4	5.5	3.9
Commodity tax	—	2.9	4.4	3.7	3.9
Customs duty	12.8	0.3	4.9	2.3	1.7
Stamp revenue	6.8	1.6	2.8	3.0	3.5
Monopoly profits[a]	16.5	20.1	3.5	2.8	2.2
Others	4.8	0.3	3.5	6.3	6.3
Total	100.0	100.0	100.0	100.0	100.0

Note: [a]From FY 1985, tobacco consumption tax.
Source: Ministry of Finance, *Zaisei kin'yū tōkei geppō*, May 1985, pp. 12–15.

historically this has not been the case. The data presented in Table 7.2 tabulates various components of national tax over a 50-year span. Immediately apparent from the data is the shift in revenue in 1934–36, from direct taxes at 34.8% and indirect at 65.2% to 71.1% and 28.9 %, respectively, in 1980. The present heavy reliance on direct taxes is inordinately large. The revenue estimates for 1985 are given in Table 7.3.

By their very nature, direct taxes make taxpayers feel their tax burden onerous. Despite Japan's fairly sophisticated tax administration, it is difficult to convince taxpayers of the fairness and reliability of the system. The taxpayers feel the burden of direct taxes keenly, and indirect taxes tend to be overlooked. In comparison with other advanced nations, Japan's tax burden (in terms of both the total national and local taxes as a percentage of national income) is low (Table 7.4).

An international comparison of taxes is made in Table 7.5, which presents tax revenue by source for six industrialized countries. The data show that the United States and Japan receive a high percentage of revenue from income and profits. Both are also similar in that tax revenues from goods and services are of relatively little importance. Among the six countries, Japan received the highest percentage of tax revenue from income and profits.

Table 7.3. Revenue from National Taxes, 1985 (¥ billion, %)

General account	38,550	97.6
Direct taxes	28,975	73.4
Income tax	15,680	39.2
Corporation tax	12,546	31.8
Inheritance tax	961	2.4
Indirect taxes	9,575	24.2
Liquor tax	1,955	5.0
Tobacco excise tax	882	2.2
Gasoline tax	1,554	3.9
Petroleum gas tax	454	1.1
Commodity tax	1,538	3.9
Securities transaction tax	475	1.2
Travel tax	77	0.2
Motor vehicle tonnage tax	445	1.1
Customs duty	688	1.7
Stamp revenue	1,366	3.5
Others	141	0.4
Special accounts	944	2.4
Local road tax	299	0.8
Petroleum gas tax	16	0.0
Aviation fuel tax	10	0.0
Motor tonnage tax vehicle	148	0.4
Special tonnage due	11	0.0
Customs duty on oil	125	0.3
Promotion of power		
resources development tax	224	0.6
Total	39,494	100.0

Note: Petroleum gas tax, aviation fuel tax, and motor vehicle tonnage tax in the special accounts are distributed to the local governments.
Source: Ministry of Finance, *Financial Statistics of Japan*, 1985, pp. 38–39.

Table 7.4. Tax Burden as Percentage of National Income (¥ billion)

	National income (A)	National tax (B)	Local tax (C)	Total (B)+(C) =(D)	B/A(%)	D/A(%)
1934–36	14.3	12.3	6.3	18.5	8.5	12.9
1950	3,382	570	188	759	16.9	22.4
1960	13,269	1,802	744	2,546	13.6	19.2
1970	60,875	7,775	3,751	11,526	12.8	18.9
1982	211,550	32,007	18,629	50,636	15.1	23.9

Source: Same as Table 7.1, p. 12.

Table 7.5. Tax Revenue of Main Headings as Percentage of Total Taxation in Industrialized Countries, 1983

	Japan	U.S.A.	U.K.	W. Germany	France	Italy
Income & profits	45.2	42.7	38.5	33.4	17.8	36.8[a]
Individual	25.6	37.1	27.7	28.3	13.4	27.9
Corporate	19.6	5.5	10.8	5.1	4.3	9.3
Social security	30.0	28.7	17.7	35.7	43.9	35.9
Payroll	—	—	1.4	—	2.4	—
Property	9.4	10.6	12.7	3.4	3.7	2.8
Goods & services	15.2	18.0	29.8	27.5	29.0	23.4
Others	0.3	—	0.0	0.0	3.2	1.1
Total	100.0	100.0	100.0	100.0	100.0	100.0

Note: Includes national and local taxes.
[a] Net of 0.5% for reimbursement of direct tax unallocable between "individual" and "corporate."
Source: OECD 1984, pp. 85–97.

Historical Background

Prior to 1868, revenues from land tax accounted for more than 80% of government revenues. A national income tax was introduced for the first time in 1887, but revenues from this tax were only 1.5% of total tax revenues. In 1899, an income tax was extended to corporations and a withholding tax on bond interest was first instituted. Around this time, indirect taxes were established, and these taxes accounted for about one-half of total tax revenues. In 1920, the income tax was completely revised. With business expansion, revenues from taxes on corporate and personal incomes increased to about 20% of total revenues; by this time revenues from land taxes decreased to less than 10% of total revenues.

Under the tax reform of 1940 taxes on income were divided into an individual income tax and a corporate income tax. Since that time, income tax refers to a tax imposed on individuals. Corporation tax refers to a tax imposed on the income of corporations. Individual income tax is progressive in nature.

Soon after the war (1946–49), various measures were instituted to curb inflation and reorient the economy. A global tax on combined income with highly progressive rates was imposed. Tax procedure was based on the American system of "self-assessment."

In 1949, an economic advisory group headed by Professor Carl S.

Shoup of Columbia University visited Japan to conduct studies which resulted in recommendations for the restructuring of the Japanese tax system in 1950. Under the Shoup reforms, the individual income tax and the corporation tax became the centerpiece of the whole tax structure. From 1950 to 1956 these tax revisions were modified to suit Japan's economic and social climate.

In the second half of the 1950s, tax revenues were much larger than estimated. This revenue surplus was due to the fast growth of the Japanese economy. In 1956, a Tax Commission was created as an advisory organ to the prime minister to review the tax structure and recommend revisions. In 1960, this commission stated that the total tax burden, excluding social security tax, should be about 20% of national income.

In 1962, the General Law of National Taxes was passed. This law provides the general principles and rules of taxation. In 1965, the government issued bonds for the first time after the war. This issuance indicated a shift in public finance from maintaining a balanced budget to playing a "counter-cyclical" role by deficit financing. Thus in 1966, an unprecedented large-scale tax reduction was put into effect.

During the period of high growth, land value increased a great deal. This phenomenon led to land speculation and to problems with urban land taxes. Thus in 1969 the taxes on land were modified. These amendments changed the treatment of capital gains from land. Long-term capital gains from sales of land were taxed at reduced rates.

During the 1970s, the Japanese economy turned from fast growth to slow growth. Breakdown of the Bretton Woods monetary agreement and the two oil crises caused major changes in Japan's economy. Personal income tax was decreased in 1971, 1973, and 1974. The income tax reduction in 1974 was the largest in history; this tax cut was accompanied by an increase in the corporate tax rate from 36.75 to 40%.

An economic recession occurred in FY 1975, causing a fall in tax revenues. The government then issued deficit-covering bonds to make up the deficit. In 1976, the government suspended the income tax cuts which had been planned. Since 1976 special tax measures, such as increases in indirect taxes, were enacted.

In 1976, an "Economic Plan for the Second Half of the 1970s" was adopted by the government. Among its many goals, this plan sought to raise the ratio of tax revenue to national income by 3%. However, the proposal met with public disapproval since direct taxes had increased as a portion of total revenue; in 1980, the share of direct taxes exceeded

70%. As an alternative, a value-added tax was proposed. This plan also failed to gain legislative approval. Since revenues were limited, curtailment of government expenditures was the only alternative. Thus great emphasis was placed on limiting government expenditures and thereby reducing the amount of deficit-covering bond issues.

In 1981, tax rates on corporations were raised by 2 percentage points to 42% and to 32% on undistributed and distributed profits, respectively. From the end of 1983 to 1984 major cuts in personal income tax were implemented.

Income Tax

Categories of Taxable Income

Japan's individual income tax is provided for in the Income Tax Law and is called "income tax"; corporate income tax is called the "corporation tax" under the Corporation Tax Law. Income tax is a global tax, under which most incomes are aggregated and taxed at highly progressive rates. The income tax is collected either by withholding at the source or by filing a tax return on the self-assessment for the income during a calendar year. Individuals are also subject to prefectural and municipal taxes (see chapter 9).

Personal incomes are classified into the following ten categories for the purposes of tax computation: (1) interest, (2) dividends, (3) real estate income, (4) business income, (5) employment income, (6) retirement income, (7) forestry income, (8) capital gains, (9) occasional income, and (10) miscellaneous income.

Under the self-assessment system, income tax liability is determined by the taxpayer's declaration as to the tax base and the tax due. However, tax is withheld at the source of income from the following items: interest, original issue discount premiums of noninterest-bearing bonds, dividends, employment and retirement payments, remuneration or fees for professional services, and fees for performance of public entertainers. Tax on wages and salaries is withheld at the source, and adjustments between withheld amounts and final tax liability are made at the last payment of such wages and salaries during the year. The majority of wage and salary earners, i.e., those with earnings of not more than ¥15 million, are not required to file a return.

Remuneration or fees are subject to withholding tax at the rate of 10% for up to ¥1 million and 20% for over ¥1 million. The rate of withholding tax on income from interest and dividends is 20%. Under the Special Taxation Measures Law, taxpayers may temporarily elect to be taxed at 35% without adding such receipts to their aggregate income. Under the same law, interest income from bank deposits, postal savings, and government bonds with a total value for principal not over ¥3 million is exempt from tax. To partially avoid double taxation, a dividend credit of 10% is allowed against income tax liability if a taxpayer's income is ¥10 million or less and 5% for that part of income which exceeds ¥10 million.

For income from the lease of real estate and income from business activities, gross receipts minus all necessary expenses are taxable. Wages paid to family employees may be deducted as necessary expenses within certain limits. A proprietor filing a blue return may elect to be treated as a corporation for tax purposes. This option has been available since 1974 and will continue until 1988. Blue returns are those filed by taxpayers who follow specified accounting procedures. One of the advantages of a blue return is that upon audit of the accounting books, the return will not be subject to reassessment unless an error is found in the entries. Those filing a blue return are also granted a special deduction of ¥100,000 and a deduction for various reserves (e.g., bad debts, price fluctuations, accelerated depreciation). They may deduct their own remuneration, to which the special deduction for employment income then applies. The "corporation income" thus obtained is taxed at the rate of 27.3% and for that part of income which exceeds ¥8 million at the rate of 37.5%.

Special deductions for employment are 5 to 40% of wages and salaries, the minimum amount deductible being ¥570,000.

Retirement income and timber income are taxed separately from other income. Japan has a custom in which an organization pays a large sum upon a person's retirement. Fifty percent of severance income, after a special deduction based on years of service, is taxed at progressive rates. The forestry industry is given special treatment because its income derived from the sale of timber differs from one year to another over a long period of time. Expenses for forestation, management, and lumbering of the forest plus a special deduction of ¥500,000 are subtracted from the gross receipts.

For capital gains the acquisition cost, other necessary expenses, and a special deduction of ¥500,000 may be deducted from the gross receipts. If such capital gains are from the sale of property which the taxpayer has owned for over five years, only half of the amount after deductions is taxable as long-term capital gains. Capital gains are added to the aggregate income to be taxed at the progressive rates. Income from the sale of stock shares is exempt from tax unless it involves 50 transactions and 200,000 shares or more during the year. There is a separate tax for capital gains on land or buildings for which the rate is 20 or 40%, depending on long or short term, according to a prescribed formula. A variety of special measures is granted on the capital gains from land and buildings for housing or other public purposes.

Aggregation of Income

All income, except the above stated types of income, is added together. Subtracted from this total income are ¥330,000 each for the basic exemption, exemption for spouse, and for each dependent. When a taxpayer, spouse, or dependent is a handicapped or aged person (65 years or older), widow, widower, or working student, an additional exemption is available.

Taking these personal exemptions into account, a family of four with an income under ¥2,357,000 is free from the national income tax. According to the Ministry of Finance estimates, this minimum taxable income compares favorably with the ¥1,863,000 of the United States, ¥984,000 of the United Kingdom, ¥1,158,000 of the Federal Republic of Germany, and ¥2,151,000 of France as of early 1985. Allowable deductions are available for the following:

1) Casualty losses in excess of 10% of income;

2) Medical expenses in excess of 5% of income or ¥50,000, whichever smaller, but up to ¥2 million;

3) Graduated percentage of life insurance premiums up to ¥50,000;

4) Fire and casualty insurance premiums up to ¥15,000 or ¥3,000 for a policy of 10 years or less;

5) Social insurance premiums; and

6) Contributions or donations which exceed ¥10,000 up to a certain amount.

Under certain conditions, income from assets (i.e., interest, dividends, and real estate income) of family members must be combined with incomes of the head of household. This is to prevent any reduction in tax liability by deliberate distribution of income among family members.

Income tax rates are graduated into 15 steps from the lowest of 10.5% for taxable income of ¥500,000 or less to the highest of 70% for income of over ¥80 million.

To alleviate the burden of progressive tax rates due to radical increases in income, income averaging may be applied to timber income, fluctuating income, or extraordinary income. By this method, the amount of tax which would apply to one-fifth of such income is determined and then multiplied by five to arrive at the total tax due. Tax credits against tax liability are as follows: 10% of dividends for taxpayers with total income of ¥10 million or less and 5% for income in excess of ¥10 million; foreign income taxes paid; and 18% of the annual house mortagage repayment in excess of ¥300,000 subject to a ceiling of ¥150,000.

Filing Income Tax Returns

Taxpayers must file a tax return by March of the following year. Persons receiving income not subject to withholding tax must pay about one-third each of their estimated income tax on the basis of the preceding year's tax. Estimated tax payments are due by July 31 and November 30 of the taxable year, and a final settlement is made at the time of filing a return.

For 1983, 7.0 million taxpayers filed a return. A percentage breakdown of the number of taxpayers by income source is as follows: 32.5% from commerce and industry; 3.8% from agriculture; 8.6% from other business activities; and 55.1% from other income. These categories account for the following percentages of reported income: 18.2% for commerce and industry; 1.4% for agriculture; 11.2% for other business activities; and 69.1% for other income.

It is commonly alleged that proprietors of small- and medium-sized businesses can minimize their tax liabilities by taking advantage of accounting practices and tax privileges. It is also alleged that farmers substantially understate their income for tax purposes. In contrast, total payments to wage and salary workers are subject to withholding as they earn.

Statistics show that in FY 1983, 87.5% of all wage and salary earners (40,980,000 persons in total), including government officials paid the national income tax. In contrast, 39.5% of those engaged in business (7,020,000 persons in total), and only 14.6% of farmers (1,370,000 persons in total) paid income tax.

Since 1950, the taxation office has posted the list of high-income tax returns for public review. This list has received wide publicity throughout Japan. This posting policy was instituted in the interest of honest and fair tax returns. The minimum amount for income to qualify for posting was raised over the years. Until 1983, persons whose annual income was more than ¥10 million (about U.S.$45,000) were put on the list. From 1984 only those who paid more than ¥10 million in taxes are listed. As a result, the number of persons on the list fell from 520,000 in 1982 to 66,000 in 1983.

Corporation Tax

Relative Importance of Corporation Tax

Corporate income tax is based on the Corporation Tax Law (Juridical Person's Tax Law). At present, it produces the second largest amount of revenue, after individual income tax, in the national tax system. Revenues from the corporation tax exceeded those from the income tax in the 18 years between FY 1957 and FY 1974, except for several years when corporation tax revenues fell due to a business recession. Estimated at 30.9% for FY 1984, the revenues from the corporation tax as a percentage of total national tax revenues are far greater than in other industrialized countries. Comparable figures for 1983 were 9.8% in the United States, 6.9% in the United Kingdom, 6.9% in the Federal Republic of Germany, 9.1% in France, and 4.5% in Italy.

The large share of the corporation tax is mainly ascribed to the relative importance of corporate activities in the national economy and to the accelerated incorporation of individual proprietorships after World War II. Tax rates for Japanese corporate taxes are not high by international standards. From April 1, 1984 to March 31, 1987, the corporation tax rates have been raised from 42 to 43.3% on undistributed profits and from 32 to 33.3% on distributed profits. For corporations with capital of less than ¥100 million, tax rates on profits up to ¥8 million have been raised from 30 to 31% if retained, and from 24 to 25% if distributed. The reduced rate of 28% is applied for cooperatives (23% on distributed earnings) and public interest corporations.

Closely held family corporations are subject to an additional tax of 10, 15, or 20% on their retained earnings under certain conditions. This added taxation is designed to maintain the tax equity between incorporated and unincorporated enterprises. Tax equity is the main concern in the administration of Japanese tax policy. In FY 1983, of the over 1,578,000 ordinary corporations in Japan, less than 0.2% had a capitalization of ¥1 billion or more, while 63.3% are capitalized at less than ¥5 million.

Tax on retained earnings of family companies is applicable to 95.2% of the total number of corporations. Of all the corporations that filed returns, 44.7% reported profits in their tax returns. They distributed 10.4% of these profits as dividends and retained 33.9%. Corporations capitalized at less than ¥5 million retained more than 40% of their profits.

At the shareholders' level, 20% of the dividend is withheld at the source, a part of which may be credited against the income tax of shareholders as mentioned earlier.

Corporations are also subject to prefectural and municipal taxes. When local taxes are taken into account, tax rates on Japanese corporations are of the same order of magnitude as the rates in other industrialized countries.

Computation of Tax

Corporations must compute their income once in each business year, any twelve-month period selected by the corporation. Returns must be filed within two months after the close of the accounting period. Interim returns must also be filed and prepayments of tax made for the first six-month period within eight months of the beginning of the period. The taxable income is broadly the excess of gross revenue over total expenses. The computation is made in accordance with generally accepted principles of business accounting. Capital gains are taxed in full. In addition, capital gains from land which corporations have owned for 10 years or less are subject to an additional tax at a flat rate of 20%. However, various reliefs are granted for capital gains on land. Dividends received from domestic corporations are, in principle, not entered in revenue. The useful life of fixed assets is legally prescribed, and the methods of depreciation and inventory valuation are specified in rules and regulations. The laws and regulations allow almost all methods utilized by standard accounting practice. Taxpayers are free to choose the accounting method, provided that a method once selected will continue to be applied.

Expense accounts for social and entertainment purposes are tax deductible only within certain limits. For corporations capitalized at ¥10 million or less, deductions of up to ¥4 million for expense accounts are allowed. For corporations capitalized between ¥10 and ¥50 million, deductions of ¥3 million are allowed. During FY 1983, corporations as a whole disbursed ¥4.02 from expense accounts for each operating revenue of ¥1,000, and 50.9% of such expenses were disallowed for taxation purposes. Especially, for the large corporations capitalized at ¥100 million or more 98.7% of their expense accounts were disallowed.

Contributions to national and local governments, and scientific, educational, cultural, and welfare organizations designated by the Ministry of Finance are deductible from taxable income. Other contributions are deductible up to a certain amount.

Income tax withheld at the source for interest, dividends, other payments to corporations, and foreign tax (both direct and indirect) are credited against the corporation tax.

For policy purposes, various tax incentive measures are provided mainly under the Special Taxation Measures Law. These incentives include accelerated depreciation, investment tax credits, and tax-free reserves. These concessions serve specific economic purposes but are granted at the cost of the principles of tax equity. At one time, these tax incentives substantially proliferated. Since 1976, the special measures for business enterprises have been carefully reassessed. Particularly, under the circumstances of government deficits, renewed endeavors are being made to minimize such concessions. Despite ongoing efforts to reduce special taxation measures, investment tax credits were instituted in 1984 as a temporary measure.

Inheritance and Gift Taxes

Inheritance and gift taxes are established by the Inheritance Tax Law. Inheritance tax was first created in 1905 as an estate tax. In 1950, it was changed to an accession-type tax. In 1953, it was divided into an inheritance tax and a gift tax. The gift tax is imposed as a transfer tax and supplements the inheritance tax.

In 1958, the inheritance tax was revised to base computation on the total value of the estate and the number of statutory heirs. Under the prior law, tax was levied on the basis of the distribution among heirs, which was prone to manipulation from tax consideration.

The inheritance tax is imposed on the recipient of assets from the decedent by inheritance, bequest, or devise. If any heir or legatee has received property by gift from the decedent within three years of death, the value of such property is added to the total taxable assets. Life and personal accident insurance payments and retirement allowances received by heirs up to a certain amount are also added to the total taxable assets.

From the value of the properties, ¥20 million as basic exemption and ¥4 million for each statutory heir are subtracted to obtain taxable value. The value thus obtained is divided among the statutory heirs in accordance with the shares provided by the Civil Code. For example, if an estate is divided between the spouse and lineal descendants, the spouse receives one-third and the rest is equally divided among the descendants. The tax rates are progressive, beginning at 10% for a taxable estate of ¥2 million or less; a maximum rate is 75% for taxable assets of over ¥500 million. The tax rates are applied to each share. The total tax on all the shares is then distributed among the heirs in proportion to the amount which they actually receive.

The gift tax previously paid on properties included in the estate and foreign taxes are credited against the tax. For a spouse of a decedent, the tax amount on whichever larger of one-half the estate or ¥40 million may be deducted from the tax of such heir. If an heir is a minor under 20 years of age or a handicapped person, his or her tax liability is reduced under a prescribed formula. On the other hand, if an heir is a person other than the decedent's spouse or lineal descendant, such heir's tax liability is increased by 20%. A tax return must be filed within six months of the death of the decedent.

The gift tax is imposed on the recipient in the calendar year of receipt. The gift from a corporation is subject to income tax as occasional income. As a basic exemption, ¥600,000 is deductible from the taxable value. In addition, a lifetime allowance of up to ¥10 million may be deducted from residential property given to a spouse who was married to the decedent for more than 20 years. The tax rates are highly progressive, ranging from 10% for value of ¥500,000 or less up to 75% for over ¥70 million. A tax return must be filed between February 1 and March 15 of the following year.

Both inheritance and gift taxes should be paid within the respective period for filing a return. However, if the tax amount exceeds ¥50,000, payment may be deferred up to five years. Depending upon the kind of property inherited, installment payments over 10 to 15 years or payment in kind may be accepted.

Tax rates for inheritance and gift taxes have not been adjusted often, but the amount of exemptions has been raised frequently. These exemptions take into consideration the number of inheritees subject to the tax. There has been no change in exemptions since 1975 when the exemptions were increased substantially. Thus, the decedents with estates of taxable value as a percentage of total decedents reported gained from 2.1% in 1975 to 5.3% in 1983, the highest percentage since 1950. The decedents with an estate valued at over ¥500 million account for 2.9% of all reported decedents, and tax revenues from this group were responsible for 42.6% of the total inheritance tax revenues for 1983.

Taxes on Consumption

Excise taxes are levied on particular commodities and services. Today, the leading items are liquor, gasoline, and automobile-related taxes. Table 7.2 shows that during the period of FY 1934 to 1936, indirect taxes on the average accounted for 65.2% of total revenues from national taxes. After World War II until the late 1960s, indirect taxes contributed about one-half of total tax revenues. Since FY 1958, when 51.3% of revenue came from indirect taxes, the percentage of total revenue from indirect taxes has steadily decreased. The estimate for FY 1985 is 26.6%.

Liquor Tax

The liquor tax is the single largest consumption tax, accounting for 18.6% of revenues from indirect taxes and 5.0% of total national tax revenues in the FY 1985 estimates. At the turn of the century, the liquor tax provided more than one-third of the total national tax revenues. During the FYs 1934 to 1936 period, the liquor tax provided on average 17.6% of total national tax revenues. After the war, the percentage rose to 18.5% in FY 1950 and then declined.

For tax purposes, liquors are classified into 10 categories such as *saké*, wine, and whiskey. An ad valorem duty is applicable on imported liquors. Effective from May 1984, the tax rates on liquors have been raised on the average by 20%. The following are illustrations of the effective tax rates on retail prices: *saké*, 40.1% for special class, and 14.1% for second class; beer, 48.8%; wine, 5.5%; and whiskey, 50.3% for special class, and 29.5% for second class.

Manufacturers or sellers of liquors must obtain a license from the taxation office. As of the end of March 1985, there were 3,539 licensed breweries and 174,439 sellers. The liquor tax is imposed on domestic liquors shipped from manufacturing premises and on imported liquors withdrawn from bonded areas.

Commodity Tax

In 1937, Japan's commodity tax was first imposed on 10 items which were considered of a luxury nature or indicative of tax-bearing capacity. During World War II, 104 items were made subject to the commodity tax. This expansion in items was to increase revenues and to curb consumption. After the war, daily necessities and business machinery were deleted from the list.

During the 1960s and 1970s, the commodity tax was revised to cope with changes in consumption and transactions occurring with rapid economic growth. As a result, the majority of taxable commodities are luxury items, expensive goods, or goods used for amusement and hobbies. By the amendment of 1984, commodity tax items were increased from 80 to 85. In FY 1985, revenues from commodity taxes accounted for 14.6% of the total indirect tax revenues. More than one-third of the commodity tax revenues is from passenger cars.

For taxation purposes, commodities are divided into two classes. Ten items, which come under class 1 commodities, are levied at the retail stage on the basis of retail price. The rates range from 10 to 15%. Under class 2, the tax is levied at the time of shipment for domestic products and at the time of receipt from bonded areas for imported items. The tax basis for domestic products is the manufacturer's selling price. Imports are taxed on the basis of the price at receipt from the bonded area. For example, tax rates on automobiles range from 5 to 30% to depending on type and size.

Other Taxes

Those who travel by certain means of transportation must pay a travel tax of 10%. In FY 1982, 94.2% of revenues from the travel tax was from air travel. Attendance at movie theaters, sports events, horse races, and the like is charged an admission tax of 10%.

The securities transaction tax is imposed partly in lieu of the tax on capital gains on stocks and bonds. Registration of real estate and others and licenses for banking and certain other businesses are subject to the registration and license tax. A stamp tax is levied on documents for transfers of assets and contracts. In the statistics, the stamp revenue includes revenues from stamp tax and registration, and license tax.

Ranking second in importance as indirect tax, revenue from the gasoline tax accounts for 15.8% of total indirect tax revenues for the FY 1985 estimates. Such revenue is earmarked for construction and improvement of roads. The revenue from the local road tax, which is collected together with the gasoline tax, and a quarter of the revenue from the motor vehicle tonnage tax are earmarked for local roads. Revenue from the petroleum tax, which is an ad valorem duty, is used for various programs to secure a stable supply of petroleum and to develop alternative energy resources.

Customs Duties

Today, customs duties in Japan are no longer levied for revenue purposes. They are primarily used to protect domestic industries against foreign competition. Hence, they are closely related to foreign economic policy as well as to domestic industrial or agricultural policy. Revenue from customs duties, as a percentage of total national tax revenues, steadily rose from 2.3% in 1874, reached the peak of 17.6% in 1912, and fell to 0.1% the year before World War II ended. After the war, it recovered from 3.3% in 1955 to the postwar high of 7.2% in 1967. Since then, the customs tariffs have been reduced remarkably due to international agreements. In FY 1985, the revenue from customs duties, including those in the special account, is estimated to account for 2.1%

of total national tax revenues. Crude oil is the single largest revenue item and accounts for more than one-sixth of the total customs revenues.

Japan's customs duties are governed by the Customs Law, Customs Tariff Law, and Temporary Tariff Measures Law. The Customs Tariff Law provides for the general rates in its Customs Tariff Schedule, the classification of which is based on the Customs Co-operation Council Nomenclature (CCCN), covering about 2,250 tariff items. The Temporary Tariff Measures Law provides for the temporary rates which take precedence over general rates. However, in application priority is given to the General Agreement on Tariffs and Trade (GATT) rates unless they are higher than general or temporary rates. In the course of import liberalization, an emergency customs duty, tariff quota system, and selective tariffs have been instituted. The List of Simplified Duty Rates, incorporating excise tax, is available for the clearance of goods carried in travelers' baggage. In an effort to ease the problems of developing countries (the so-called North-South problem), Japan grants preferential tariff rates to goods from developing countries under the Generalized System of Preferences (GSP).

As a result of all-out tariff cutting efforts, in conformity with both Kennedy and Tokyo Rounds of multilateral tariff negotiations, the average tariff rate measured by the total amount of duties collected as a percentage of total import value has been reduced sharply from 7.7% in FY 1964 to 2.6 and 2.5% in FYs 1982 and 1983, respectively. The FY 1982 figure compares favorably with 3.6% of the United States, 2.7% of the EC, 4.3% of Canada, and 9.3% of Australia.

In terms of tariff items, about 18% are now free of duty. However, since many of these commodities are important to Japan, they account for more than one-third of the total import value. A majority of the rates are ad valorem. About 4% of the items are of specific duty but they cover such important items, including sugar and oil, that they contribute to about one-third of the total customs revenues. About a half of the items concentrates on tariff rate brackets from 5 to 10%. Under the philosophy of tariff escalation, the rates for raw materials and primary products are low and the rates rise as the degree of processing increases. To illustrate some items of interest, automobiles, watches, and semiconductors were made duty-free from 1978, 1983, and 1984, respectively. Recently the tariffs have been reduced to 20% on chocolate cookies; 20 or 24% on biscuits; 21.5% on cocoa; 20% (if converted to ad valorem) on cigarettes, 17.5% (between April and September) and 35% (between October and March) on bananas (GSP); and 6.6% on perfumery.

The effective tariffs on other major items of interest are as follows: 25% on beef; 20% (between June and November) and 40% (between December and May) on oranges; 35% on butter and cheese; 37 to 80% (in FY 1983, if converted to ad valorem) on refined and raw sugar; the lesser of 36% or ¥332 per liter, subject to a minimum duty of ¥299 per liter, on whiskey.

The Customs and Tariff Bureau of the Ministry of Finance is responsible for both tariff policy and customs administration. Revision of the rates of customs duty and other important related matters have to be referred to the Customs Tariff Council, an organ attached to the Ministry of Finance. For administration purposes, the country is divided into nine districts, in each of which there is one custom house (headquarters) and several branch offices and guard posts.

Customs duty is to be paid, in principle, under the self-assessment system. However, the official assessment system is applied to customs duties on goods accompanied or unaccompanied by persons entering Japan, on postal items, and some other specific items. The system of bonded areas and transportation in bond are available to ensure the correct procedures for customs clearance of goods as well as to facilitate transaction of imported goods, and to promote the transit and processing trade.

International Aspects of Japanese Tax

Nonresidents and Foreign Corporations

Nationality has little relevance with respect to foreign taxpayers. The important distinction is the classification of residents and nonresidents and limited and unlimited tax liabilities. Those foreigners who reside in Japan for less than a year are classified as "nonresidents" and subject to limited tax liability. All others are "residents" and are subject to unlimited tax liability. Unlimited taxpayers pay taxes on all sources of income wherever derived. Limited taxpayers pay tax only on the income derived from Japanese sources. Japanese sources of income are from business activities or income from property located in Japan. A special category of "nonpermanent resident" covers those individuals who do not intend to remain in Japan for more than five years. A nonpermanent resident's foreign income is not taxed as long as the foreign income is not remitted to Japan. Foreign corporations or nonresidents who have a fixed place of business in Japan are subject to aggregate income taxation at the normal rates for income from sources within Japan.

Taxable income and tax amount for foreign corporations and non-residents are computed in the same way as their domestic counterparts. However, while not all the deductions and credits are allowed, tax on undistributed profits and special additional tax on family corporations are not levied and certain exceptions are made for interest income. Income from sources in Japan is subject to 20% withholding at the source. A nonresident or foreign corporation who is subject to aggregate income taxation must file a return in the same way as a resident or domestic corporation.

Foreign Tax Credit

In order to eliminate double taxation, foreign taxes levied on domestic corporations or residents may be credited against their tax liability. Limits on the credit are based on the ratio of foreign income to total income. Also taking into consideration the OECD Council Recommendation on Tax Avoidance and Evasion (1977), taxation on the undistributed profits of foreign subsidiaries was instituted in 1978. Undistributed income of foreign subsidiaries located in 33 countries or territories designated as tax havens must be included in the gross income of the domestic corporation.

Double Taxation Conventions

Japan has tax treaties with regard to double taxation with 35 capitalist and socialist states. In general, these tax treaties are based on the principles adopted by the OECD in 1963 and modified in 1977, with due regard given to the United Nations Model Covention of 1980.

Most of Japan's treaties with developing countries feature the tax-sparing credit. Under this device, Japanese investors may deduct from their own tax in Japan an amount corresponding to a tax which would have been paid to these developing countries but for the tax concessions granted. This credit is allowed to enable developing nations to achieve their objectives of tax incentive measures for economic development.

Tax Administration

Organization of Tax Administration

While the Tax Bureau of the Ministry of Finance is responsible for tax policy, the National Tax Administration (NTA) is in charge of tax administration. The Tax Bureau prepares tax legislation on the basis of the recommendations of the Tax Commission. The commission studies and makes recommendations on long-range tax policy as well as yearly changes in the tax systems.

The NTA was established in 1949 as an affiliated agency of the Ministry of Finance and is in charge of the enforcement of the tax laws. Under the National Office of the NTA are 11 Regional Taxation Bureaus and the Okinawa Regional Taxation Office. These organizations have jurisdiction over their respective regions and the 512 taxation offices which administer the subdivisions within the regions.

The National Office issues rulings to the regional bureaus and offices but does not audit taxpayers. The regional organizations supervise each taxation office and may intervene in some cases. For example, cases involving audits of large corporations or cases of tax fraud, evasion, or arrearage may be handled by a regional bureau. The size of taxation offices differs, the smallest with 30 officers and the largest almost 300.

As of July 1985, tax officials totaled 52,852. Almost 80% of them are assigned to the taxation offices. By type of duty, 52.4% are engaged in direct taxes, 4.6% in audit and intelligence, 8.3% in indirect taxes, 14.5% in tax collection, and the rest in disposition of disputes, training of staff, administration, and other activities. In the last decade, the number of tax officials has leveled off while the persons filing returns have increased by some 40%. As a result of cost-cutting efforts and the increase in tax revenues, the cost for raising every ¥100 of national tax was halved from ¥2.79 in FY 1950 to ¥1.13 in FY 1985.

Self-assessment Taxation and Tax Withholding

The self-assessment system replaced the official assessment system in 1947; each taxpayer computes the tax base and tax amount and files a return with the taxation office. The taxation office examines the returns and, if found incorrect, such returns are subject to reassessment or correction by the director of the taxation office. Returns are divided into blue and white returns. In 1984, nearly 2.9 million people were eligible to file a blue return, and nearly 1.5 million actually filed a return. Nearly 1.8 million corporations, 91.1% of eligible corporations, filed a blue return. Those filing a white tax return may seek guidance from tax officials at the taxation offices.

The tax withholding system plays a vital role in the self-assessment system. Withholding enhances taxpayer compliance, ensures tax revenues, serves the taxpayer's convenience, and improves efficiency in tax administration. As of June 1983, there were 5.7 million tax-withholding agents of which 55.8% were for employment income. Owing to the unique mechanism of year-end adjustment by the withholding agent, out of 34.9 million wage and salary earners, only 3.8 million filed a return. During FY 1983, 72.8% of tax withheld was from employment income. In FY 1985, almost 80% of income tax is estimated to be withheld at the source.

About 26,000 or 0.3% of the total taxpayers were reassessed by the taxation offices in 1983. The amount of increase by such reassessment was ¥4.3 billion or 0.2% of the total revenues for the self-assessed income tax.

Corporation Tax

In FY 1984, of the total 2.0 million corporations liable to file a return, 89.9% did so. This represents an increase from the 58.5% that filed in FY 1950. Audits of corporation tax returns are classified according to the amount of the corporation's capital. Corporations with capital of ¥100 million or more as well as foreign corporations fall under the jurisdiction of the Regional Tax Bureaus. These large corporations totaling only 21,000 in number paid 67.1% of the total corporation tax in FY 1982. All other corporations are under the jurisdiction of the taxation offices.

Field audits were conducted on 192,100 cases at the taxation office level in FY 1984. This figure represented 9.9% of the total number of corporations. For 82.4% of the field audit cases, a correction or determination was made, and for 26.4% of the cases willfully false reportings were found. Tax payments by self-assessment in FY 1984 accounted for 96.6% in contrast to 68.9% in FY 1950.

Appeals

When a taxpayer wishes to protest the action of the tax authorities with regard to tax matters, an administrative protest (called a request for reinvestigation) may be filed with the agency which made the original disposition. A suit may not be brought in court unless an administrative decision has been made on the request. If the taxpayer is dissatisfied with the decision, a request for reconsideration can be filed with a higher level of the administrative agency. In the case of the national tax, the request for reconsideration is filed with the National Tax Tribunal, an organization attached to the NTA. The Tribunal was established in 1970 to protect the rights of taxpayers. It has 12 Regional Tribunals and 7 branch offices. The president is appointed by the commissioner of the NTA with the approval of the Ministry of Finance. The judges are appointed from among experienced judges of civil courts, tax officials, or high-ranking officials in the civil service.

8 | Government Bonds

Masazo Ohkawa

Government-bond issues have increased in recent years, and bonds
have become an important financing instrument. Originally these
bonds were used to finance construction projects. Lately, a bond to
finance government deficits has evolved. Increasing use of these deficit-
covering bonds entails the danger of leading to inflation. This chapter
discusses the development and use of government bonds in the postwar
period. As background, a brief history of government bonds in the
postwar era is presented. Methods of issuing bonds and distribution
of bondholders are then described. Finally, the consequences of the
government's present bond policy are discussed.

A Brief History of Postwar Government Bonds

Since the end of World War II, the government has undergone dramatic changes in the financing of its expenditures. These changes have been,
in part, due to cyclical business conditions and due in part to the political pressures both inside and outside government. During the 1960s
and the first half of the 1970s, Japan had a high rate of economic
growth. The government enjoyed high tax revenues and could finance
increased expenditures as well as reduce tax rates. However, in the
second half of the 1970s the government could no longer depend on
increasing tax revenues. The oil crisis resulted in depressed business
conditions, and tax revenues in FY 1975 fell far below the original
budget estimates. The government was in a serious financial situation,
and bonds to finance the deficit were issued for the first time.

Some Keynesian economists have advocated a policy of budget
deficits to stimulate effective demand. They have strongly recommended
the issuance of government bonds to fill the revenue deficit, thus causing an expansionary budget. Since 1975, the government has justified
issuing bonds by declaring efficiency and equity in the financing of its

123

investment expenditures. Financing deficits by issuing bonds does not necessarily shift the burden of government expenditures to future generations. However, the government has tried to convince the public of the efficient and equitable relations between present and future generations. The future generations which will enjoy the benefits of government investment will also be required to pay the debt-servicing expenditure including interest payment and capital-refunding. If the whole of government investment expenditures is financed by taxes collected from the present generation, an unequal burden is imposed. Taxation of the present generation may lead to inefficiency in government investment. Until 1974, the total government bond issue did not exceed the total government investment (for construction works) in the general account budget. Thus the government bonds issued were called "construction" bonds. The issuance of government bonds for the general account budget were lawful in such special cases as when the revenues raised were used for government investments.

Deficit-Covering Bonds to Finance Current Consumption Expenditures

Toward the end of FY 1975, the government faced a critical financial situation due to tax revenues far below the original budget estimate. To cover the large revenue deficit, the government issued construction bonds and a new type of deficit-covering bond, the latter to finance the government deficit. Table 8.1 lists the amount of deficit-covering bonds,

Table 8.1. Transition in the Issue of Government Bonds, 1975–82 (General Account) (¥ billion, %)

	Amount of bond issue (A)	% of (A) to total expenditures	Amount of deficit-covering bond issue (B)	% of (B) to current expenditures	Government debt outstanding (C)	% of (C) to GNP
1975	5,280.5	25.3	2,290	13.9	14,973.1	9.9
1977	9,561.2	32.9	4,957	21.6	31,902.4	16.9
1979	13,472.0	34.7	6,917	22.4	56,251.3	25.3
1981	12,899.9	27.5	5,860	15.3	82,273.4	32.3
1982	14,044.7	29.7	7,309	18.9	96,482.2	36.1

Source: Extracted from Zaisei Seisaku Kenkyūkai 1984, Table 5, p. 114.

the total amount of bonds issued, and government debt as a percentage of the GNP.

Until 1975 the Public Finance Law, which regulates the preparation and execution of government budgets, did not permit the issuance of deficit-covering bonds. Based on the wartime experience of war bonds and the resultant hyperinflation, the postwar Public Finance Law mandated a balanced budget based on principles of sound finance. However, construction bonds were legal though limited by the amount of government investment expenditures. For deficit-covering bonds, it was feared that there would be no means to control the deficits.

The business community argued emphatically for increased government expenditures financed by government bond issues. Facing a lack of private investment, the government reacted by initiating a "big government" policy. Bond issues approached and exceeded legal limits. The government authorized expanded bond issues by passing the Exceptional Law on Bond Issues. Every year since 1975, outstanding governmental debt has increased, amounting to a total of ¥96,482.2 billion by the end of FY 1982. Of the total, deficit-covering bonds occupy 41.8%, equivalent to ¥40,330.1 billion.

In the 1980s, nearly all developed countries resorted to deficit financing. Their financial difficulties have been a result of static or decreased tax revenues combined with political pressure for increased government expenditures. The Japanese government has been faced with the most difficult financial condition. This difficulty is apparent by examining the percentage of total bonds issued to total budget expenditures. Table 8.2 presents this ratio for the United States, the United Kingdom, West Germany, and Japan. Japan has had the highest percentage every year with a variation between 25 and 35%. Can such a high ratio of bond issuance to government expenditure be justified? Surprisingly, about 20% of current revenues have been defrayed by revenue from bond issues.

The high percentage of government bond issues violates the principles of sound finance and a balanced budget, foundations for stable capitalistic development. Violation of economic principles in democratic societies seems common. Politicians are elected by the public and are motivated to support large expenditures while minimizing taxes. They must satisfy voters to be elected, and the voters may have only short-term interests in mind.

Desiring a balanced budget, the Ministry of Finance has tried to narrow the gap between expenditures and tax revenues. As a whole, it has not approached the desired goal. The increased rates of expendi-

Table 8.2. International Comparison of Government Bonds (%)

Country	Year	Bond issue / Total expenditures	Interest payment / Total expenditures	Long-term debt / GNP
Japan	1979	34.7	8.5	30.5
	1980	32.6	10.1	34.5
	1984	25.0	17.5	47.7
U.S.A.	1980	10.3	9.1	27.5
	1984	20.9	12.9	
	1985	19.2	13.2	
U.K.	1979	10.9	6.8	43.8
	1980	13.1	6.6	46.1
	1984	5.2	6.6	
West Germany	1979	12.8	5.5	13.9
	1980	12.8	6.5	15.1
	1984	13.1	(11.4)	

Source: Same as Table 8.1, p. 183.

tures have been reduced from nearly 20% in 1975 to a single-digit percentage figure since 1980. However, the deficit is so large that controlling expenditures will not solve the problem. A number of academics, fearing financial difficulties, believe that tax increases should be implemented. However, some major obstacles must be overcome for the introduction of a general consumption tax.

Political parties understand the economic necessity for returning to a balanced budget. However, these parties oppose any tax increase which may place an additional burden on their political supporters. Following the interests of their voters, political parties generally favor bills which promise voters visible benefits but which carry invisible burdens. Little attention is paid to bills with invisible benefits to the general voters, but there is vigorous opposition to any bill with visible burdens to the voters. A tax burden is clearly visible in the eyes of the voters, but a bond burden is less visible. Thus political parties are not inclined to introduce new taxes to replace the present bond burden. As to expenditures, politicians avoid reducing social-welfare expenditures which are clearly visible benefits. Politicians can then be considered the main promoters of big government.

In spite of these political inclinations against increased taxes and reduced expenditures, the need for tax increases has gradually become accepted among intelligent, non-political people. A portion of the population clearly recognizes the undesirable effects of present bond issue policy on the national economy. Present bond issue policy has two undesirable effects. First, the percentage of interest payments and other debt servicing has increased dramatically. In FY 1984 the percentage of interest payments and debt-servicing costs to total government expenditures amounted to more than 18%. Rapid growth of these obligatory expenditures naturally leads to a rigidity in budget-making. In other words, the government has been losing the fiscal ability to cope with new social needs. Second, there is a fear of inflation since there will be keener competition between the government and the private sector for the limited supply of monetary funds. The likely result will be a rise in interest rates.

Government Bond Issuance and Distribution of Bond Holders

Presently, there are three methods of issuing new government bonds depending upon the classification of the underwriter. Underwriters are divided into three groups: (a) the underwriting syndicate; (b) the Trust Fund Bureau; and (c) the general public. When postwar government bonds were first issued, most were underwritten by the so-called syndicate consisting of a variety of financial institutions. As the amount of government bonds has increased each fiscal year, the ratio underwritten by the Trust Fund Bureau and by the general public has increased. The continuous, large-scale growth of government bond issues has placed strong pressure on the domestic financial market.

Underwriting by the Syndicate

The underwriting syndicate was formed to assist in the marketing of the large volume of government bonds. Through consultation with the Ministry of Finance and the Bank of Japan, the syndicate is responsible for determining the total amount of government bonds issued per year, the issuing terms, and the amount to be issued per month.

The financial institutions listed in Table 8.3 form the underwriting syndicate. The procedure for marketing of government bonds is as follows. First, the total amount is divided between the securities firms and other syndicate members. The securities firms are responsible for distributing their underwritten share of government bonds to individuals, non-financial firms, and associations. The rest of the government bonds are allocated to each of the ten groups of financial institutions according to an established allocation. Table 8.4 presents the allocation shares for FY 1982. The part allocated to each group is allocated further to each member of the group. The allocation share by the group of

8.3. Government Bond Underwriting Share and Available Fund Share by Type of Financial Institution

Financial institution	No.	Underwriting share 1982 (%)	Available fund share 1980 (%)
City banks	13	42.2	30.3
Long-term credit banks	3	10.1	7.9
Local banks (representatives)	5	19.8	21.8
Trust banks (representative)	1	6.7	1.9
Mutual banks (representative)	1	5.0	9.6
National Union of Credit Union	1	5.6	12.5
Central Cooperative Bank for Agriculture and Forestry	1	4.4	4.0
Life insurance companies (representative)	1	5.1	9.6
Non-life insurance companies (representative)	1	1.1	2.3
Securities firms (representatives)	6		
Total	33	100.0	100.0

Note: The classification of banks into city and local banks is not made in the Banking Law but for convenience for the administration of the banks by the government. City banks are characterized as having much more funds available, nationwide networks of branch offices, and larger-enterprise customers. In contrast, local banks are characterized as having less funds available, business in a limited and local area, and smaller-enterprise customers.
Source: Suzuki 1983, pp. 64, 67.

financial institutions has been determined in proportion to the amount of available funds held in each group. In reality, the allocation share does not always correspond to the available funds share listed in Table 8.3. City banks, in particular, have been complaining about their heavier burden.

Underwriting by the Trust Fund Bureau

The main function of the Trust Fund Bureau has been to supply low-interest funds for the Fiscal Investment and Loan Program (FILP). Since the first postwar issuance of government bonds in 1965, another function has been added to the Trust Fund Bureau. Table 8.4 lists the total amount of government bond issues and the percentage distribution of these issues among the syndicate, the Trust Fund Bureau, and by open bidding. Table 8.5 shows that the importance of the Trust

Table 8.4. Transition in the Underwriting Ratios by Method of Underwriting Government Bonds

Year	Total revenue from government bonds issuance (¥ billion)	Syndicate (%)	Trust Fund Bureau (%)	Open bidding (%)
1970	347.2	91.4	8.6	
1975	5,280.5	84.1	15.9	
1978	10,674.0	87.8	2.8	9.4
1979	13,472.0	72.5	19.8	7.7
1980	14,170.2	59.8	28.0	12.2
1981	12,899.9	49.7	34.3	16.0
1982	14,345.0	55.6	25.8	18.6

Source: Same as Table 8.3, p. 62.

Table 8.5. Distribution of Government Bond Holders (%)

Holder \ Year	1975	1977	1978	1979	1980	1981
Private financial institutions	36.3	45.7	48.6	42.0	32.1	29.0
(City banks)	(16.3)	(19.2)	(19.3)	(14.0)	(9.2)	(7.4)
(Others)	(20.0)	(26.5)	(29.3)	(28.0)	(22.8)	(21.6)
Individuals, etc.	7.8	19.2	21.9	27.8	38.3	40.9
Trust Fund Bureau	19.7	15.5	10.1	14.4	16.9	20.3
Bank of Japan	36.2	19.5	19.3	15.8	12.8	9.9
Total	100.0	100.0	100.0	100.0	100.0	100.0

Source: Same as Table 8.3, pp. 94–95.

Fund Bureau as an underwriter has been growing while the share of underwriting by the syndicate has been declining. Thus private financial institutions have steadily been freed from the less profitable burden imposed by the deficit policy of the government. As more of the available funds go through the Trust Fund Bureau to underwrite government bonds, less funds are available for the FILP. This means there are less funds available for public works like highway construction, flood control, and airport construction. A part of the burden of deficit-covering bonds on the people manifests itself in lower public works expenditures.

Open Bidding

Unlike syndicate underwriting, which is half-compulsory, open bidding can be characterized as a voluntary underwriting, voluntary in the sense that financial investors for government bonds competitively participate in the subscription without government pressure. Open bidding was introduced experimentally in June 1978 in hopes of making the issuance of medium-term bonds easier. Open bidding is desirable because the issuing terms and total amounts of bond issues are determined by supply and demand in the financial markets. However, open bidding cannot be relied upon as a stable source of revenue. Depending on conditions prevailing in the money market, the amounts of revenue raised may be less than desired. Table 8.4 shows that the percentage of total bond issuance by open bidding has increased since 1979. The increase indicates that the government has allowed the issuing terms for medium-term bonds to be determined by market interest rates.

Distribution of Government Bonds Holders

Table 8.4 shows the rising percentage of bonds underwritten by the Trust Fund Bureau and by open bidding. The ratio of bonds underwritten by financial institutions in the syndicate has been declining proportionally. This shift leads to changes in the distribution of bond holders.

City banks have been asked to underwrite a greater percentage of government bonds than their percentage in distribution of available funds. Thus city banks are naturally motivated to sell these less profitable bonds back to the Bank of Japan (BOJ) as soon as they are allowed to. Government-issued bonds are purchased by the BOJ to supply as much money as required for stable growth. This buying operation by the BOJ should result in the decline of city banks as bond holders and a corresponding increase in the BOJ share.

However, Table 8.5 shows that the ratio of bonds held by the Bank of Japan has been rapidly declining over the years. The table presents the percent holding of government bonds by financial institutions, individuals, the Trust Fund Bureau, and the BOJ. One reason for the decline in the BOJ share is that the BOJ has followed a strict money supply policy. Another reason is that the holdings by the Trust Fund Bureau and individuals have been growing. Corporations and non-profit corporations are included in the "individuals" category.

The growth of individuals as bond holders can be ascribed to the favorable terms for these bonds in the bond circulation market. The circulation market has been active since April 1981 when city banks were allowed to sell government bonds on hand subject to the condition that sale occurred after 100 days after underwriting. Financial institutions, particularly city banks, have not willingly assumed the business of underwriting government bonds. If possible, they want to part with these less-attractive securities. Presently the transfer of government bonds from city banks to individuals has not resulted in difficulties. However, a time may come when the BOJ may be asked to buy the bonds being sold in the circulation market.

Government Bond Policy in the Future

The large total of outstanding government bonds, nearly ¥141 trillion, results in a high debt-servicing expenditure. This debt-service expenditure totaled ¥8,865.7 billion in FY 1984, equivalent to 17.5% of all government expenditures. Debt-servicing expenditures are obligatory and must be paid prior to other expenditures. This results in a growing rigidity in government finance. To overcome such rigid financial constraints, the government is apt to depend on other government bonds. Thus there is the danger of creating a vicious circle of debt-servicing expenditures and government-bond revenues. To escape this vicious circle the government has tried to control expenditures while increasing tax revenues. It has partly succeeded in controlling expenditures but has not succeeded in raising tax revenues.

From FY 1985 on, the government must redeem expired bonds, an additional expenditure for a government already plagued by deficits. In preparing the budget for FY 1985, the Ministry of Finance intends to refund nearly all of the expired bonds. According to the original regulations, construction bonds have a 10-year term with an authorization to refund the bonds 5 times (to account for the 60-year life of construction assets). Deficit-covering bonds cannot be refunded and must be redeemed at expiration without exception. Presently, the government intends to break the traditional rule of redeeming deficit-covering bonds at expiration. Refinancing deficit-covering bonds can have an inflationary impact, and we must guard ourselves against taking steps that lead to inflation.

9 | The Local Public Finance System

Nobuo Ishihara

An Overview of Local Public Finance

Local autonomy is guaranteed by the constitution, in chapter VIII on local self-government. The Local Autonomy Law, the basic statute concerning the local government system, contains provisions for local tax and finance administration, and various other laws, such as the Local Finance Law, the Local Tax Law, and the Local Allocation Tax Law, delineate the finer points of local finance and taxation.

Local public finance has two dimensions: One dimension is the separate financial activities of 3,302 local government bodies (including 47 prefectures), each with their individual characteristics. (See p. 33n.) A second dimension is the macro local public finance operation as a single entity comparable to the national government.

Status of Local Public Finance

The net size of local public finance using the ordinary accounts for FY 1982 was as follows:

Revenue   ¥52,167.7 billion
Expenditure   ¥51,133.3 billion

National government expenditure for FY 1982 was ¥47,245.1 billion. Thus local government expenditures were 8% larger than that of the national government.

The gross breakdown of revenue and expenditure for prefectures and municipalities (including transfers to these bodies) was:

Prefectures	Revenue	¥27,731.4 billion
	Expenditure	¥27,424.3 billion
Municipalities	Revenue	¥27,149.6 billion
	Expenditure	¥26,422.2 billion

In size, the financial activities of the 47 prefectural governments were almost equal to those of the 3,255 municipal governments. This equivalence does not mean similarity of function, for their respective roles are different.

In terms of financial size the Tokyo metropolitan government (TMG) was the largest among the prefectures. TMG's expenditure in FY 1982 amounted to ¥3,277.7 billion, and Tottori prefecture was the smallest with an expenditure of ¥240.4 billion in the same year. Among municipalities, the largest was Osaka with ¥989.8 billion expenditure, and the smallest was a village in Aichi prefecture that had an expenditure of ¥0.35 billion.

Besides the ordinary accounts listed above, the finances of local public enterprises are very large. In FY 1982, the final accounts for 7,853 enterprises totaled ¥10,737.2 billion (Table 9.6).

The total national expenditure for FY 1982 is presented in Figure 9.1. Gross national expenditure amounted to ¥267,351 billion which was divided in part as follows: ¥216,782 billion for private expenditure and ¥50,569 billion for public expenditure. Of the total private expenditure, ¥179,336 billion was for household expenditure and ¥34,784 billion for corporate expenditures. Of the total public expenditure, local expenditure accounted for ¥36,431 billion, while national government expenditure accounted for ¥13,664 billion. With respect to total national expenditure, local government was responsible for 13.6% and the national government was responsible for 5.1%. Thus in terms of final expenditures, local public bodies are much larger than the national government. Local public finance has been expanding at a pace exceeding that of the national economy. The local expenditure index for FY

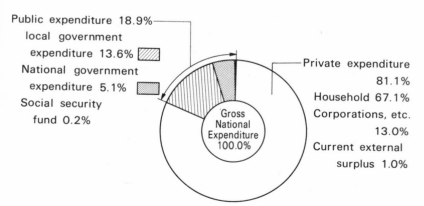

Fig. 9.1. The Gross National Expenditure, 1982
Source: Ministry of Home Affairs, *Chihō zaisei hakusho*, 1984.

1982 was 2,138 (base of 100 for FY 1961), which far exceeded the fiscal 1982 GNP index of 1,347, using the same fiscal base.

National Public Finance and Local Public Finance

Financial Relationship Between the National and Local Governments

The national government and local governments are expected to perform their functions based on a division of roles and an attitude of mutual cooperation. However, financial relationships among the different levels of government are becoming increasingly complex, due in part to the current socio-economic milieu. Of great importance is the guarantee of autonomous management for local public finance. The financial relationship between the national and local governments is specified in the Local Finance Law: "The central government shall endeavor to promote the self-dependence and soundness of local finance, and refrain from any action prejudicial to the financial autonomy of local governments or from shifting its burden upon local governments" (Local Finance Law, Article 2 (2)). Under this article, financial intervention by a higher level of government is limited to maintaining the sound operation of public finance.

The Local Finance Law provides for the burden of expenses as follows: Article 9 provides that all expenses for the affairs of the local body or its organs shall be borne by such local public body. However, this rule has exceptions for certain expenses enumerated in Article 10, subsections (10) (ii) through (10) (iv), which prescribe the cases in which all or part of the expenses must be borne by the national government:

(1) expenses which affect both national and local interests but are performed by the local body according to law (the national government bears such expenses to assure smooth performance);

(2) expenses for construction projects (as provided by law or by cabinet order) carried out under integrated plans for the national economy;

(3) expenses for measures related to disasters; and

(4) all expenses solely affecting the national government (e.g., expenses for national elections.

The purposes, standards for computing division of expenses, and the exact proportion of expenses to be borne by the national and local public bodies are determined by the law or by cabinet order. Obviously, the national government may grant subsidies to local public bodies only if such subsidies are found especially necessary for national policies or only for the finance of local public bodies.

Distribution of Revenues

Revenues are distributed between the different levels of government so that each level of government can perform its own tasks in a proper way. The present system of revenue distribution consists of the following four parts:

(1) Taxes are divided into national and local taxes, imposed by the national and local governments, respectively;

(2) Revenues from a number of national taxes are transferred (in whole or in part) to local governments;

(3) National disbursements are paid to local governments to finance a part of or all of the expenses related to specific expenditure programs;

(4) Payments by local governments to the national government to finance a number of special programs run by the national government.

Scale of Expenditures

A comparison between national government expenditures in the general account and local government expenditures in the ordinary account is presented in Table 9.1. Gross expenditures for the national government and local governments are nearly equal in the years listed. However, when these gross expenditures are adjusted by transfer payments between bodies, the importance of local governments is apparent. Adjustments for transfers results in total net expenditures of ¥80,402.8 billion in FY 1982. Net expenditures of all local governments account for 62.9% of total net expenditures (both local and national). Net total expenditures for local governments accounted for 18.9% of gross national expenditures (GNE).

Table 9.1. Expenditures by the National Government
and Local Governments (¥ billion)

	1982	1980	1975	1970
Gross expenditure				
National (A)	50,546.5	46,006.5	22,758.4	8,626.6
Local (B)	51,133.3	45,780.8	25,654.5	9,814.9
Transfers				
from national (C)	20,755.1	19,132.2	10,601.5	3,999.9
from local (D)	521.9	460.1	266.8	126.2
Net expenditure	80,402.8	72,195.0	37,544.6	14,315.4
National (A) – (C)	29,791.4	26,874.3	12,156.9	4,626.7
Local (B) – (D)	50,611.4	45,320.7	25,387.7	9,688.7
Gross national				
expenditures	267,350.9	240,847.0	151,797.0	75,091.6

Source: Ministry of Home Affairs, *Chihō zaisei hakusho.*

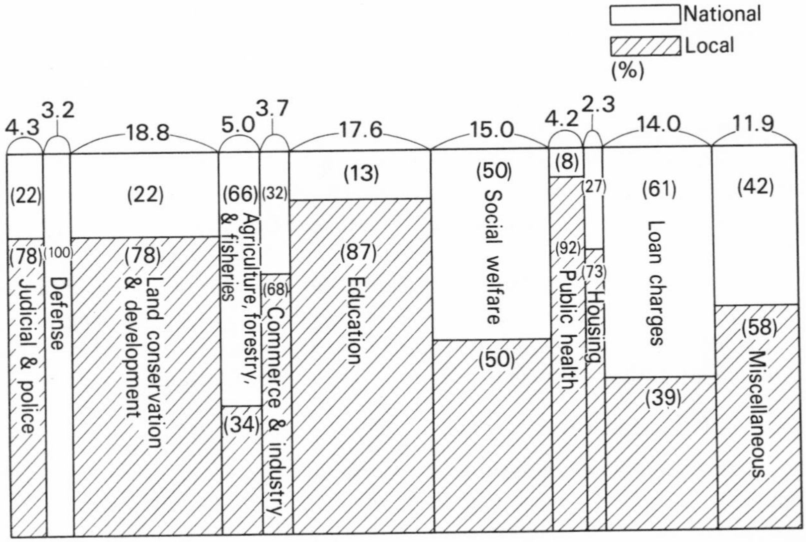

Fig. 9.2. Ratio of Expenditures of National and Local Governments in Specific Fields

Note: Parentheses indicate the ratio of national and local expenditures.

Source: Same as Fig. 9.1.

Figure 9.2 presents the ratio of expenditures by national and local governments in specific fields of government services. The data are presented in bar chart form with the shaded area representing the share of local governments. Most of the public services, except for national defense and some others, are executed by the local governments.

Outline of Expenditures

The composition of expenditure varies by prefecture, municipality, size of the local government body, and by the nature of the community it serves. However, the composition of the macro local expenditure indicates the general condition of local public finance and the characteristics that distinguish it from national finance.

Expenditure by Purpose

Figure 9.3 presents local government expenditures (all local public entities, prefectures, and municipalities) analyzed by purpose, given as percentages of total expenditures. Seven categories (general admin-

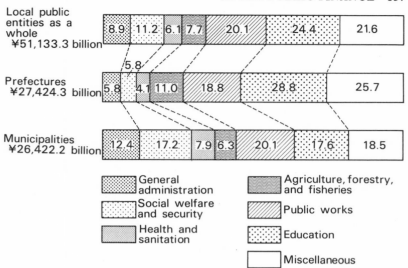

Fig. 9.3. Local Government Expenditures Analyzed by Purpose, 1982
Source: Same as Fig. 9.1.

istration, social welfare and security, health and sanitation, agriculture, forestry and fisheries, public works, education, and miscellaneous) are compared. Net settlement of accounts is calculated by deducting expenditures duplicated by prefectural and municipal accounts.

Expenditure for all local public entities in FY 1982 was ¥51,133.3 billion. This total includes the following expenditures: education ¥12,454.7 billion or 24.4% of total expenditures; public works ¥10,261.6 billion or 20.1%; and social welfare ¥5,745.3 billion or 11.2%. The high percentage for education expenditure is attributable to the fact that compulsory education and high school education are mainly financed by local governments.

The percentage for public works expenditure has fluctuated in the past fifteen years. These fluctuations were as follows: A decrease in public works expenditure between FY 1973 and FY 1976; an upward tendency in 1977 as a result of expanded public works designed to reflate the economy; and a decrease again in FY 1979.

Percentages for social welfare expenditures increased until FY 1976 and have stabilized at around 11%. Specifically, the percentage for social welfare was only 7% until FY 1971, then reached 9.9% in FY 1973, reflecting the rapid increase in expenditures, such as free medical care, for the aged.

Percentages for local loan charges have been increasing rapidly in recent years, the result of large increases in local loan issues to make up for the fiscal deficits of local governments. The increase in local fiscal deficits has occurred since FY 1975.

Figure 9.3 also shows the breakdown of expenditures at the prefectural and municipal levels, again based on settlement of accounts. At the prefectural level, the percentage of education expenditure is the highest at 28.8 %, followed by public works with 18.8 % and agriculture, forestry, and fisheries with 11.0 %. At the municipal level, the percentage for public works expenditure (20.1 %) is the highest, then education expenditures (17.6 %), and social welfare expenditures (17.2 %) are third. The percentage of education expenses is high at the prefectural level because the prefectures pay the education-related personnel costs, representing about 60 % of the total cost of education.

Expenditure by Nature

Figure 9.4 presents the expenditure of local public bodies classified by the nature of expenditure, based on settlement of accounts. These items of expenditure are divided into obligatory expenditure, capital expenditure, and other expenditure. Obligatory expenditure consists of personnel expenditure, such as salaries, social assistance expenditure (e.g., livelihood protection), and loan charges for redemption of principal and interest payments. Once expanded, obligatory expenditure is difficult to reduce as it affects fiscal flexibility. Its percentage is regarded as an important index in the analysis of a local public body's financial stability. In FY 1982, obligatory expenditure amounted to ¥24,113.6 billion (47.2 % or nearly half the total), and capital expenditure reached ¥15,977.3 billion (31.2 %). The percentage of obligatory expenditure reached its highest in FY 1976. After 1977 it began to decrease because of decreases in personnel expenditure, although the percentage of local loan charges is still increasing.

In terms of specific expenditure categories for all local bodies, personnel expenditures were highest at 31.1 % of total expenditure, followed by ordinary construction expenditure with 29.1 %. About 70 % of obligatory expenditure was personnel expenditure. Comparing prefectural and municipal obligatory expenditures, prefectural percentages (47.3 %) exceed that of municipalities (42.6 %). This difference results from the higher percentage of personnel expenditures (including education) at prefectural governments (36.2 %).

LOCAL PUBLIC FINANCE 139

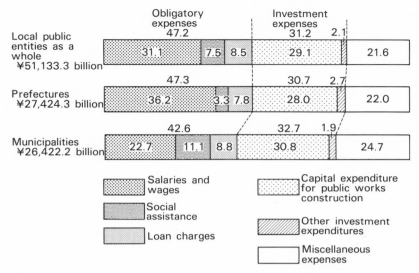

Fig. 9.4. Local Government Expenditures Classified by Nature, 1982
Source: Same as Fig. 9.1.

Outline of Revenues

Categories of Revenues

Revenue of local public bodies can be divided generally into six categories: local taxes, local allocation tax, local transfer taxes, national
government disbursements, local public loans, and miscellaneous
items. Table 9.2 presents the settled accounts of revenue (FY 1982)
for these various categories for the prefectures, municipalities, and
total revenue.

Local Taxes   The principal method of financing government expenditures is by taxation. Thus, local taxes are the fundamental method by
which local public bodies gain financial resources. However, local
public bodies can no longer depend upon local taxes because of the
economic disparities among different regions. In addition there has
been a growing demand for equalization of administrative services
throughout the country. As a result of this public pressure, a local tax
allocation system was established.

Local Allocation Tax   Local allocation tax is levied to secure equitable distribution of financial resources among local public bodies and
to guarantee sufficient revenue to execute planned administration in
each locality. Under this system, the national government reserves a

Table 9.2. Settled Accounts of Revenue, 1982 (¥ billion, %)

Items	Prefectures		Municipalities		Total	
Local taxes	9,206.1	33.2	9,422.5	34.7	18,628.6	35.7
Local transfer taxes	183.4	0.7	276.6	1.0	460.1	0.9
Local allocation tax	4,977.2	17.9	4,200.4	15.5	9,177.6	17.6
Tax transfers	—	—	281.8	1.0	—	—
(General revenue)	14,366.8	51.8	14,181.4	52.2	28,266.3	54.2
Shares defrayments	381.5	1.4	386.5	1.4	517.9	1.0
Charges, fees	587.3	2.1	623.8	2.3	1,211.1	2.3
National government disbursements	7,112.3	25.6	3,953.4	14.6	11,065.7	21.2
Special traffic safety grant	30.8	0.1	20.9	0.1	51.7	0.1
Prefectural government disbursements	—	—	1,585.2	5.8	—	—
Income from properties	278.7	1.0	512.8	1.9	791.5	1.5
Contributions	14.8	0.1	157.8	0.6	169.1	0.3
Transfer	213.3	0.8	505.6	1.9	718.9	1.4
Adjusting funds	273.1	1.0	615.2	2.3	888.3	1.7
Miscellaneous	2,119.5	7.6	1,612.8	5.9	3,568.3	6.8
Local public loans	2,351.8	8.5	2,677.5	9.9	4,918.9	9.4
Others	1.4	0.0	316.8	1.2	—	—
Total revenues	27,731.4	100.0	27,149.6	100.0	52,167.7	100.0

Note: National government disbursements include government shares to municipalities where specific government properties are located.
Source: Same as Table 9.1.

certain ratio of national tax revenues as a common fund for local bodies. It then distributes funds to each local public body according to their needs and local revenue sources, based on a detailed equation determined by the national government.

The total amount granted as local allocation tax in one fiscal year is fixed at 32% of the revenues from specified national taxes (personal income tax, corporation tax, and liquor tax). There is virtually no constraint on the use of the local allocation tax distribution, and local bodies may use the monies for whatever purpose they choose.

Local Transfer Taxes   Local transfer taxes are collected by the national government and transferred to local public bodies. Distribution of revenues are based on a simple formula (e.g., total area of public roads).

Revenues from local taxes, local allocation tax, and local transfer taxes are not earmarked for specific uses. Thus these three types of tax revenues are labelled general revenue sources.

The ratio of tax revenue to total revenue for local public bodies is about one to three. The tax revenue for the national government is a little less than 70% of the total revenue. The amount of revenue for the local allocation tax is about one-half of the local tax. General revenue sources account for 54.2% of total revenue.

National Government Disbursements for Specific Purposes The largest specific revenue source to local public bodies is the national government disbursement for specific purpose which accounts for 21.2% of total revenue. The relative weight of national government disbursement is much higher in the total revenue of prefectures than in municipalities. These disbursements are usually classified into two broad categories: (1) disbursements for national functions delegated to local public bodies, their executive organs, or administered by them; (2) disbursements for part or all of the costs of local functions to promote national objectives. Disbursements for delegated tasks are termed national treasury payments for agential tasks. Disbursements for specific local functions are further divided into two categories: (1) disbursements to local public bodies to bear part or all of specific local expenditures; and (2) disbursements to execute specific services or to render financial assistance. In the Local Finance Law, the former is termed national treasury obligatory share, and the latter is termed national treasury grants-in-aid. Obligatory shares constitute the largest in terms of total amounts disbursed.

Local Public Loans Public loans are issued to overcome revenue shortages. A local public loan is a debt incurred in the form of a certificate or bill with a redemption period of more than two fiscal years. Dependency upon local public loans is increasing, accounting for 9.4% of total revenue.

Miscellaneous Revenue Miscellaneous revenue includes incomes from properties, shares, reimbursements, contributions, charges, and fees. The ratio of miscellaneous revenues to total revenue is not small (6.8%) and is an important source of revenue to local public bodies.

Local Taxes

Local taxes represent a major part of local government revenue. Local taxes are either prefectural taxes imposed by the 47 prefectural governments, or municipal taxes imposed by over 3,000 municipal governments. As appropriations, these taxes are classified as ordinary taxes for general expenditure or purpose taxes earmarked for specific expenditure. The Local Tax Law and its amendments provide the legal basis for imposition and collection of local taxes and serves as a guideline for the local tax system. Actual tax obligations are based on by-laws passed by local public bodies. These by-laws provide tax items, tax objects, tax bases, tax rates, and other details within the framework of the Local Tax Law.

While local codes function as implementing regulations, the Local Tax Law prescribes the basic framework of local taxation. National involvement in local taxation can be explained as follows: (1) The constitution (Article 94) requires that regulations by local public bodies be fixed by law; and (2) national legislation is necessary to avoid economic disorder.

The leeway in local taxation which public bodies enjoy varies from tax to tax. The greatest freedom for local public bodies is in the area of discretionary taxes. The Local Tax Law allows local governments to levy taxes, on the basis of their own legislation, other than statutory taxes with the permission of the minister of home affairs. Some examples of discretionary taxes currently in force are: merchandise certificate tax, advertisement tax, and nuclear fuel tax.

The present local tax system has two important characteristics. First, the present local tax system follows the principle of independent taxes. Local surtaxes, which played an important role in prewar Japan, have been abandoned. Under the prewar surtax system, local taxes were imposed on the same tax base as higher levels of government. Responsibility for administration was vague. In principle, each level of government now levies its own taxes.

Second, the working of the present local tax system is based upon the close cooperation established between the three levels of government: municipal, prefectural, and national. For example, both the prefectural and municipal inhabitant tax (counterpart of the U.S. local income tax) levied upon an individual is collected by the municipal government. The amount due to the prefecture is transferred by the municipal government. Another example is the tax basis for real property. The tax base for the real property acquisition tax (a prefectural tax) is the same as the assessed value of real property for the fixed assets tax (a municipal tax). Intergovernmental cooperation aims to reduce the cost of tax management through simplified administration.

Table 9.3 presents a breakdown of local tax revenue for FY 1982 by prefectures and municipalities. For prefectures, the inhabitant tax and the enterprise tax (counterpart of the state business tax in the U.S.) account for two-thirds of the total amount of revenue. For municipalities, the inhabitant tax and the fixed assets tax account for more than 80 % of the total tax revenue.

Local Inhabitant Tax The prefectural and the municipal inhabitant taxes are usually referred to as the local inhabitant tax. The American counterpart would be state and local income taxes. The local inhabitant tax is one of the most important local taxes, along with the enterprise tax and the fixed assets tax (real estate tax in the United States).

The local inhabitant tax can be divided into the individual inhabitant tax and the corporate inhabitant tax. The former is levied on an individual who has a domicile, office, or place of business within the jurisdiction (municipal or prefectural). January is the date upon which tax liability is decreed. Corporate inhabitant tax is levied on a corporation which has its office or place of business within the jurisdiction (prefecture or municipality). If a corporation has an office (or place of business) within the jurisdiction of two or more prefectures (or municipalities), the tax base for corporate inhabitant tax purposes is allocated to the prefecture (or municipalities) based on the number of employees working in each office (or place of business).

The individual inhabitant tax rate is composed of a per capita tax rate and an income tax rate. Similarly, the corporate inhabitant tax rate is composed of a per capita rate based on the number of employees and the amount of the capital, and a corporate income tax rate whose tax base is the amount of the national corporate tax. The inhabitant income tax has a less progressive rate structure than the national income tax. However, the inhabitant income tax levied on an individual is similar to the national income tax, as the tax base is basically the same.

Enterprise Tax The enterprise tax, the most important prefectural tax, accounts for less than 40 % of the total prefectural tax revenue. This tax is levied both on corporations and unincorporated businesses. In terms of tax revenues, the corporate enterprise tax collects a far greater share than individual enterprise tax does.

Corporation enterprise tax is, in principle, based on net income for most enterprises, and gross income for electricity or gas supply companies and insurance companies. Net income is calculated for each fiscal year of the business enterprise. The tax base for the individual enterprise tax is net income, regardless of the type of business, and is calculated on the basis of income of the preceding calendar year. If a taxpayer has an office or a place of business within the jurisdiction of two or more prefectures, the tax base is allocated to all prefectures concerned. The allocation is made on the basis of number of employees

Table 9.3 Local Tax Revenue, 1982
Prefectural taxes

Tax items	¥ billion	%
Ordinary taxes	7,572.1	90.9
Statutory taxes	7,563.5	90.8
Prefectural inhabitant tax	2,387.2	28.6
Individual	1,771.0	21.3
Corporation	616.2	7.4
Enterprise tax	3,176.3	38.1
Individual	104.9	1.3
Corporation	3,071.4	36.9
Real property acquisition tax	335.6	4.0
Prefectural tobacco consumption tax	277.7	3.3
Amusement tax	89.8	1.1
Meals and hotel tax	439.9	5.3
Automobile tax	844.6	10.1
Mine-lot tax	.9	0.0
Hunter's license tax	3.0	0.0
Prefectural fixed assets tax	8.5	0.1
Prefectural discretionary taxes	8.7	0.1
Purpose taxes	760.8	9.1
Automobile acquisition tax	293.2	3.5
Light oil delivery tax	465.4	5.6
Hunting tax	2.2	0.0
Total	8,332.9	100.0

continued on next page

or other pertinent indicators of the scale of business activities (e.g., value of fixed assets).

Personal allowances (e.g., dependents' deductions) are not allowed in individual enterprise tax, but ¥2.4 million is deducted in computing taxable income. The flat rate of 5% (3% or 4% for a number of business enterprises) is applied to taxable income after the entrepreneur deduction.

A flat rate of 1.5% is applied to corporate taxpayers where the basis of the tax is gross receipts. Tax rates for corporations taxed on net income are summarized as follows:

(1) A flat rate of 12% (8% for a number of special corporations) is applied to taxable net income of corporations which are capitalized at ¥10 million or over and have an office or place of business within the jurisdiction of three or more prefectural governments;

Table 9.3—*Continued*
Municipal taxes

Tax items	¥ billion	%
Ordinary taxes	9,550.9	92.8
Statutory taxes	9,543.0	92.7
Municipal inhabitant tax	5,184.7	50.4
Individual per capita rate	56.5	0.5
Individual income rate	3,612.3	35.1
Corporation per capita rate	42.0	0.4
Corporation tax rate	1,473.8	14.3
Fixed assets tax	3,320.4	32.3
Land	1,372.3	13.3
Buildings	1,230.9	12.0
Tangible business assets	601.5	5.8
Charges on the national government's and public corporations' assets	115.7	1.1
Light motor vehicle tax	48.2	0.5
Municipal tobacco consumption tax	487.8	4.7
Electricity tax	422.4	4.1
Gas tax	11.0	0.1
Mineral products tax	4.5	0.0
Timber delivery tax	2.8	0.0
Special land-holding tax	61.2	0.6
Municipal discretionary taxes	8.0	0.1
Purpose taxes	744.8	7.2
Spa tax	13.2	0.1
Business office tax	176.9	1.7
City planning tax	554.4	5.4
Water utility and land profit tax	0.3	0.0
Common facilities tax	—	—
Taxes based on laws currently not in force	0.0	0.0
Total	10,295.7	100.0

Source: Same as Table 9.1.

(2) A progressive tax rate for most corporations is shown below:

annual income up to ¥3.5 million	6%
annual income between ¥3.5 million and ¥7 million	9%
annual income over ¥7 million	12%

The tax rates described so far are called standard tax rates which prefectural governments are expected to levy. The Local Tax Law allows a prefectural government to increase the tax rate up to 110% of the standard tax rates.

Fixed Assets Tax The fixed assets tax is a municipal tax imposed on fixed assets (land, buildings, and tangible business assets) located within the jurisdiction of a municipality. This tax is based on the benefit principle. For municipalities, the fixed assets tax is one of the most important taxes along with the municipal inhabitant tax. The fixed assets tax meets the requirements of a local tax because the tax produces fairly stable revenue and the distribution of fixed assets is evenly spread throughout the country.

An owner listed in the tax register book as of January 1 is required to pay the fixed assets tax for the following fiscal year starting April 1. The tax is based on an assessment made by municipal assessors under guidelines determined by the minister of home affairs. Assessments of land and buildings are made every three years, while tangible business assets are assessed annually. The standard tax rate is 1.4% of assessed value. A municipal government may increase the tax rate up to 2.1% (150% of the standard tax rate). A taxpayer may petition for review of an assessment to the Fixed Assets Assessment Commission of each municipality.

Although the fixed assets tax, in principle, is a municipal tax, there is a limit placed on revenues. The municipal taxation limit (on revenues from the fixed assets tax) is determined by the Local Tax Law, based on the population of the municipality. This limit is used to redistribute tax revenues because the geographical distribution of business assets is highly uneven.

Automobile-Related Taxes   The number of automobiles has increased since the 1950s, and a significant part of national and local tax revenues comes from nine automobile-related taxes: (1) the gasoline tax; (2) the local road tax; (3) the light oil delivery tax; (4) the petroleum gas tax; (5) the automobile tax; (6) the light motor vehicle tax; (7) the commodity tax; (8) the automobile acquisition tax; and (9) the motor vehicle tonnage tax. The first four are classified as consumption taxes. The next two (5 and 6) are classified as property taxes. The following two (7 and 8) are classified as consumption or turnover taxes. The last (9) is considered a privilege tax. Among them, the automobile tax, the light motor vehicle tax, the light oil delivery tax, and the automobile acquisition tax are local taxes. The local road tax, the petroleum gas tax, and the motor vehicle tonnage tax are imposed and collected by the national government, but the revenues thereof are partially or totally transferred to local governments.

The automobile tax is imposed on a person who owns an automobile as of April 1 by the prefectural government where the automobile is registered. This tax has the dual characteristic of being a tax on property and a payment for road use. The standard tax rate of the automobile tax is provided in the Local Tax Law according to type of automobile, use, and cylinder displacement. Taxes levied on the compact private passenger car range between ¥30,000 and ¥40,000.

The light motor vehicle tax is imposed on the owner of a motor vehicle, light automobile, or two-wheeled motor vehicle (about ¥2,000 to ¥4,000 per vehicle). This tax is imposed by the municipality where the vehicle is registered. This tax also has a dual characteristic similar to the automobile tax. Maximum tax rates for the automobile and light motor vehicle taxes are set at 120% of standard tax rates.

The light oil delivery tax is imposed on a person who receives light oil from wholesalers. This tax is imposed by the prefecture where the wholesaler's office is located. The tax rate is ¥24,300 per kiloliter. Revenues from the light oil delivery tax are earmarked for road expenditure. A part of the revenue is transferred to the designated cities* in the prefecture in which the seller's office is located.

The automobile acquisition tax is a prefectural tax imposed on a person who buys an automobile. Revenue from this tax is also earmarked for road expenditure. The tax base is the selling price, and the tax rate is 5%. Part of the revenue (66.5%) is transferred to municipalities in the prefecture according to the length and width of roads in each municipality. Transfers are also made to cities responsible for maintaining national roads.

Local Transfer Taxes

The local transfer tax system is a financial arrangement in which revenues raised through national taxes are transferred to local governments based on an objective standard. The tax revenue transferred is inherently considered local government revenue sources. Theoretically, these taxes should be collected by local governments. However, taxpayer convenience, efficiency of tax collection, and regional disparity of tax base make national tax collection preferable to collection by the local governments.

Currently, there are five transfer taxes, listed in Table 9.4: (1) local road transfer tax; (2) petroleum gas transfer tax; (3) aviation fuel transfer tax; (4) motor vehicle tonnage transfer tax; and (5) special tonnage transfer tax. Revenue from the special tonnage transfer tax is classified as general revenue. Revenues from the other four are ear-

---

* Cities with populations over 500,000 and designated by cabinet order. They have more administrative and financial power than ordinary cities. Today they number ten: Sapporo, Kawasaki, Yokohama, Nagoya, Kyoto, Osaka, Kōbe, Hiroshima, Kitakyūshū, and Fukuoka.

Table 9.4. Local Transfer Taxes, 1982 (¥ billion)

Items	Prefectures	Municipalities	Total
Local road transfer tax	168.0	117.6	285.7
Petroleum gas transfer tax	12.7	2.2	14.9
Special tonnage transfer tax	0.3	10.2	10.5
Motor vehicle tonnage transfer tax	—	140.2	140.2
Aviation fuel transfer tax	2.4	6.4	8.8
Total	183.4	276.6	460.1

Source: Same as Table 9.1.

marked as revenue to be used for expenditures related to roads and airports. Thus the local transfer taxes are quite different from specific grants-in-aid, which are subject to many conditions.

Revenues from the local road transfer tax, derived from local road taxes levied on benzene and naphtha (gasoline), are transferred to prefectures and municipalities. Sixty-four percent of the local road tax revenue is distributed to prefectures and designated cities in proportion to length and area of national and prefectural roads. Thirty-six percent is distributed proportionally to municipalities on the basis of the total area of municipal roads.

The motor vehicle tonnage tax is a national tax levied on owners of motor vehicles through vehicle test certificates or by weight of the vehicle. One-fourth of the revenue of this tax is transferred to municipalities as a motor vehicle tonnage transfer tax, in proportion to length and area of municipal roads.

Local Loans

Article 5 of the Local Finance Law provides that the expenditure of local public bodies must be financed by revenue other than local loans. At the same time, it also restricts the expenditures which may be financed by local loans. Expenditures eligible for local loans are as follows:

(1) expenditure relating to local government enterprises, such as transportation, gas supply, and water supply;

(2) investments and loans;

(3) repayment of previous loans;

(4) emergency measures, restoration work, and relief measures in time of disaster;

(5) construction work of public facilities and other facilities for official use; and

(6) other expenditures prescribed by specific laws as eligible for local loans.

When issuing loans, a local public body must include in its annual budget such items as the purpose of the issue, planned interest rates, and conditions of repayment. These items must by approved by the local government assembly. In addition, prefectures and designated cities must obtain permission for receiving local loans from the minister of home affairs. Municipalities must obtain permission from the prefectural governor. The reasons for establishing such a loan permission procedure are as follows:

(1) smooth operation of national financial markets necessitate incorporation of local financial needs in the national plan and comprehensive fund adjustments between the public and private sector;

(2) prevention of funds concentrating in wealthier local public bodies and to further equitable distribution among all local public bodies;

(3) maintenance of appropriate limits for the total amount of local loans so that heavy financial burdens are not left to future years.

Permission for the issuance of local loans is based on the Local Loan Program and on the Policies of the Local Loans Permits. The Policies of Local Loans Permits and circulars of operation based on it delineate the detailed policies in granting permission for local loans. The minister of home affairs specifies the conditions which must be met by local public bodies applying for permission. Permission is not granted to any local public body which is in default of redemption of existing loans.

The minister bases loan permit approval on an item called the loan charge ratio. This loan charge ratio is the amount of general revenue expended on loan charges to the total amount of general revenue represented by the average of the past three fiscal years. Where the loan charge ratio is between 20% and 30%, local loans for general work projects without national subsidies and loans for recreation, sports, and social-welfare facilities are not permitted. Where the loan charge ratio is 30% and over, loans are not approved except for natural disaster restoration, local public enterprise expenses, and other specified expenditure.

An approved local loan is usually a portion of the local share of burden. Local share of burden is defined as the total amount of related expenditure less specific or earmarked revenues such as national subsidies. The ratio of local loans to the total amounts of local shares of burden is called an appropriation ratio. Appropriation ratios are prescribed in the circulars for each of the different kinds of projects to be financed by local loans.

There are two kinds of funds for local borrowing, domestic funds and external funds. Domestic funds are further divided into: government funds, funds of the Japan Finance Corporation for Municipal Enterprises (JFM), private funds, and bonds issued in lieu of cash payments. Government funds consist mainly of funds held by the Trust Fund Bureau and funds held by the Post Office Life Insurance. Funds held by the Trust Fund Bureau are drawn mainly from postal savings and trust funds. These funds are managed by the minister of posts and telecommunications. The JFM is a government agency under the supervision of the Ministry of Home Affairs. This corporation is established to provide stable, low-interest rate funds to local public enterprises.

Management of Local Public Finance

The Local Public Finance Program

Each year the national government must make an official estimate of expenditures and revenues of all local governments (Article 7 of the Local Allocation Tax Law). This estimate and the national government policies based on this estimate are consolidated into the Local Public Finance Program. The program estimates of revenues and expenditures are considered "ideal" or "standard" targets based on officially approved criteria. This program seeks to guarantee sufficient financial revenues to local governments and to provide guidelines for local governments to manage their financial affairs.

One example is tax revenue. The official estimate takes no account of tax revenue due to tax rates higher than the standard tax rates published as guidelines. National government disbursements and the local allocation tax are based on the national budget. Local bond issues are based on the Local Loan Program, and therefore loans not based on the program or donations are excluded. The same principle is applied to expenditure. For example, the salaries and wages paid to local government employees is calculated in accordance with salaries and wages paid to national government employees; that part in excess of the national government standard is excluded.

The above-mentioned procedures result in an estimate of total expenditures which is less than actual expenditures. The amount of expenditures estimated in the program was ¥47,054.2 billion in FY

LOCAL PUBLIC FINANCE 151

1982. Net total expenditures in the ordinary accounts of all local governments in the same fiscal year were ¥51,133.3 billion or 8.7% more than the programmed expenditures.

The functions of the Local Public Finance Program can be summarized as follows:

(1) Guarantee of sufficient local financial resources. Prefectural and municipal governments are required by law to bear responsibility for a number of tasks. Local governments are also expected to provide a certain level of services regardless of tax revenues. The demand for services has been increasing in recent years, making it necessary for the national government to guarantee financial resources to the local governments. The Local Public Finance Program helps the national government in balancing revenues and expenditures. It also indicates whether the local allocation tax rate should be revised, or whether any reform in local public finance is necessary.

Thus the program is not only an official estimate but an important procedure whereby sufficient financial resources are guaranteed to local governments. When there is a gap between revenue and expenditure estimates for a fiscal year, measures to balance the two items must be taken to guarantee smooth management of local governments.

(2) Coordination of national and local public finance policies. Local and national government public finance play important roles in the national economy. In order to establish national budget policy and evolve a national budget, proper coordination is essential. Local public finance is an aggregation of annual budgets formed separately by 3,302 autonomous bodies. Only through the Local Public Finance Program is the coordination of local public finance, national government finance, and macroeconomic policy achieved.

(3) Setting guidelines for local government financial management. National policies related to local governments are stated in the program. These policies include almost all estimated local government expenditures and provide an overall picture of local governments' activities. These policies serve as guidelines for local decision-making and financial management.

Present Condition of Local Public Finance

Local public finance has had a chronic shortage of financial resources since 1975. The principal reasons for this shortage include the failure of local taxes and local allocation tax grants to increase. The decrease in revenues has been due to a stagnant economy. As revenues have decreased, the expenditure structure has increased in rigidity. This rigidity is due to the increase in obligatory expenditures.

Shortages in local public finance have been covered by issuing local bonds and by increasing the amount of local allocation tax of the special account by borrowing from other funds. Due to chronic revenue shortages, local governments have reviewed their administrative and financial operations and have instituted reforms in expenditures.

However, at the beginning of FY 1985, borrowings of all local public bodies in the ordinary account amounted to about ¥50,700 billion; the central government's borrowings from the special account to increase the amount of the local allocation tax grants amounted to ¥5,700 billion totaling about ¥56,400 billion, almost 1.1 times the local public expenditures for a single year. These borrowings must be repaid from the future resources in the local tax and local allocation tax account.

The percentage of total expenditure required for repayment of the local public loan in the general revenue resources is 12.7% (average of all local governments). A rule of thumb is that 15% for loan repayment is a warning level. For the local governments, 1,484 out of 3,302 have exceeded this 15% level. Five hundred forty-five (545) local governments have exceeded the 20% level. Twenty percent (20%) is considered to be dangerous, and any local government over this level is not permitted to issue local loans. Dependence upon local loans has already reached the limit of the local government's ability to repay.

Consequently, the most important and urgent problem for local public finance is to make its financial structure sound. One way toward this goal is by reviewing and reducing expenditures enlarged in the age of the high-growth economy. In addition, local governments must become less dependent upon loans. Along with these measures, local public finance must endeavor to expand its own revenue sources in order to meet public needs.

Local Public Enterprises

Characteristics and Roles of Local Public Enterprises

Local public enterprises are enterprises operated by local public bodies to provide services and thereby contribute to the promotion of the welfare of the residents. In this respect, they do not differ from general public administration financed mainly by taxes. Services provided by local public enterprises benefit specific individuals, and therefore such services are financed by charges based on the extent of the benefit.

The main reasons why local public bodies operate local public enterprises are as follows:

(1) Certain services must be provided in response to the needs of the community residents. Such services should not be left entirely to private enterprise which puts the highest priority on profitability. Additionally, local governments provide services, such as water supply, highly technical or specialized medical treatment, and medical care in isolated islands or mountain areas, in order to meet the basic needs of the people.

(2) Some facilities, for example, water supply, sewage facilities, subways, require substantial advance investment. Private companies would have difficulty in managing this initial outlay of capital and the accompanying loan repayment.

Number and Financial Status of Local Public Enterprises

Table 9.5 shows the total number of local public enterprises at the end of FY 1983. Three hundred forty-seven (347) were managed by joint associations established by municipalities and prefectures. Each pre-

Table 9.5. Number of Local Public Enterprises, 1983

	Pre-fecture	Desig-nated city	Munici-pality	Associ-ation	Total	Ratio (%)
Water supply	30	10	1,760	97	1,897	24.2
Industrial water supply	40	7	40	4	91	1.2
Transportation	6	19	105	7	137	1.7
Electricity	32	0	1	0	33	0.4
Gas	2	0	68	3	73	0.9
Hospitals	47	10	572	95	724	9.2
Smaller-scale water supply	1	1	1,709	31	1,742	22.2
Sewerage	48	10	963	25	1,046	13.3
Harbor improve-ment	64	11	107	5	187	2.4
Market	8	10	152	14	184	2.3
Slaughterhouse	3	8	208	38	257	3.3
Sightseeing facilities	17	7	732	18	774	9.9
Housing site preparation	38	11	416	4	469	6.0
Toll roads	24	2	3	0	29	0.4
Parking lot	7	3	151	3	164	2.1
Others	10	0	33	3	46	0.5
Total	377	109	7,020	347	7,853	100.0

Source: Same as Table 9.1.

fecture operates an average of about eight enterprises, and each municipality operates about two enterprises. The dominant enterprise was water supply with 3,639 operations (1,897 water supply and 1,742 small-scale water supply) accounting for 46.4% of the total number of enterprises. Then came sewerage with 1,046 enterprises (13.3%), sightseeing facilities with 774 (9.9%), followed by hospitals with 724 (9.2%).

Local public enterprises have expanded and developed every year, both in number and scale. This expansion has been in proportion to socio-economic progress and improved living standards. Table 9.6 presents the settled accounts for local public enterprise for FY 1982.

The magnitude of expenditure (the total expenditures of running costs and investment) of local public enterprises was ￥10,737.2 billion, equivalent to 21% of the total general administration expenditure (Table 9.6). In terms of national expenditure, sewerage was the largest with ￥2,908.3 billion accounting for 27.1%. This large figure is attributable to the low diffusion ratio of sewerage systems (32%) relative

Table 9.6. Expenditures of Local Public Enterprises, 1982 (￥ billion)

Type of service	Expenditures	%	Total costs	%	Capital expenditures	%
Water supply	2,777.2	25.9	1,729.1	30.3	1,280.5	23.5
Industrial water supply	193.5	1.8	98.0	1.7	113.1	2.1
Transport	1,061.4	9.9	687.3	12.1	448.9	8.2
Electricity	81.5	0.8	48.4	0.8	41.3	0.8
Gas	89.0	0.8	69.3	1.2	26.5	0.5
Hospitals	2,001.2	18.6	1,718.8	30.1	360.9	6.6
Sewerage	2,908.3	27.1	850.0	14.9	2,112.7	38.8
Harbor improvement	300.0	2.8	83.7	1.5	209.3	3.8
Market	134.1	1.2	71.9	1.3	60.7	1.1
Sightseeing facilities	105.9	1.0	66.7	1.2	34.7	0.6
Housing site preparation	932.7	8.7	207.3	3.6	683.6	12.5
Others	152.5	1.4	72.1	1.3	80.7	1.5
Total	10,737.2	100.0	5,702.7	100.0	5,452.9	100.0

Note: Figures for "Expenditures" are calculated by deducing depreciations for law-applicable enterprises, and by adding reserves and advanced appropriations for law-inapplicable enterprises.

Source: Same as Table 9.1.

to population. Expanding sewage facilities require high capital investment. The next largest expenditure is for water supply, which is now attaining maturity, with ¥2,777.2 billion or 25.9%. Next is hospitals with ¥2,001.2 billion (18.6%), followed by transportation with ¥1,061.4 billion (9.9%).

Settled accounts may be divided broadly into capital expenditure (representing the scale of construction investment) and other expenditure (suggesting the extent of ordinary business activities). A breakdown of specific activities and number of enterprises is given in Table 9.5. Sewerage enterprises are predominant in capital expenditure because of the high expenses for construction of the facilities.

The present status of management varies with local conditions, the local enterprise, and other factors. For FY 1982, the national total of the settled accounts of all the local public enterprise reveals a surplus of ¥87.3 billion for those using the accrual method of accounting; and ¥22.6 billion for those enterprises using a cash basis. Analyzed by type of service, two sectors show a deficit: The transport sector, which is suffering a decline in bus usage, shows a deficit of ¥33.1 billion; hospitals, showing a gap between public medical benefits and actual income, incurred a deficit of ¥24.9 billion.

10 | Financial Relations Between National and Local Governments

Junshichirō Yonehara

This chapter describes the financial relations between the national and local governments. Transfers between these organs have been described in previous chapters on a macroscopic level. A more detailed description of these transfers follows. General characteristics of the financial relations, its vertical imbalance, are stated in the first section. The specific transfers which occur are then delineated. The extent of national government control is discussed. The section on general characteristics concludes with a discussion of the policy of the equalization of fiscal capacity.

The second section looks at various aspects of the local allocation tax. The size of the system is examined and the two types of allocation tax, ordinary and special, are then examined in detail.

The third and final section examines the national government disbursements for specific purposes or the national specific purpose grant system. This section is divided into three parts with the first part describing the features of the national disbursements. The second part examines the allocation of these disbursements. The third part of this section looks at the various classifications for these disbursements.

General Characteristics

Vertical Imbalance

Financial relations between the national and local governments are marked by a vertical financial imbalance. In recent years the national government has received tax revenues that exceed twice the amount that it spends for its activities. In contrast, the tax revenue of local governments is far less than the amount necessary to perform their functions. This imbalance can be seen by examining Table 10.1, which

156

Table 10.1. Vertical Financial Imbalance (%)

Year	Tax revenue received by		Tax revenue expended by	
	National government	Local governments	National government	Local governments
1965	67.9	32.1	30.4	69.6
1970	67.5	32.5	33.9	66.1
1975	64.0	36.0	23.4	76.6
1980	64.1	35.9	23.1	76.9
1982	63.2	36.8	26.7	73.3

Source: Ministry of Home Affairs, *Chihō zaisei hakusho*.

presents the relative share of all tax revenues and expenditures of the two levels of government. As suggested by the table, the national government has collected more than 60% of the total tax revenue every fiscal year since 1965, while it has expended less than 35% of the total tax revenue.

Specifically in FY 1982, the total tax revenues amounted to ¥50,636 billion. Of this amount, the national government received ¥32,007 billion and the local governments received ¥18,629 billion. Expenditures by the national government were only ¥13,005 billion, and the remaining ¥19,002 billion were transferred to local governments. Local governments also transferred a part of their tax revenue to the national government. Local government transfers were the cost-sharing contribution to public works constructed by the national government. But the amount of this reverse transfer was only ¥522 billion. By subtracting this ¥522 million from the ¥19,002 billion, we find the net transfer from the national government to local governments was ¥18,480 billion. Thus, in FY 1982, the total tax receipts of ¥50,637 billion was finally distributed as follows: ¥13,527 billion to the national government and ¥37,109 billion to local governments.

However, both the national and local governments raise a considerable amount of funds from sources other than taxes. Some of these sources have been discussed in previous chapters. In recent years, all levels of government have utilized "loans" to increase revenues. These non-tax revenues have rarely been transferred between levels of government. Since 1975 the national government has raised a considerable amount of revenues by borrowing through public bond issues. A part of this loan revenue has been transferred to local governments. National revenue gains through borrowing have occurred in part to supplement the deficiency of national tax revenue that is transferred to local governments. Total transfers, including transfers from non-

tax revenues, in FY 1982 was ¥20,755 billion. This amount was
¥1,735 billion greater than tax revenue transfers.

Specific Transfers to Local Government

There are five transfers from the national government to local governments: the local allocation tax; national government disbursements;
local transfer taxes; special traffic safety grants; and the transfer as a
substitution of fixed property tax. Of these transfers, the local allocation tax and national government disbursements are the two dominant
transfers. (See Table 10.2.) These two comprise almost all of the
transfer from the national government to local governments. The local
allocation tax is allocated to local governments to equalize their
financial capacity and to ensure sufficient funds for the public services
local governments are required to provide.

National government disbursements total the largest transfer category, the number of disbursements exceeding one thousand. These
disbursements cover almost all fields of local government activities
including education, social welfare, public works, transportation, and
regional development. Details of these two major categories will be
presented in the following sections.

The last transfer listed in Table 10.2, the transfer as a substitution of
fixed property tax, is not a transfer in the true sense of the word. In
fact, it is a tax payment on the national government's property. The tax
is imposed on properties that are not used directly for governmental
administration. Housing for government employees, dormitories at

Table 10.2. Fiscal Transfers in 1982 (¥ billion)

	Transfers from tax revenue	Transfers from other funds	Total
Local allocation tax	7,424.5	1,753.1	9,177.6
National government disburse-ments for specific purposes	11,035.6	0.0	11,035.6
Specific traffic safety grant*	51.7	0.0	51.7
Local transfer taxes	460.1	0.0	460.1
Transfers as substitution of fixed property tax	30.1	0.0	30.1
Total	19,002.0	1,753.1	20,755.1

*Fines imposed for violation of traffic regulations are included in the tax
revenue in this grant.
Source: Same as Table 10.1.

national universities, and land and buildings in civil aviation airports are examples of taxable property.

Ambiguities exist in classifying local transfer taxes in the transfers from the national government. In fact these taxes are levied by the national government, which imposes them as local rather than national taxes. The national government collects these taxes on behalf of local governments because of advantages in assessment and collection. In a sense, local transfer taxes can be said to be local taxes that are delegated to the national government for their exaction and collection.

The special traffic safety grant is a kind of national specific-purpose disbursement, but it is separated from other disbursements because it is funded by fines imposed for violations of traffic regulations. No revenues from tax or borrowing are appropriated for this transfer.

National Government Control

Local governments are under the detailed control of the national government. When a local government undertakes an agency-delegated function, it becomes an agency of the national government and executes functions as directed. Agency-delegated functions are essentially the responsibility of the national government but are delegated to local governments for administrative convenience. The number of agency-delegated functions has increased significantly. At present, more than half of the functions performed by prefectural governments are agency-delegated.

The national government also tries to control functions other than agency-delegated functions. For almost all activities of local governments, it sets guidelines, standards, and regulations, even for functions which are inherently the responsibility of local governments. Observation of the national guidelines and directions is expected, and various inducements are also provided. In this respect, the national government disbursements for specific purposes are the most important instrument for the national government. These disbursements are distributed on condition that the recipient follow the directives issued by the national government. If a local government fails to observe national directives, it is requested to refund the disbursement in whole or in part.

A basic principle which underlies national government control seems to be uniformity throughout the country. The national government seeks to standardize local taxation as well as the distribution of public services. As a policy, the national government tries to treat all local governments equally. When a department of the national government distributes a specific-purpose disbursement, it takes great care not to discriminate against any local government.

The local allocation tax also plays a very important role in standardizing the level of public services among local jurisdictions. This program equalizes the fiscal capacity among local governments by supplementing the shortage of tax revenue. The allocation tax enables local governments to provide public services at the level prescribed by the national government. When a local government does not maintain the level prescribed for public services, or has paid an excessive amount for the services, the national government may reduce the local allocation tax for that local government.

Local Allocation Tax

Equalization of Fiscal Capacity

With the exception of a few minor national specific-purpose disbursements distributed to local governments of poor fiscal capacity, the local allocation tax is the only equalization scheme in Japan. It is allocated both to prefectures and municipalities in the same way. Table 10.3 presents the distribution of the local allocation tax to prefectures and municipalities. The amount allocated to prefectures is slightly larger than the amount allocated to municipalities.

In the United States of America, the federal government distributes revenue-sharing grants as equalization grants. The local allocation tax is similar to revenue sharing in the sense that both are fiscal equalization schemes from the central government. But Japan's allocation tax is much more important. In recent years, Japan's local allocation tax was more than 16% of the total revenue of local governments; the U.S. government revenue sharing was less than 2% of the total revenue of state and local governments. In the United States, fairly large amounts of funds are being transferred for purposes of fiscal equalization by the states to the local county and city governments. In Japan, there is no

Table 10.3. Distribution of Local Allocation Tax to Prefectures and Municipalities (¥ billion)

Year	Prefectures	Municipalities	Total
1970	963.2	835.1	1,798.2
1975	2,392.2	2,078.8	4,471.1
1980	4,324.4	3,789.6	8,114.0
1982	4,977.2	4,200.4	9,177.6

Source: Same as Table 10.1.

equivalent transfer between prefectures and municipalities. (The one exception is a transfer between the Tokyo metropolitan government and the special wards in Tokyo.)

The local allocation tax in Japan is similar to General Revenue Assistance in Australia. Both distributions are tax-sharing grants and are transferred to prefectures (states in Australia) as well as municipalities. Moreover, the guidelines used to determine the amount to be transferred to a specific government are very similar. Both Japan and Australia consider local tax-raising capacity and local financial needs.

The fiscal capacity of a government depends upon two factors: tax-raising capacity and the cost of providing public services. A government which enjoys a high tax-raising capacity and has a low cost for providing government services is considered a government of strong fiscal capacity.

An index of fiscal capacity is used to measure fiscal strength. The index of fiscal capacity is calculated as the ratio of the basic financial revenue divided by the basic financial needs. Table 10.4 presents the index of fiscal capacity, per capita tax revenue, per capita local allocation tax, and the sum of the tax revenue and allocation tax. Generally, local governments situated within large metropolitan areas have strong fiscal capacity when compared to those governments situated in rural areas. Among the 47 prefectures, in FY 1981, Tokyo had the highest index of fiscal capacity followed by Aichi, Kanagawa, and

Table 10.4. Distribution of Local Allocation Tax among Prefectures (Per capita base), 1981

	Index of fiscal capacity	Per capita tax revenue (A) (¥)	Per capita local allocation tax (B) (¥)	Sum (A)+(B) (¥)
High-capacity group				
Tokyo	1.198	159,070	—	159,070
Aichi	1.054	82,800	—	82,800
Kanagawa	0.997	70,594	129	75,723
Osaka	0.957	79,077	2,881	81,958
Low-capacity group				
Okinawa	0.246	32,515	82,595	115,110
Kōchi	0.247	40,850	113,646	154,496
Shimane	0.261	43,398	116,534	159,932
Tottori	0.261	46,263	112,592	158,855

Sources: Ministry of Home Affairs, *Chihō zaisei tōkei nempō*, 1983; Ministry of Home Affairs, *Chihō zaisei yōran*, 1983.

Osaka prefectures. The low-capacity group are Okinawa, Kōchi, Shimane, and Tottori prefectures in order of lowest index of fiscal capacity. Table 10.4 shows the per capita local allocation tax to these prefectures. The stronger prefectures receive little or no allocation tax, and the low-capacity prefectures receive a large per capita allocation tax. In this table, the top four prefectures and the bottom four prefectures in the ranking of index of fiscal capacity are listed for purposes of comparison.

Size of Local Allocation Tax

The local allocation tax is essentially a tax-sharing grant. Article 6 of the Local Allocation Tax Law provides that this tax is 32% of the three major national taxes (income tax, corporation tax, and liquor tax). However, the rate of transfer is flexible. Paragraph 2 of article 6(3) provides that if the amount of the local allocation tax is insufficient, the rate of transfer may be increased. In fact, when the local allocation tax was introduced in 1954, the rate of transfer was only 20%. Since 1954, the rate has been increased until the present rate of 32% was reached in 1966.

Since 1975, the national budget has shown a large deficit. Thus the national government has resisted an increase in the rate of transfer. The national government deficit was due to an unexpected slowdown in the rate of increase in tax revenue, which has resulted in insufficient local allocation tax, linked to national tax revenues. In FY 1977, for example, ¥6,692 billion was the estimated revenue necessary to ensure each local government reasonable funds. The actual amount available based on 32% of the three national taxes was only ¥4,622 billion. Thus all local governments, as well as the Ministry of Home Affairs, requested that the Ministry of Finance increase the rate of transfer. However the Ministry of Finance declined, stating that the national budget was strained more severely than the budgets of local governments. The Ministry of Finance stated it could not afford transferring additional tax revenue to local governments.

The national government has the responsibility of providing local governments with the revenue necessary to maintain local public services at the level prescribed. Every fiscal year since 1975, the national government has chosen to adopt an ad hoc program rather than raise the rate of transfer. This ad hoc program has consisted of three measures. First, an extra lump sum transfer in excess of the 32% of the three national taxes has been distributed. This extra transfer is called the extra allocation grant. Second, the trust fund to distribute the local allocation tax raises loans and the funds thus acquired are added to the

32% amount from the national taxes. This fund has previously been referred to as a national transfer from borrowing. Third, the national government authorizes local governments to generate revenue by borrowing more than usual. The increment in loan authorization is equal to the deficiency of the local allocation tax after lump sum transfers and trust fund loan raising.

In FY 1977, the extra allocation grant was ¥95 billion, the borrowing of the trust fund was ¥940 billion, and the increase in local loans was ¥1,035 billion. In recent years the local allocation tax is far from being a total tax-sharing scheme.

Ordinary Local Allocation Tax

The local allocation tax is distributed partly (94%) as an ordinary allocation tax and partly (6%) as a special allocation tax. The ordinary allocation tax is paid to local governments whose basic financial needs exceed their basic financial revenue. As a rule, the amount of the ordinary allocation tax is equal to the excess of the basic financial needs over the basic financial revenue. No ordinary allocation tax is distributed to local governments whose basic financial needs are less than their basic financial revenue. These local governments are entitled to retain the excess.

Basic financial need is not equivalent to the actual expenditure of local government. This need represents a fair and standardized amount necessary to provide public services at the level prescribed by the national government. The total financial need of a local government is the sum of the basic financial need for each item of public service. These services include such items as police service, fire protection service, compulsory education, and construction of roads and bridges. The basic financial need for each public service is calculated according to the following equation:

$$\text{basic financial need} = \begin{matrix} \text{unit of} \\ \text{measurement} \end{matrix} \times \begin{matrix} \text{modification} \\ \text{coefficient} \end{matrix} \times \begin{matrix} \text{unit} \\ \text{cost} \end{matrix}$$

In this equation, the unit of measurement is a figure which provides an appropriate measure for the cost of the particular service. For example, the number of police for police protection, population for fire protection service, or the area of road for maintenance of roads are instances of units of measurement.

A single measure is inadequate to measure the amount needed to provide a given public service. The cost of providing public services is affected by various factors, such as geographical, social, economic, and institutional characteristics of each locality. Thus modification coefficients are applied to the equation to allow for these various factors.

The final variable in the equation used to calculate basic financial need is the unit cost. The unit cost is recalculated each fiscal year, taking into account the change in price level and the change in the people's demand for the particular public service.

Basic financial revenue is defined as general revenue which can be appropriated to meet the basic financial need. Basic financial revenue is calculated as the sum of the local transfer tax and a prescribed percentage of the standardized local tax revenue, 80% for prefectures and 75% for municipalities. Note that total tax revenue is not included in basic financial revenue. The reason for this is as follows: First, inclusion of the total financial needs of all the various local governments within a uniform formula is difficult, if not impossible. Many local governments have their own peculiar financial needs requiring a certain amount of tax revenues. Second, if total tax revenue is included in the calculation of basic financial revenue, any increase in local tax revenue would reduce the local allocation tax by the same amount. Obviously, this would discourage local governments from developing their areas and enlarging the tax base within their territories.

Special Local Allocation Tax

The special local allocation tax compensates for shortfalls in the ordinary local allocation tax. Transfers are made in the following circumstances.

1) Where special financial needs not included in the basic financial needs require distribution. Examples of special financial needs are expenditures for local assembly election, which takes place every four years, expenditures for protection of historical properties, or expenditures for natural disaster relief.

2) When local government tax revenue estimates are greater than actual local tax revenue. This condition occurs because the national government computes estimated local tax revenue based on a prescribed equation. Overestimates of local tax revenue result in a decrease in the local allocation tax. The shortfall is supplied by the special local allocation tax.

3) When unforeseen local government financial needs not included in the ordinary allocation tax arise. The tax is determined before the end of August, and sometimes financial needs arise after that date. For example, a typhoon in September may cause damages requiring heavy expenditures. Such special cases also result in transfer by a special local allocation tax.

National Government Disbursement for Specific Purposes

Features

As discussed above, the specific-purpose disbursements from the national government constitute a fairly large portion of the total revenue of local governments. For prefectural governments, the disbursement constitutes about a quarter of total revenue. Thus if we assume that the average matching rate of the national specific-purpose disbursement is one to one (i.e., the rate of subsidy is 50%), about half of the prefectural government expenditures are for subsidized activities.

Table 10.5 outlines the distribution of the national specific-purpose disbursement by categories established by the Ministry of Home Affairs. About 40% of the total national specific disbursement (to both prefectural and municipal governments) consists of subsidies for ordinary construction. These subsidies include grants for roads, bridges, parks, river banks, harbors, and housing for the poor. As a single program, one which subsidizes the salaries of teachers engaged in compulsory education is the largest. In Table 10.5 this grant program is included in the subsidy for compulsory education disbursed

Table 10.5. Distribution of National Government Disbursements for Specific Purposes, 1982 (¥ billion, %)

	Prefectures		Municipalities		Net total	
Subsidy for compulsory education	2,267.6	31.9	19.3	0.5	2,287.0	20.7
Cash benefit for the poor	226.3	3.2	857.6	21.8	1,083.9	9.8
Welfare allowances for children	126.9	1.8	308.1	7.8	435.1	3.9
Medical expenses of tuberculosis patients	27.7	0.4	14.2	0.4	41.8	0.4
Expenses for mentally ill patients	77.2	1.1	—	—	77.2	0.7
Welfare allowances for the aged	85.9	1.2	139.6	3.6	225.5	2.0
Medical expenses of the aged	—	—	340.1	8.7	340.1	3.1
Ordinary construction outlays	2,988.2	42.0	1,551.0	39.5	4,539.2	41.1
Restoration work after disasters	463.6	6.5	153.2	3.9	616.9	5.6
Others	848.8	11.9	545.1	13.9	1,393.9	12.6
Total	7,112.3	100.0	3,928.3	100.0	11,040.5	100.0

Source: Same as Table 10.1.

to prefectures. For municipalities, the largest disbursement is the subsidy for cash payments to the poor.

Almost all national specific-purpose disbursements are cost-sharing. The rate of subsidy differs from one program to another. For instance, the disbursement for teachers' salaries in primary and junior high schools subsidizes 50% of expenditures. The disbursement for cash payments to the poor subsidizes 80% of expenditures, while that for construction of swimming pools subsidizes 33.3% of construction outlays. Generally speaking, the subsidized share of the outlay is large for those programs which impose a heavy financial burden on local governments or for which the national government has a strong interest. Conversely, the subsidizing share is small for programs which are inherently the functions of local governments.

Allocation

Most of the national specific-purpose disbursements are allocated among local governments at the discretion of the national government; there are only a few formula disbursements. Therefore, every local government seeks to obtain specific-purpose disbursements to the maximum extent possible. To that end, local governments expend much time and energy. Allocations for a particular specific-purpose program are usually made on the following basis:

First, a local government submits an application for a disbursement to the national government. The application describes the project and explains the reasons for its importance. The national government assesses all of the applications submitted by local governments and selects those projects to which payments will be given. During this selection process, the national government often requires modifications to a project so that it will conform with national government standards. Needless to say, almost all local governments accept the conditions required. Conditions accompanying the allocation of a specific-purpose disbursement provide the national government with a powerful method of control over the activities of the local governments.

Classification

As we noticed in the previous chapter, national government disbursements for specific purposes can be grouped into two broad categories: (1) grant programs for agency-delegated functions and (2) grant programs for local government functions. The former programs are usually termed national treasury payments for agential tasks. As the objects of these grant programs are inherently national government functions, the cost should duly be borne wholly by the national government.

However some grant programs which come under this category are subsidized at a rate less than 100 %. Examples of functions which result in the national treasury payment include: election of national assembly members, compiling of statistics and research for the benefit of the national government, registration of aliens, quarantine activities, administration of health insurance, and the provision of national pension.

The grant programs for local government functions are subdivided into two categories: (1) obligatory share of the national government and (2) grants-in-aid. Obligatory shares of the national government are not fiscal assistance but payments by the national government for costs which should inherently be borne by it. Therefore, obligatory shares pay for those functions for which the national government is partly responsible. Generally these functions have a large spill-over effect and thus benefit people living outside the jurisdiction of the local government which undertakes the task, or in which the national government is deeply interested and in which it seeks to standardize the level of activity. Obligatory shares of the national government are itemized according to the type of expenditure for which they are intended: ordinary shares, contribution for construction works, and shares for disaster relief.

Ordinary shares, which are detailed in Article 10 of the Local Finance Law, cover shares in expenditures on education, health, welfare, assistance to agriculture, and other matters. The expenditure items which attract this share are strictly defined in the Local Finance Law. They include salaries of teachers in compulsory education, expense for poor relief, medical expenses under national health insurance, and welfare allowances for children.

Contribution for construction works is set out in Article 10 (2) of the Local Finance Law. It covers contributions to capital expenditure on civil engineering works. These shares provide financial assistance for projects which may benefit people in an area extending beyond that of the local government undertaking the expenditure. Most of these constructions are directed to public works which are undertaken in accordance with the five-year programs prepared by the national government. They include construction of important civil engineering projects such as those involving roads, parks, river banks, harbors, and construction of such public buildings for nursery schools, low-income housing, and welfare housing for the aged.

Shares for disaster relief expenditure are set out in Article 10 (3) of the Local Finance Law. These shares are directed to expenditures resulting from disasters and include disaster-relief projects and the restoration of public facilities damaged in disasters.

Grants-in-aid by the national government. Article 16 of the Local Finance Law provides that the national government may grant subsidies to local governments when necessary for the execution of its policies (the incentive subsidy) or for the financing of the local government (the financial subsidy). Incentive subsidies are used to encourage local government to perform specific functions which the national government deems important. There are a large number of incentive subsidies. Every section of the national government has at least one such subsidy to ensure that its directions are observed by local governments. Financial subsidies are seldom used because financial assistance to local governments is generally provided by the local allocation tax grant.

Appendix 1. Organizational Charts

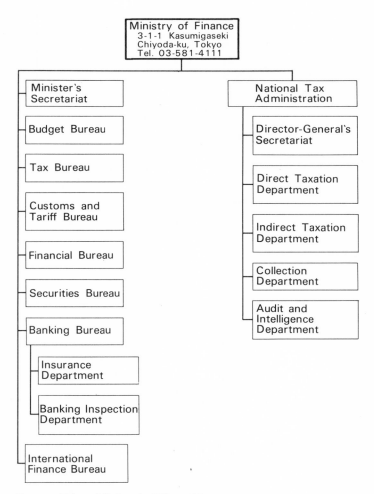

Source: Prime Minister's Office 1985.

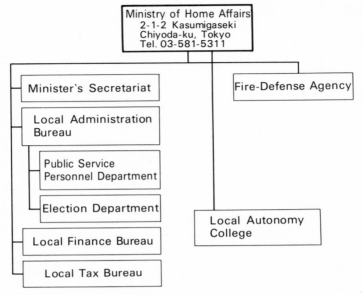

Source: Prime Minister's Office 1985.

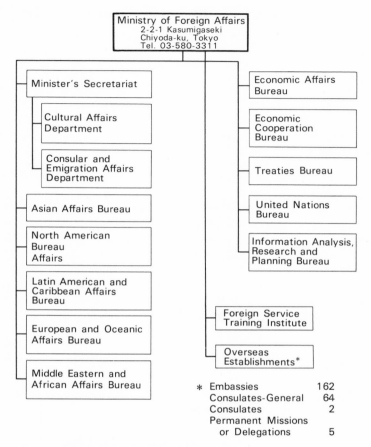

Ministry of Foreign Affairs
2-2-1 Kasumigaseki
Chiyoda-ku, Tokyo
Tel. 03-580-3311

Minister's Secretariat

Cultural Affairs Department

Consular and Emigration Affairs Department

Asian Affairs Bureau

North American Bureau Affairs

Latin American and Caribbean Affairs Bureau

European and Oceanic Affairs Bureau

Middle Eastern and African Affairs Bureau

Economic Affairs Bureau

Economic Cooperation Bureau

Treaties Bureau

United Nations Bureau

Information Analysis, Research and Planning Bureau

Foreign Service Training Institute

Overseas Establishments*

* Embassies   162
  Consulates-General   64
  Consulates   2
  Permanent Missions
    or Delegations   5

Source: Prime Minister's Office 1985.

Appendix 2. The Constitution of Japan (Excerpts)

Chapter IV
The Diet

Article 60. The budget must first be submitted to the House of Representatives.

Upon consideration of the budget, when the House of Councilors makes a decision different from that of the House of Representatives, and when no agreement can be reached even through a joint committee of both Houses, provided for by law, or in the case of failure by the House of Councilors to take final action within thirty (30) days, the period of recess excluded, after the receipt of the budget passed by the House of Representatives, the decision of the House of Representatives shall be the decision of the Diet.

Chapter V
The Cabinet

Acticle 73. The Cabinet, in addition to other general administrative functions, shall perform the following functions:

. . . .

(v) Prepare the budget, and present it to the Diet.

. . . .

Chapter VII
Finance

Article 83. The power to administer national finances shall be exercised as the Diet shall determine.

Article 84. No new taxes shall be imposed or existing ones modified except by law or under such conditions as law may prescribe.

Article 85. No money shall be expended, nor shall the State obligate itself, except as authorized by the Diet.

Article 86. The Cabinet shall prepare and submit to the Diet for its consideration and decision a budget for each fiscal year.

Article 87. In order to provide for unforeseen deficiencies in the budget, a reserve fund may be authorized by the Diet to be expended upon the responsibility of the Cabinet.

The Cabinet must get subsequent approval of the Diet for all payments from the reserve fund.

Article 88. All property of the Imperial Household shall belong to the State. All expenses of the Imperial Household shall be appropriated by the Diet in the budget.

Article 89. No public money or other property shall be expended or appropriated for the use, benefit, or maintenance of any religious institution or association, or for any charitable, educational or benevolent enterprises not under the control of public authority.

Article 90. Final accounts of the expenditures and revenues of the State shall be audited annually by a Board of Audit and submitted by the Cabinet to the Diet, together with the statement of audit, during the fiscal year immediately following the period covered.

The organization and competency of the Board of Audit shall be determined by law.

Article 91. At regular intervals and at least annually the Cabinet shall report to the Diet and the people on the state of national finances.

Chapter VIII
Local Self-Government

Article 92. Regulations concerning organization and operations of local public entities shall be fixed by law in accordance with the principle of local autonomy.

Article 93. The local public entities shall establish assemblies as their deliberative organs, in accordance with law.

The chief executive officers of all local public entities, the members of their assemblies, and such other local officials as may be determined by law shall be elected by direct popular vote within their several communities.

Article 94. Local public entities shall have the right to manage their property, affairs and administration and to enact their own regulations within law.

Article 95. A special law, applicable only to one local public entity, cannot be enacted by the Diet without the consent of the majority of the voters of the local public entity concerned, obtained in accordance with law.

Bibliography

Ackley, G., and H. Ishi. 1976. "Fiscal, Monetary, and Related Policies." In *Asia's New Giant*. See Patrick and Rosovsky 1976.

The Bank of Japan. 1978. *The Japanese Financial System.*

———. *Kokusai hikaku tōkei* (Comparative international statistics). Published annually.

Bieda, K. 1970. *The Structure and Operations of the Japanese Economy.* Sydney: John Wiley.

Boltho, A. 1975. *Japan: An Economic Survey 1953–1973.* London: Oxford University Press.

Campbell, J.C. 1976. "Japanese Budget Baransu." In *Modern Japanese Organization and Decision Making*, E. Vogel, ed. Berkeley and Los Angeles: University of California Press.

———. 1977. *Contemporary Japanese Budget Politics.* Berkeley and Los Angeles: University of California Press.

Denison, E.F., and W.K. Chung. 1976. *How Japan's Economy Grew So Fast: The Sources of Post-War Expansion.* Washington, D.C.: The Brookings Institution.

Economic Council of Canada. 1982. *Intervention and Efficiency.*

Economic Planning Agency. *Annual Report on National Accounts.* Published annually.

———. *Keizai hakusho* (Economic white paper). Published annually.

———. *Keizai yōran* (Economic manual). Published annually.

———. *Kokumin keizai keisan nempyō* (National economic statistics annual report). Published annually.

———. 1982. *2000 nen no Nihon.* (Japan in the year 2000).

Federation of Bankers Association of Japan. 1982. *Banking System in Japan.*

Foreign Press Center. 1982. *Japan: A Pocket Guide.*

Gomi, Y. *Guide to Japanese Taxes.* Zaikei Shōhōsha. Published annually.

175

Haitani, K. 1976. *The Japan Economic System.* Lexington, Mass.: D.C. Heath.

Ishi, H. 1982. "Financial Institutions and Markets in Japan." In *Financial Institutions and Markets in the Far East,* M.T. Scully, ed. London: Macmillan.

―――. 1983. "An Overview of Postwar Tax Policies in Japan." *Hitotsubashi Journal of Economics* 23(2).

Japan Development Bank. *Annual Report.* Published annually.

Jichi Sogo Centre. 1982. *Local Public Finance in Japan.*

Johnson, C. 1978. *Japan's Public Policy.* Washington, D. C.: American Enterprise Institute.

Keizai Kōhō Center. *Japan: An International Comparison.* Published annually.

Lockwood, W.W., ed. 1965. *The State and Economic Enterprise in Japan.* Princeton: Princeton University Press.

Ministry of Finance. Budget Bureau. *The Budget in Brief Japan.* Published annually.

―――. Customs and Tariff Bureau. 1983. *Customs Administration in Japan 1983.* Japan International Cooperation Agency.

―――. National Tax Administration. *An Outline of Japanese Tax Administration.* Published annually.

―――. Research and Planning Division. *Financial Statistics of Japan.* Published annually.

―――. *Quarterly Bulletin of Financial Statistics.* Published quarterly until 1982.

―――. *Zaisei kin'yū tōkei geppō* (Monthly statistics of government finances and banking). Published monthly.

―――. Tax Bureau. *An Outline of Japanese Taxes.* Published annually.

Ministry of Home Affairs. *Chihō zaisei hakusho* (White paper on local public finance). Published annually.

―――. Local Finance Bureau. *Chihō zaisei tōkei nempō* (Statistical yearbook of local public finance). Chihō Zaimu Kyōkai. Published annually.

―――. *Chihō zaisei yōran* (Handbook of local public finance). Published annually.

―――. *Chihōzei ni kansuru sankō keisū shiryō* (Statistical data for local taxes). Published annually.

Ministry of Labor. *Rōdō tōkei yōran* (A survey of labor statistics). Published annually.

Mizoguchi, T. 1969. *Personal Savings and Consumption in Postwar Japan.* Tokyo: Kinokuniya.

Noguchi, Y. 1979. "Decision Rules in the Japanese Budgetary Process." *Japanese Economic Studies* 7(4).

———. 1980. "A Dynamic Model of Incremental Budgeting." *Hitotsubashi Journal of Economics* 20(2).

———. 1981. "Restructuring Public Finances." *Economic Eye* 2(1).

———. 1982a. "Japan's Fiscal Crisis." *Japanese Economic Studies* (Spring).

———. 1982b. "The Government-Business Relationship in Japan: The Changing Role of Fiscal Resources." In *Policy and Trade Issues*. See Yamamura 1982.

———. 1983a. "Problems of Public Pensions in Japan." *Hitotsubashi Journal of Economics* 24(1).

———. 1983b. "The Failure of Government to Perform Its Proper Task: A Case Study of Japan." *ORDO* 34.

———. 1984. "Governmental Reform of Industrial Society." *World Futures* 19(3/4).

———. 1985a. "Failing of the Income Tax." *Japan Echo* XII(1).

———. 1985b. "Tax Structure and Saving-Investment Balance." *Hitotsubashi Journal of Economics* 26(1).

OECD. 1978. *Public Expenditure Trends, OECD Studies in Resource Allocation.*

———. 1981. *National Accounts of OECD Countries, 1962-1979.*

———. 1984. *Revenue Statistics of OECD Member Countries, 1965-1984.*

Ohkawa, M. 1985. "The Role of Political Parties and Executive Bureaucrats in Governmental Budget-Making: The Case of Japan." In *Staat und politsche okonomie heute*, Halusch, Roskamp, and Wiseman, eds. Stuttgart: Gustav Fishcher.

Ōkura Zaimu Kyōkai. 1985. *Zaisei kaikei roppo* (Legal handbook for public finance and accounts).

Ōshima, H.T. 1965. "Meiji Fiscal Policy and Economic Progress." In *State and Economic Enterprise*. See Lockwood 1965.

Ōuchi, H., et al. 1971. *Nihon keizai zusetsu* (A charted survey of the Japanese economy). Iwanami.

Patrick, H.T. 1965. "Cyclical Instability and Fiscal-Monetary Policy in Postwar Japan." In *State and Economic Enterprise*. See Lockwood 1965.

———. 1968. "Financing of the Public Sector in Postwar Japan." In *Economic Growth: The Japanese Experiences since the Meiji Era*, K. Ohkawa and L. Klein, eds. Homewood, Ill.: R.D. Irwin.

———. 1970. "The Phoenix Risen from the Ashes: Postwar Japan." In *Modern East Asia: Essays in Interpretation*, J.B. Crowley, ed.

New York: Harcourt, Brace and World.

Patrick, H.T., and H. Rosovsky, eds. 1976. *Asia's New Giant: How the Japanese Economy Works.* Washington, D.C.: The Brookings Institution.

Peacock, A.T., and J. Wiseman. 1967. *The Growth of Public Expenditure in the United Kingdom.* New ed. London: George Allen and Unwin.

Peckman, J.A., and K. Kaizuka. 1976. "Taxation." In *Asia's New Giant.* See Patrick and Rosovsky 1976.

Prime Minister's Office. *Kokusai tōkei yōran* (International statistics manual). Published annually.

————. 1985. *Organization of the Government of Japan,* 1984 ed.

Sakakibara, E., and Y. Noguchi. 1977. "Dissecting the Finance Ministry-Bank of Japan Dynasty." *Japan Echo* IV(4).

Shibata, T. 1976. *Gendai Toshiron* (Theory of modern cities). Tokyo: University of Tokyo Press.

————. 1985. "Tokyo: Bright Present, Foreboding Future." *Japan Quarterly* 32 (4).

Shibata, T., and C. Cleaver. 1972. "Japan." In *Lands and People,* vol. 2. New York: Grolier.

Shibata, T., and I. Hayashi. 1978. "The Braking of Urban Expansion." In *Urban Growth in Japan and France,* I. Kobori, ed. Japan Society for the Promotion of Science.

Social Insurance Agency. 1981. *Outline of Social Insurance in Japan 1981.* Yoshida Finance and Social Security Law Institute.

Sugimura, S. 1982. *Zaisei Hō* (Public finance law). Tokyo: Yūhikaku.

Suzuki, T. 1983. *Kokusai no hanashi* (About government bonds). Tokyo: Tōyō Keizai Shimpo.

Takahashi, M. 1967. "The Development of War-time Economic Controls." *Developing Economies* 5(4).

————. 1979. "Lo sviluppo dei controlli in economia di guerra." In *Il capitalismo giapponese,* F. Mazzei, ed. Naples: Liguori Editore.

————. 1980. "Economic Development and Fiscal Policy in the Meiji Era." *Keizai shirin* 48(1).

Takeda, T., et al. 1983. *Nihon zaisei yōran* (Outline of Japanese public finance), rev. ed. Tokyo: University of Tokyo Press.

Tokyo Astronomical Observatory. *Rika nempyō* (Science almanac). Published annually.

The Tokyo Chamber of Commerce. *Statistical Manual about Japan's Economy in Comparison with Foreign Countries.* Published annually.

Tokyo Metropolitan Government. *Sekai daitoshi hikaku tōkei nempyō* (Comparative statistics of major world cities). Published annually.

————. *Tokyo Municipal News.* Published quarterly.

Trezise, P. H. 1983. "Industrial Policy Is Not the Major Reason for Japan's Success." *The Brookings Review* (Spring).

Trezise, P.H., and Y. Suzuki. 1976. "Politics, Government, and Economic Growth in Japan." In *Asia's New Giant.* See Patrick and Rosovsky 1976.

Tsuji, K. ed. 1983. *Public Administration in Japan.* Tokyo: University of Tokyo Press.

Tsuneta-Yano Memorial Society, ed. *Nihon kokusei zue* (A charted survey of Japan). Kokuseisha. Published annually.

————. *Nippon: A Charted Survey of Japan.* Kokusei-sha. Published annually.

U.S. Government. 1971. International Economic Report of the President.

————. 1978–81. Economic Report of the President.

————. 1983. The Budgets for Fiscal Year 1984, Special Analysis D.F.

Wallich, H.C., and H.I. Wallich. 1976. "Banking and Finance." In *Asia's New Giant.* See Patrick and Rosovsky 1976.

Yamamura, K. 1967. *Economic Policy in Postwar Japan.* Berkeley and Los Angeles: University of California Press.

————. ed. 1982. *Policy and Trade Issues of the Japanese Economy: American and Japanese Perspectives.* Seattle: University of Washington Press; Tokyo: University of Tokyo Press.

Zaisei Seisaku Kenkyūkai, ed. 1984. *Korekara no zaisei to kokusai hakkō* (Government finance and bond issue hereafter). Ōkura Zaimu Kyōkai.

Glossary

Accounts Law: 会計法 (Kaikei Hō)
Ad Hoc Council on Administrative
Reform: 臨時行政調査会 (Rinji
Gyōsei Chōsakai)
agency
Economic Planning Agency: 経済
企画庁 (Keizai Kikaku Chō)
Hokkaidō Development Agency:
北海道開発庁 (Hokkaidō Kaiha-
tsu Chō)
National Land Agency: 国土庁
(Kokudo Chō)
Okinawa Development Agency:
沖縄開発庁 (Okinawa Kaihatsu
Chō)
agency-delegated function, agential
task: 機関委任事務 (kikan inin
jimu)
Agricultural Land Development
Public Corporation: 農用地開発公
団 (Nōyōchi Kaihatsu Kōdan)
Agriculture, Forestry and Fisheries
Finance Corporation: 農林漁業金
融公庫 (Nōrin Gyogyō Kin'yū
Kōko)
Airport Improvement (Special
Account): 空港整備特別会計
(Kūkō Seibi Tokubetsu Kaikei)
airport user charge: 空港使用料
(kūkō shiyō ryō)
Alcohol Monopoly (Special
Account): アルコール専売事業特別
会計 (Arukōru Senbai Jigyō
Tokubetsu Kaikei)
Allotment of Local Allocation Tax
and Local Transfer Tax (Special
Account): 交付税及び譲与税配付金
特別会計 (Kōfu-zei Oyobi Jōyo-zei
Haifukin Tokubetsu Kaikei)

banks
Bank of Japan: 日本銀行 (Nippon
Ginkō)
Central Cooperative Bank for
Agriculture and Forestry: 農林
中央金庫 (Nōrin Chūō Kinko)
city bank: 都市銀行 (toshi ginkō)
Export Bank of Japan: 日本輸出銀
行 (Nihon Yushutsu Ginkō)
Export Bank of Japan Law: 日本
輸出銀行法 (Nihon Yushutsu
Ginkō Hō)
Export-Import Bank of Japan: 日
本輸出入銀行 (Nihon Yushutsu-
nyū Ginkō)
Hokkaidō Development Bank: 北
海道拓殖銀行 (Hokkaidō Taku-
shoku Ginkō)
Industrial Bank of Japan: 日本興
業銀行 (Nihon Kōgyō Ginkō)
Japan Development Bank: 日本開
発銀行 (Nihon Kaihatsu Ginkō)
Kangyō Bank of Japan: 日本勧業
銀行 (Nihon Kangyō Ginkō)
local bank: 地方銀行 (chihō ginkō)
long-term credit bank: 長期信用銀
行 (chōki shin'yō ginkō)
mutual bank: 相互銀行 (sōgo
ginkō)
Reconstruction Finance Bank: 復
興金融金庫 (Fukkō Kin'yū
Kinko)
Shoko Chukin Bank: 商工組合中央
金庫 (Shōkō Kumiai Chūō
Kinko)
trust bank: 信託銀行 (shintaku
ginkō)
basic financial needs: 基準財政需要額
(kijun zaisei juyō gaku)

basic financial revenue: 基準財政収入
額 (kijun zaisei shūnyū gaku)
Board of Audit: 会計検査院 (Kaikei
Kensa In)
Audit Commission: 会計検査官会
議 (Kaikei Kensa-kan Kaigi)
Commissioner: 会計検査院検査官
(Kaikei Kensa In Kensa-kan)
General Executive Bureau: 会計
検査院事務総局 (Kaikei Kensa
In Jimu Sōkyoku)
Board of Audit Law: 会計検査院法
(Kaikei Kensa In Hō)
bonds
appropriation ratio: 充当率 (jūtō
ritsu)
bond dependence ratio, ratio of
bond revenue to total revenue:
公債依存度 (kōsai isondo)
construction bonds: 建設債 (kensetsu sai)
deficit-covering (deficit-financing)
bonds: 赤字国債 (akaji kokusai)
Exceptional Law on Bond Issues:
公債の発行の特例に関する法律
(Kōsai No Hakkō No Tokurei
Ni Kansuru Hōritsu)
Government Bonds Consolidation Fund (Special Account): 国
債整理基金特別会計 (Kokusai
Seiri Kikin Tokubetsu Kaikei)
Government Guaranteed Bonds
and Borrowings: 政府保証債・政
府保証借入金 (Seifu Hoshō-sai,
Seifu Hoshō Kari-ire Kin)
Law Concerning Government
Bonds: 国債ニ関スル法律 (Koku-
sai Ni Kansuru Hōritsu)
loan charge ratio: 償還率 (shōkan
ritsu)
local (public) loans: 地方債 (chihō
sai)
Local Loan Program: 地方債計画
(Chihō Sai Keikaku)
Policies of the Local Loans Permits: 地方債許可方針 (Chihō Sai
Kyoka Hōshin)
public bonds / debts / loans: 公債
(kōsai)
redemption / consolidation of
government bonds: 国債の償

還・整理 (kokusai no shōkan /
seiri)
budget
approved carry-over expense: 繰
越明許費 (kurikoshi meikyo hi)
budget examiner: 主計官 (shukei
kan)
continued expense: 継続費 (keizo-
ku hi)
contract authorization: 国庫債務負
担行為 (kokko saimu futan kōi)
divisions: 予算の区分 (yosan no
kubun)
department: 主管 (shukan)
part: 部 (bu)
title: 款 (kan)
item: 項 (kō)
sub-item: 目 (moku)
sub-sub-item: 目の細分 (moku
no saibun)
general budget provisions: 予算総
則 (yosan sōsoku)
initial budget: 当初予算 (tōsho
yosan)
MOF draft: 大蔵省原案 (Ōkura-
shō gen'an)
provisional budget: 暫定予算 (zantei yosan)
report of estimate: 概算見積書
(gaisan mitsumorisho)
reserve fund: 予備費 (yobi hi)
settlement adjustment fund: 決算
調整資金 (kessan chōsei shikin)
settlement of expenditure and revenue: 歳出・歳入決算 (saishutsu
sainyū kessan)
supplementary budget: 補正予算
(hosei yosan)

capital-refunding: 元本償還 (ganpon
shōkan)
charges: 使用料 (shiyō ryō)
Coal Mining and Petroleum or
Alternative Energy to Petroleum
Industry (Special Account): 石炭
並びに石油及び石油代替エネルギー
対策特別会計 (Sekitan Narabini
Sekiyu Oyobi Sekiyu Daitai
Enerugī Taisaku Tokubetsu
Kaikei)
contributions: 寄附金 (kifukin)

Council on Economic Affairs: 経済
審議会 (Keizai Shingi Kai)
customs
ad valorem duty: 従価税 (jūka zei)
customhouse: 税関 (zeikan)
Customs Co-operation Council
Nomenclature: 関税協力理事会品
目表 (Kanzei Kyōryoku Riji
Kai Hinmoku Hyō)
customs duty: 関税 (kanzei)
Customs Law: 関税法 (Kanzei
Hō)
Customs Tariff Law: 関税定率法
(Kanzei Teiritsu Hō)
Customs Tariff Schedule: 関税率
表 (Kanzei Ritsu Hyō)
Generalized System of Preferences: 一般特恵関税制度 (Ippan
Tokkei Kanzei Seido)
simplified duty rates: 簡易税率
(kan'i zei ritsu)
specific duty: 従量税 (jūryō zei)
Temporary Tariff Measures Law:
関税暫定措置法 (Kanzei Zantei
Sochi Hō)
Customs Tariff Council: 関税率審議
会 (Kanzei Ritsu Shingi Kai)

debt-servicing expenditure: 利払費
(ribarai hi)
designated city: 政令指定市 (seirei
shitei shi)

Electric Power Development Com-
pany: 電源開発株式会社 (Dengen
Kaihatsu Kabushiki Kaisha)
Employer Security Fund: 雇用安定資
金 (Koyō Antei Shikin)
Employment Adjustment Fund: 雇
用調整給付金 (Koyō Chōsei Kyūfu
Kin)
Environmental Sanitation Business
Financing Corporation: 環境衛生
金融公庫 (Kankyō Eisei Kin'yū
Kōko)
extra allocation grant: 特例交付金
(tokurei kōfu kin)

fees: 手数料 (tesū ryō)
Finance for Urban Development
(Special Account): 都市開発資金融

通特別会計 (Toshi Kaihatsu Shikin
Yūzū Tokubetsu Kaikei)
financial public enterprise: 公的金融
機関 (kōteki kin'yū kikan)
fiscal capacity: 財政力 (zaisei ryoku)
Fiscal Investment and Loan agen-
cies: 財政投融資機関 (Zaisei
Tōyūshi Kikan)
Fiscal Investment and Loan Pro-
gram (FILP): 財政投融資計画
(Zaisei Tōyūshi Keikaku)
Fiscal System Council: 財政制度審議
会 (Zaisei Seido Shingi Kai)
Fixed Assets Assessment Commis-
sion: 固定資産評価審査委員会
(Kotei Shisan Hyōka Shinsa
Iinkai)
Flood Control (Special Account): 治
水特別会計 (Chisui Tokubetsu
Kaikei)
Foodstuff Control (Special
Account): 食糧管理特別会計 (Sho-
kuryō Kanri Tokubetsu Kaikei)
Foreign Exchange Fund (Special
Account): 外国為替資金特別会計
(Gaikoku Kawase Shikin
Tokubetu Kaikei)
Foreign Trade Fund (Special
Account): 貿易資金特別会計
(Bōeki Shikin Tokubetsu Kaikei)
Forest Development Corporation:
森林開発公団 (Shinrin Kaihatsu
Kōdan)

general account(s): 一般会計 (ippan
kaikei)
General Agreement on Tariffs and
Trade (GATT): 関税及び貿易に関
する一般協定 (Kanzei Oyobi Bōeki
Ni Kansuru Ippan Kyōtei)
General Law of National Taxes: 国
税通則法 (Kokuzei Tsūsoku Hō)
Government Bond Issue Advisory
Group: 国債発行懇談会 (Kokusai
Hakkō Kondan Kai)
gross national product (GNP): 国民
総生産 (kokumin sō seisan)

Hanshin Expressway Public Corporation: 阪神高速道路公団 (Han-
shin Kōsoku Dōro Kōdan)

Harbor Improvement (Special Account): 港湾整備特別会計 (Kōwan Seibi Tokubetsu Kaikei)

Hokkaidō-Tōhoku Development Corporation: 北海道東北開発公庫 (Hokkaidō-Tōhoku Kaihatsu Kōko)

Honshū-Shikoku Bridge Authority: 本州四国連絡橋公団 (Honshū-Shikoku Renraku Kyō Kōdan)

Housing and Urban Development Corporation: 住宅・都市整備公団 (Jūtaku Toshi Seibi Kōdan)

Housing Loan Corporation: 住宅金融公庫 (Jūtaku Kin'yū Kōko)

Housing Supply Corporation: 住宅供給公社 (Jūtaku Kyōkyū Kōsha)

Industrial Investment (Special Account): 産業投資特別会計 (Sangyō Tōshi Tokubetsu Kaikei)

insurance

Agricultural Mutual Aid Reinsurance (Special Account): 農業共済再保険特別会計 (Nōgyō Kyōsai Saihoken Tokubetsu Kaikei)

Day Laborers' Insurance: 日雇労働者保険 (Hiyatoi Rōdōsha Hoken)

Earthquake Reinsurance (Special Account): 地震再保険特別会計 (Jishin Saihoken Tokubetsu Kaikei)

Employment Insurance: 雇用保険 (Koyō Hoken)

Export Insurance (Special Account): 輸出保険特別会計 (Yushutsu Hoken Tokubetsu Kaikei)

Fishing Boat Reinsurance and Fishery Mutual Aid Insurance (Special Account): 漁船再保険及漁業共済再保険特別会計 (Gyosen Saihoken Oyobi Gyogyō Kyōsai Saihoken Tokubetsu Kaikei)

Forest Insurance (Special Account): 森林保険特別会計 (Shinrin Hoken Tokubetsu Kaikei)

Health Insurance: 健康保険 (Kenkō Hoken)

Laborer's Insurance (Special Account): 労働保険特別会計 (Rōdō Hoken Tokubetsu Kaikei)

life insurance: 生命保険 (seimei hoken)

National Health Insurance: 国民健康保険 (Kokumin Kenkō Hoken)

non-life insurance: 非生命保険 (hi-seimei hoken)

Post Office Life Insurance and Postal Annuity (Special Account): 簡易生命保険及郵便年金特別会計 (Kan'i Seimei Hoken Oyobi Yūbin Nenkin Tokubetsu Kaikei)

Reinsurance Compensation for Motorcar Accidents (Special Account): 自動車損害賠償責任再保険特別会計 (Jidōsha Songai Baishō Sekinin Saihoken Tokubetsu Kaikei)

Seamen's Insurance (Special Account): 船員保険特別会計 (Sen'in Hoken Tokubetsu Kaikei)

Small Business Credit Insurance Corporation: 中小企業信用保険公庫 (Chū-shō Kigyō Shin'yō Hoken Kōko)

social insurance: 社会保険 (shakai hoken)

social insurance premium: 社会保険料 (shakai hoken ryō)

Welfare Annuity Insurance: 福祉年金 (Fukushi Nenkin)

Welfare Insurance (Special Account): 厚生保険特別会計 (Kōsei Hoken Tokubetsu Kaikei)

Japan Atomic Energy Research Institute: 日本原子力研究所 (Nihon Genshiryoku Kenkyūjo)

Japanese National Railways: 日本国有鉄道 (Nihon Kokuyū Tetsudō)

Japan Finance Corporation for Municipal Enterprises: 公営企業金融公庫 (Kōei Kigyō Kin'yū Kōko)

GLOSSARY 185

Japan Highway Public Corporation:
日本道路公団 (Nihon Dōro Kōdan)
Japan Housing Corporation: 日本住
宅公団 (Nihon Jūtaku Kōdan)
Japan National Oil Corporation: 日
本石油公団 (Nihon Sekiyu Kōdan)
Japan Private School Promotion
Foundation: 私学振興財団 (Shiga-
ku Shinkō Zaidan)
Japan Railway Construction Public
Corporation: 日本鉄道建設公団
(Nihon Tetsudō Kensetsu Kōdan)
Japan Raw Silk and Sugar Price
Stabilization Agency: 蚕糸砂糖類
価格安定事業団 (Sanshi Satō Rui
Kakaku Antei Jigyōdan)
Japan Regional Development Cor-
poration: 地域振興整備公団 (Chiiki
Shinkō Seibi Kōdan)
Japan Scholarship Foundation: 日本
育英会 (Nihon Ikuei Kai)
Japan Tobacco and Salt Public Cor-
poration: 日本専売公社 (Nihon
Senbai Kōsha)
jigyōdan 事業団

kikin 基金
kōdan 公団
kyōkai 協会

Law Concerning Management of
National Credits: 国の債権の管理等
に関する法律 (Kuni No Saiken No
Kanri Tō Ni Kansuru Hōritsu)
Law Concerning the Budget and
the Settlement of Accounts of
the Financing Corporations: 公庫
の予算及び決算に関する法律 (Kōko
No Yosan Oyobi Kessan Ni Kansuru Hōritsu)
Livestock Industry Promotion Corporation: 畜産振興事業団 (Chiku-
san Shinkō Jigyōdan)
Local Autonomy Law: 地方自治法
(Chihō Jichi Hō)
Local Finance Law: 地方財政法 (Chihō Zaisei Hō)
Local Public Finance Program: 地方
財政計画 (Chihō Zaisei Keikaku)

Maritime Credit Corporation: 船舶

整備公団 (Senpaku Seibi Kōdan)
Medical Care Facilities Financing
Corporation: 医療金融公庫 (Iryō
Kin'yū Kōko)
Metropolitan Expressway Public
Corporation: 首都高速道路公団
(Shuto Kōsoku Dōro Kōdan)
Ministry of Agriculture, Forestry
and Fisheries: 農林水産省 (Nōrin
Suisan Shō)
Ministry of Finance (MOF): 大蔵省
(Okura Shō)
Budget Bureau: 主計局 (Shukei
Kyoku)
Customs and Tariff Bureau: 関税
局 (Kanzei Kyoku)
National Tax Administration: 国
税庁 (Kokuzei Chō)
Okinawa Regional Taxation
Office: 沖縄国税事務所 (Oki-
nawa Kokuzei Jimusho)
regional taxation bureau: 国税
局 (kokuzei kyoku)
taxation office: 税務署 (zeimu
sho)
National Tax Tribunal: 国税不服審
判所 (Kokuzei Fufuku Shinpan
Sho)
Tax Bureau: 主税局 (Shuzei
Kyoku)
Ministry of Health and Welfare: 厚
生省 (Kōsei Shō)
Ministry of Home Affairs: 自治省
(Jichi Shō)
Ministry of International Trade and
Industry (MITI): 通商産業省
(Tsūshō Sangyō Shō)
Ministry of Posts and Telecom-
munications: 郵政省 (Yūsei Shō)
Mint Bureau (Special Account): 造
幣局特別会計 (Zōhei Kyoku
Tokubetsu Kaikei)
Motorcar Inspection and Registra-
tion (Special Account): 自動車検査
登録特別会計 (Jidōsha Kensa
Tōroku Tokubetsu Kaikei)

National Forest Service (Special
Account): 国有林野事業特別会計
(Kokuyū Rin'ya Jigyō Tokubetsu
Kaikei)

National Goods Management Law: 物品管理法 (Buppin Kanri Hō)

national government disbursements for specific purposes: 国庫支出金 (kokko shishutsu kin)

national treasury grants-in-aid: 国庫補助金 (kokko hojo kin)

national treasury obligatory share: 国庫負担金 (kokko futan kin)

national treasury payments for agential tasks: 国庫委託金 (kokko itaku kin)

National Hospitals (Special Account): 国立病院特別会計 (Kokuritsu Byōin Tokubetsu Kaikei)

National Officials Law: 国家公務員法 (Kokka Kōmuin Hō)

National Property Law: 国有財産法 (Kokuyū Zaisan Hō)

National Property Special Consolidation Fund (Special Account): 特定国有財産整備特別会計 (Tokutei Kokuyū Zaisan Seibi Tokubetsu Kaikei)

National Schools (Special Account): 国立学校特別会計 (Kokuritsu Gakkō Tokubetsu Kaikei)

National Space Development Agency of Japan: 宇宙開発事業団 (Uchū Kaihatsu Jigyōdan)

National Union of Credit Union: 全国信用組合連合会 (Zenkoku Shin'yō Kumiai Rengō Kai)

New Tokyo International Airport Authority: 新東京国際空港公団 (Shin Tokyo Kokusai Kūkō Kōdan)

Nippon Telegraph and Telephone Public Corporation: 日本電信電話公社 (Nihon Denshin Denwa Kōsha)

nonfinancial public enterprise: 非公的金融機関 (hi-kōteki kin'yū kikan)

obligatory expenditure: 義務的経費 (gimu teki keihi)

Ocean Science Technology Center: 海洋科学技術センター (Kaiyō Kagaku Gijutsu Sentā)

Official Development Aid (ODA): 政府開発援助 (Seifu Kaihatsu Enjo)

Okinawa Development Finance Corporation: 沖縄振興開発金融公庫 (Okinawa Shinkō Kaihatsu Kin'yū Kōko)

Overseas Economic Cooperation Fund: 海外経済協力基金 (Kaigai Keizai Kyōryoku Kikin)

Patent (Special Account): 特許特別会計 (Tokkyo Tokubetsu Kaikei)

pensions
Employees' Pension: 厚生年金 (Kōsei Nenkin)
National Pensions (Special Account): 国民年金特別会計 (Kokumin Nenkin Tokubetsu Kaikei)

People's Finance Corporation: 国民金融公庫 (Kokumin Kin'yū Kōko)

Petroleum Public Corporation: 石油公団 (Sekiyu Kōdan)

Post Office: 郵便局 (Yūbin Kyoku)

Postal Savings (Special Account): 郵便貯金特別会計 (Yūbin Chokin Tokubetsu Kaikei)

Postal Services (Special Account): 郵政事業特別会計 (Yūsei Jigyō Tokubetsu Kaikei)

Power Reactor and Nuclear Fuel Development Corporation: 動力炉核燃料開発事業団 (Dōryokuro Kakunenryō Kaihatsu Jigyōdan)

Printing Bureau (Special Account): 印刷局特別会計 (Insatsu Kyoku Tokubetsu Kaikei)

Priority Production Policy: 傾斜生産方式 (Keisha Seisan Hōshiki)

Promotion of Electric Power Resources Development (Special Account): 電源開発促進対策特別会計 (Dengen Kaihatsu Sokushin Taisaku Tokubetsu Kaikei)

public assistance: 生活保護 (seikatsu hogo)

Public Finance Law: 財政法 (Zaisei Hō)

Registration (Special Account): 登記特別会計 (Tōki Tokubetsu Kaikei)
Reinforcement of Agricultural Management Condition (Special Account): 農業経営基盤強化措置特別会計 (Nōgyō Keiei Kiban Kyōka Sochi Tokubetsu Kaikei)
Road Improvement (Special Account): 道路整備特別会計 (Dōro Seibi Tokubetsu Kaikei)

securities firms: 証券会社 (shōken kaisha)
Small Business Finance Corporation: 中小企業金融公庫 (Chū-shō Kigyō Kin'yū Kōko)
social welfare: 社会福祉 (shakai fukushi)
Social Welfare and Medical Care Enterprise: 社会福祉・医療事業団 (Shakai Fukushi, Iryō Jigyōdan)
Special Measures for Establishment of Landed Farms (Special Account): 自作農創設特別措置特別会計 (Jisaku-nō Sōsetsu Tokubetsu Sochi Tokubetsu Kaikei)
Specific Land Improvement (Special Account): 特定土地改良工事特別会計 (Tokutei Tochi Kairyō Kōji Tokubetsu Kaikei)
specific traffic safety grant: 交通安全対策特別交付金 (kōtsū anzen taisaku tokubetsu kōfu kin)
super balancing policy: 超均衡政策 (chō kinkō seisaku)

tax
admission tax: 入場税 (nyūjō zei)
advertisement tax: 広告税 (kōkoku zei)
amusement tax: 娯楽施設利用税 (goraku shisetsu riyō zei)
assessed value: 評価額 (hyōka gaku)
assessors: 評価員 (hyōka in)
automobile acquisition tax: 自動車取得税 (jidōsha shutoku zei)
automobile tax: 自動車税 (jidōsha zei)
aviation fuel tax: 航空機燃料税

(kōkūki nenryō zei)
basic exemption: 基礎控除 (kiso kōjo)
business office tax: 事業所税 (jigyō-sho zei)
capital gains: 譲渡所得 (jōto shotoku)
certified tax account: 税理士 (zeiri shi)
city planning tax: 都市計画税 (toshi keikaku zei)
commodity tax: 物品税 (buppin zei)
common facilities tax: 共同施設税 (kyōdō shisetsu zei)
consumption tax: 消費税 (shōhi zei)
corporation (corporate income) tax: 法人税 (hōjin zei)
correction: 更正 (kōsei)
deduction: 控除 (kōjo)
discretionary tax: 法定外税 (hōtei gai zei)
double taxation: 二重課税 (nijū kazei)
electricity tax: 電気税 (denki zei)
enterprise tax: 事業税 (jigyō zei)
exemption: 控除／免除 (kōjo / menjo)
fixed assets tax: 固定資産税 (kotei shisan zei)
building: 家屋 (kaoku)
land: 土地 (tochi)
national governmet and public corporation assets: 交付金・納付金 (kōfu kin, nōfu kin)
tangible business assets: 償却資産 (shōkyaku shisan)
gasoline tax: 揮発油税 (kihatsuyu zei)
gas tax: ガス税 (gasu zei)
general consumption tax: 一般消費税 (ippan shōhi zei)
gift tax: 贈与税 (zōyo zei)
hunter's license tax: 狩猟者登録税 (shuryōsha tōroku zei)
hunting tax: 入猟税 (nyūryō zei)
income tax: 所得税 (shotoku zei)
inhabitant tax, municipal: 市町村民税 (shi-chō-son min zei)
corporation, per capita rate: 法

tax (*continued*)
　人均等割 (hōjin kintō wari)
　corporation, tax rate: 法人税割
　　(hōjin zei wari)
　individual, income rate: 所得割
　　(shotoku wari)
　individual, per capita rate: 個人
　　均等割 (kojin kintō wari)
　inhabitant tax, prefectural: 道府県
　　民税 (dō-fu-ken min zei)
　inheritance tax: 相続税 (sōzoku
　　zei)
　light motor vehicle tax: 軽自動車
　　税 (keijidōsha zei)
　light oil delivery tax: 軽油引取税
　　(keiyu hikitori zei)
　liquor tax: 酒税 (shu zei)
　local allocation tax: 地方交付税
　　(chihō kōfu zei)
　　modification coefficient: 補正係
　　　数 (hosei keisū)
　　ordinary: 普通交付税 (futsū kōfu
　　　zei)
　　special: 特別交付税 (tokubetsu
　　　kōfu zei)
　　unit cost: 単位費用 (tan'i hiyō)
　　unit of measure: 測定単位
　　　(sokutei tan'i)
　Local Allocation Tax Law: 地方交
　　付税法 (Chihō Kōfu Zei Hō)
　local road tax: 地方道路税 (chihō
　　dōro zei)
　local tax: 地方税 (chihō zei)
　Local Tax Law: 地方税法 (Chihō
　　Zei Hō)
　local transfer tax: 地方譲与税 (chi-
　　hō jōyo zei)
　　aviation fuel transfer tax: 航空
　　　機燃料譲与税 (kōkūki nenryō
　　　jōyo zei)
　　local road transfer tax: 地方道路
　　　譲与税 (chihō dōro jōyo zei)
　　motor vehicle tonnage transfer
　　　tax: 自動車重量譲与税 (jidōsha
　　　jūryō jōyo zei)
　　petroleum gas transfer tax: 石油
　　　ガス譲与税 (sekiyu gasu jōyo
　　　zei)
　　special tonnage transfer tax: 特
　　　別とん譲与税 (tokubetsu ton
　　　jōyo zei)

　meals and hotel tax: 料理飲食等
　　消費税 (ryōri inshoku tō shō-
　　hi zei)
　merchandise certificate tax: 商品
　　切手発行税 (shōhin kitte hakkō
　　zei)
　mine-lot tax: 鉱区税 (kōku zei)
　mineral products tax: 鉱産税
　　(kōsan zei)
　motor vehicle tonnage tax: 自動車
　　重量税 (jidōsha jūryō zei)
　nuclear fuel tax: 核燃料税 (kaku-
　　nenryō zei)
　ordinary tax: 普通税 (futsū zei)
　petroleum gas tax: 石油ガス税
　　(sekiyu gasu zei)
　petroleum tax: 石油税 (sekiyu zei)
　promotion of power resources
　　development tax: 電源開発促進
　　税 (dengen kaihatsu sokushin
　　zei)
　property tax: 財産税 (zaisan zei)
　purpose tax: 目的税 (mokuteki
　　zei)
　real property acquisition tax: 不動
　　産取得税 (fudōsan shutoku zei)
　registration and license tax: 登録
　　免許税 (tōroku menkyo zei)
　reserves: 準備金 (junbi kin)
　return
　　blue return: 青色申告 (ao-iro
　　　shinkoku)
　　final return 確定申告 (kakutei
　　　shinkoku)
　　interim return 中間申告 (chūkan
　　　shinkoku)
　　self-assessment: 申告納税
　　　(shinkoku nōzei)
　　white return: 白色申告 (shiro-iro
　　　shinkoku)
　securities transaction tax: 有価証
　　券取引税 (yūka shōken torihiki
　　zei)
　spa tax: 入湯税 (nyūtō zei)
　special land-holding tax: 特別土地
　　保有税 (tokubetsu tochi hoyū
　　zei)
　Special Taxation Measures Law:
　　租税特別措置法 (Sozei Toku-
　　betsu Sochi Hō)
　special tax measures: 租税特別措置

(sozei tokubetsu sochi)
stamp tax: 印紙税 (inshi zei)
standard tax rate: 標準税率 (hyō-
jun zeiritsu)
statutory tax: 法定税 (hōtei zei)
sugar excise tax: 砂糖消費税 (satō
shōhi zei)
surtax: 付加税 (fuka zei)
tax credit: 税額控除 (zeigaku kōjo)
tax rates: 税率 (zeiritsu)
tax sparing credit: みなし税額控除
(minashi zeigaku kōjo)
tax treaty, tax convention: 租税条
約 (sozei jōyaku)
timber delivery tax: 木材引取税
(mokuzai hikitori zei)
tobacco consumption tax: たばこ
消費税 (tabako shōhi zei)
travel tax: 通行税 (tsūkō zei)
value-added tax: 付加価値税 (fuka
kachi zei)
water utility and land profit tax:
水利地益税 (suiri chieki zei)
withholding income tax: 源泉徴収
所得税 (gensen chōshū shotoku
zei)

year-end adjustment: 年末調整
(nenmatsu chōsei)
Tax Commission: 税制調査会 (Zeisei
Chōsa Kai)
Teito Rapid Transit Authority: 帝都
高速度交通営団 (Teito Kōsokudo
Kōtsū Eidan)
transfer as substitution of fixed
property tax: 固定資産税に代わる交
付金 (kotei shisan zei ni kawaru
kōfu kin)
treasury bill: 大蔵省短期証券 (Ōkura-
shō tanki shōken)
Trust Fund Bureau (Special
Account): 資金運用部特別会計
(Shikin Un'yōbu Tokubetsu
Kaikei)

Water Resources Development
Corporation: 水資源開発公団
(Mizu Shigen Kaihatsu Kōdan)

Yokinbu: 預金部

Index

accounting, unified, 52
Accounts Law, 51, 52
Ad Hoc Council on Administrative
   Reform, 47, 101
admission tax, 117
advertisement tax, 142
agency-delegated functions, 141,
   159, 166–67
aging society, 18, 29–30
agriculture: farm size, 8–9; government aid, 75–76; labor surplus, 8
Agriculture, Forestry and Fisheries
   Finance Corporation, 63, 91,
   95–96
Airport Improvement Special
   Account, 75
Alcohol Monopoly, 31
approved carry-over expense, 55
Audit Commission, 64–65, 66
audit system, 64–66
automobile acquisition tax, 146, 147
automobile tax, 146
aviation fuel transfer tax, 147

balanced budget, 38, 125, 126
Bank of Japan, 54, 60, 65, 90, 98,
   127, 130–31
Board of Audit, 61, 64–66
Board of Audit Law, 51, 64
budget: classifications, 55–56, con-
   stitutional provisions, 50; contents, 53–55, 67–71; definitions,
   52; Diet deliberation, 59–60; execution, 60; formulation, 56–59

city banks, 128, 129, 130
Civil Code, 114
commodity tax, 116–17, 146

communications, 16
constitution; on budget, 50, 56, on
   local government, 132
consumption tax, 115–17, 146
continued expense, 55
contract authorization, 54, 55
corporate income tax. See corporation tax
corporate inhabitant tax, 143
corporation tax, 40, 41, 46, 106,
   107, 108, 112–14, 122
Corporation Tax Law, 108, 112
crime, 18, 30
Customs Co-operation Council
   Nomenclature, 118
customs duties, 117–19
Customs Law, 118
Customs Tariff Council, 119
Customs Tariff Law, 118

Day Laborers' Insurance, 70
defense budget, 78
designated cities, 147
Diet: budget deliberation, 51, 54,
   59–60; settlement deliberation, 66
disaster prevention, government
   programs, 75
Dodge Plan, 37, 38, 39, 90
double taxation, 120

economic cooperation, 77–78
economic development, postwar,
   8–11
Economic Planning Agency, 58
Economic Rehabilitation in Occupied Area, 90
education, 9; budget, 71–72, 137,
   138

eidan, 99, 100
Electric Power Development Co., 92
Employees' Pension, 41, 48, 70, 83
Employer Security Fund, 71
Employment Adjustment Fund, 71
Employment Insurance, 71
energy: research in, 76; sources, 10
enterprise tax, 143–45
environmental pollution, 18–19
Environmental Sanitation Business Financing Corporation, 63, 97
excise taxes, 115
Export Bank of Japan, 39, 90– 91
Export Bank of Japan Law, 90
Export-Import Bank of Japan, 63, 78, 91, 97

final consumption expenditure, 32
financial public enterprises, 31, 39, 83, 97
financial reforms, postwar, 27, 36–38, 89–92, 106–7
fiscal burden, 28
fiscal capacity, 160–62
fiscal deficit, 35; analysis, 44–45; cause, 43–44, 162
Fiscal Investment and Loan agencies, 93, 95
Fiscal Investment and Loan Program (FILP), 31, 63, history, 88–92; scope, 81–84; sources of, 85–86, 128, 129; uses, 40, 79, 86–88, 93–94
fiscal reconstruction, 46–48
fiscal size, 26–27, 28–29
Fiscal System Council, 58
fiscal year, 51–52
fixed assets tax, 145–46
Foodstuff Control Special Account, 76
Foreign Trade Fund Special Account, 90

gasoline tax, 117, 146
General Agreement on Tariffs and Trade, 118
general consumption tax, 46, 48, 126
Generalized System of Preferences, 118

General Law of National Taxes, 107
geography, 3–5
gift tax, 114
global tax, 106
Government and Relief in Occupied Area, 90
Government Bond Issue Advisory Group, 58
government bonds, 52–53, 54, 79–80; construction bonds, 52, 53, 79, 124, 131; deficit-covering bonds, 53, 107, 108, 124–25, 131; dependence ratio, 38, 43, 47; history, 123–24; holders, 127–31; interest payments, 127, 131; international comparison, 125; issuance, 35, 48, 123–24, 125; open bidding, 129–30; reduction, 47
Government Bonds Consolidation Fund Special Account, 52
government credit program. *See* Fiscal Investment and Loan Program
government employees, 28
Government Guaranteed Bonds and Borrowings, 83, 86
government investment: industrial, 11, 36–37; in low-productivity sectors, 39
government party, and budget formulation, 58–59
government size, 27–28, 43, 45–46, 47, 48
gross domestic product (GDP), 12, 44, 45
gross national expenditures (GNE), 133, 135
gross national product (GNP): historical comparison, 25–26; international comparison, 11–12, 24

Harbor Improvement Special Account, 75
health and sanitation, 70–71
Health Insurance, 70
history, 6–8
Hokkaidō Development Bank, 89
Hokkaidō-Tōhoku Development Corporation, 63, 97

housing, 17, 73
Housing and Urban Development
Corporation, 101
Housing Loan Corporation, 63, 73,
95–96

income tax, 38, 46, 106, 107,
108–11
Income Tax Law, 108
individual inhabitant tax, 143
Industrial Bank of Japan, 89, 90
Industrial Investment Special
Account, 83, 85, 86
industrial products, 12–13, 19
industry: financing of, 10, 37; postwar reconstruction, 36–37; two-
tier system, 14
inflation, 37, 127
inheritance tax, 114–15
Inheritance Tax Law, 114
intergovernment fiscal relations,
32–33, 79, 134, 135, 147–48, 151,
156. See also local allocation tax

Japan Atomic Energy Research In-
stitute, 76
Japan Development Bank, 39, 63,
90, 91, 93, 97
Japanese National Railways, 31, 47,
63, 83, 86, 101–2
Japan Finance Corporation for
Municipal Enterprises, 63, 150
Japan Housing Corporation, 73,
101
Japan Incorporated, 24–25
Japan Private School Promotion
Foundation, 72
Japan Scholarship Foundation, 72
Japan Tobacco and Salt Public Cor-
poration, 31, 63, 101, 102
jigyōdan, 86, 100

Kangyō Bank of Japan, 89
kikin, 86
kōdan, 86, 99, 100
kyōkai, 86

labor force, 13–15; and migration,
9, 11, 30
land prices, 17
land tax, 106

Law Concerning Government
Bonds, 51, 52
Law Concerning Management of
National Credits, 51
Law Concerning the Budget and
the Settlement of Accounts of
the Financing Corporations, 64
leisure, 17–18
license tax, 117
life expectancy, 6
light motor vehicle tax, 146, 147
light oil delivery tax, 146, 147
liquor tax, 116
List of Simplified Duty Rates, 118
living standards, 15
local allocation tax, 79, 139–40,
150, 151, 152, 158, 160–64
Local Allocation Tax Law, 132,
150, 162
Local Finance Law, 132, 134, 141,
148, 167, 168
local govenment: expenditure, 26,
132, 133, 135–38; finance, 79,
134; number, 132; obligatory expenditure, 138, 151, 167; tax revenues, 33, 139–50. See also intergovernment fiscal relations
local inhabitant tax, 143
Local Loan Program, 149
local loans, 141, 148–50, 152, 157;
charges, 138, 149–50
local public authorities, 83
local public enterprises, 152–55; expenditures, 133
Local Public Finance Program, 150
local road tax, 117, 146
local road transfer tax, 147, 148
local taxes, 139, 141–47
Local Tax Law, 132, 142, 147
local transfer tax, 140–41, 147–48,
158, 159

Medical Care Facilities Financing
Corporation, 63
medical insurance, 41, 42
merchandise certificate tax, 142
migration, urban, 8, 9, 30
military expenditure, 26–27
minister of finance: bond issuance
and, 53; budget execution, 60;
settlement of accounts, 61, 64–65

Ministry of Finance: Budget Bureau, 56–57, 59; budget formulation, 21–22, 56–59; Customs and Tariff Bureau, 119; Export Bank and, 91; FILP and, 87–88; government bonds and, 125; Tax Bureau, 120; Yokinbu and, 88
Ministry of Posts and Telecommunications, 98
Mint Bureau, 31
motor vehicle tonnage tax, 117, 146
motor vehicle tonnage transfer tax, 147, 148
municipalities, 33, 132–33. *See also* local allocation tax

National Forest Service, 83
National Goods Management Law, 51
national government: expenditure, 26, 31–33, 34, 132, 133, 135–36; income, 33, 48. *See also* intergovernment fiscal relations
national government control, 159–60
national government disbursements for specific purposes, 141, 150, 158, 165–68
National Health Insurance, 70
National Pension, 41, 48, 70, 83
National Property Law, 51
National Schools Special Account, 72
National Space Development Agency of Japan, 73
National Tax Administration, 120–21, 122
National Tax Tribunal, 122
national treasury grants-in-aid, 141, 167, 168
national treasury obligatory share, 141
New Tokyo International Airport Authority, 75
New Town Development Corporation, 101
Nippon Telegraph and Telephone Public Corporation, 31, 47, 63, 92, 101, 102
nonfinancial public enterprises, 98–100

nuclear fuel tax, 142

Ocean Science Technology Center, 73
Official Development Aid, 77
oil crisis, effects of, 29, 34–35, 42–43, 83, 101, 107, 123
Okinawa Development Finance Corporation, 63
Overseas Economic Cooperation Fund, 78

pensions, 47, 48, 70, 83
People's Finance Corporation, 63, 78, 91, 93, 95–96
petroleum gas tax, 146
petroleum gas transfer tax, 147
Petroleum Public Corporation, 76
petroleum tax, 117
Policies of the Local Loans Permits, 149
population, 5–6, 29. *See also* migration
Postal Annuity, 31
postal savings, 31, 88–89, 97–98; and FILP, 40
Postal Services, 31
Post Office Life Insurance, 31, 83, 86, 150
Power Reactor and Nuclear Fuel Development Corporation, 76
prefectures, 33, 132–33. *See also* local allocation tax
Printing Bureau, 31
Priority Production Policy, 36
privilege tax, 146
property tax, 146
public amenities, 17–18, 74
public assistance, 69
public corporations, 63–64, 83, 100; dual structure, 31
public finance, future problems, 21–23
Public Finance Law, 51–52, 53, 56, 61, 73, 79, 125
public sector, comparison, 27–28
public works expenditure, 73–76, 137, 138

rapid-growth era, 37, 38–41, 71, 107

Reconstruction Finance Bank, 37, 39, 89–90, 91
registration tax, 117
rice control, 76–77
roads, public programs, 74–75

savings, as investment funds, 10, 37, 44. *See also* postal savings
science and technology budget, 72–73
securities firms, 127
securities transaction tax, 117
settlement, of accounts, 61, 66
Shoko Chukin Bank, 76
Shoup, Carl S., 38, 106–7
small businesses, government aid to, 78–79
Small Business Credit Insurance Corporation, 63
Small Business Finance Corporation, 63, 78, 91, 93
social insurance, 69–70
social security, 41–42; expenditures, 44, 45, 48, 67–71; quality, 47; ratio, 32; taxes, 107
social welfare, 69; expenditure, 137, 138
Social Welfare and Medical Care Enterprise, 63
special accounts, 61–63, 83, 99–100, 152
Special Taxation Measures Law, 109, 114
special tonnage transfer tax, 147
special traffic safety grants, 158, 159
super balancing policy, 37
Supreme Commander for the Allied Powers (SCAP), 89, 91
syndicates, 127

tax: appeals, 122; computation, 113; deductions, 109, 113, 115, 145; direct, 38, 46, 103–4, 107–8; exemptions, 110, 114; history, 106–8; incentives, 114; increase, 48, 126; indirect, 103–4, 115; international comparison, 104, 112; local, 103–4; national, 103–4; on foreign corporations, 119–20; policy, 40–41; rates, 108, 115, 121; reforms, 38; returns, 111; revenues, 44, 45–46, 157; revenues, automatic increases, 29, 39, 42, 46; self–assessment, 108, 121; special treatment, 40; transfers, 33–34, 135
taxation office, 111, 116
Tax Commission, 56, 59, 107, 120
tax-free reserves, 40
taxpayers, 111; foreign, 119–120
Temporary Tariff Measures Law, 118
Tokyo, 5, 9; fiscal capacity, 161; government expenditures, 133
trade, 19–21
transfer as a substitution of fixed property tax, 158–59
transportation, 15–16
travel tax, 117
Trust Fund Bureau, 40, 83, 91; and government bonds, 127, 128–29, 130

unemployment, 18, 30, 71
unions, 14–15
U.S. Counterpart Fund, 90, 91

value-added tax, 108

wages, 14
withholding tax, 113, 121–22

Yokinbu, 88, 91